GREENBERG'S® GUIDE TO
MARX TOYS

Volume II

By
Maxine A. Pinsky

Edited by
Marcy Damon and Leslie Greenberg

Cover photograph: The 1930 Whoopee Car is the only Marx Eccentric Car to have female figures perched on its trunk. Photograph by Robert Grubb.

Copyright © 1990

Greenberg Publishing Company, Inc.
7566 Main Street
Sykesville, MD 21784

(301) 795-7447

Manufactured in the United States of America

Greenberg Publishing Company, Inc. offers the world's largest selection of Lionel, American Flyer, LGB, Ives, and other toy train publications as well as a selection of books on model and prototype railroading, dollhouse miniatures, and toys. For a copy of our current catalogue, please send a large self-addressed stamped envelope to the address above.

Greenberg Shows, Inc. sponsors the world's largest public train, dollhouse, and toy shows. They feature extravagant operating model railroads for N, HO, O, Standard, and 1 Gauges as well as a huge marketplace for buying and selling nearly all model railroad equipment. The shows also feature a large selection of dollhouses and dollhouse furnishings. Shows are currently offered in metropolitan Baltimore, Boston, Ft. Lauderdale, Cherry Hill in New Jersey, Long Island in New York, Philadelphia, Pittsburgh, and Tampa. Greenberg Auctions, a division of Greenberg Shows, Inc., offers nationally advertised auctions of toy trains and toys. Please contact Joseph Armacost at (301) 795-7447 for further information. To receive our current show listing, please send a self-addressed stamped envelope marked "Show Schedule" to the address above.

ISBN: 0-89778-100-7

Library of Congress Cataloging-in-Publication Data

Pinsky, Maxine A.

    Greenberg's guide to Marx Toys.

    Vol. 2 edited by Marcy Damon and Leslie Greenberg.
    Includes bibliographies and index.
      1. Toys—United States.   2. Louis Marx & Co.
I. Suehle, MaryAnn S.   II. Damon, Marcy.
III. Greenberg, Leslie.   IV. Greenberg Publishing Company.
V. Guide to Marx toys.
TS2301.T7P48   1988   688.7'2'0973   87-30250
ISBN 0-89778-027-2 (v. 1).

TABLE OF CONTENTS

Dedication

To the memory of two unique people: Stewart Bearn, the kindest and most patient of men, and my Aunt May Pinsky. No matter how ill, dear Aunt May maintained her interest in my work.

And, I dedicate this book to my husband, Edward, without whose tremendous support, encouragement and love I would never have even attempted such a project.

ACKNOWLEDGMENTS

Many people contributed greatly to each chapter of the book and it is a pleasure to take this opportunity to thank them.

SPECIAL CONTRIBUTORS

The following people deserve special recognition for their considerable help:

Particularly outstanding was **Malcolm Kates, M.D.**, past National President of Antique Toy Collectors of America. He spent many hours recording clear and extremely detailed information, answering questions, and even lending toys to be photographed more than once from his outstanding collection. He was particularly helpful with Marx airplanes, motorcycles, and automobiles.

Hillel Don Lazarus, D.D.S., past National President of Toy Train Operating Society, sent numerous catalog pages which I am still using, and also helped me to realize the importance of patents. His constant encouragement saw me through some difficult periods.

John S. Newbraugh loaned valuable original catalogs, answered questions, and to this day continues to send useful information.

Trip Riley donated large quantities of very useful information, reviewed the manuscript, and also allowed toys from his fine collection to be photographed. He devised a system of organizing the trucks by type and contributed his specific knowledge of Marx airplanes, buses, trucks, automobiles, and tanks.

John S. Ritter did practically everything. He gave new meaning to the word "reader" with his wonderfully detailed notes, especially on Marx airplanes and tanks, as well as providing prices. John spent many hours covering information

and in addition, sent many letters with in-depth explanations, photos, and beautiful drawings.

Philip Rolin spent many hours with me under adverse conditions, while I studied his collection, and willingly transported numerous boxes of toys which he also allowed to be photographed.

Cheryl A. Weber, R.N., and **Charles W. Weber, Ph.D.**, lent their toys for long periods in order for their interesting collection to be studied and photographed. Charles, as well as being a reader, never lost his patience with all the questions I asked him.

INFORMATION CONTRIBUTORS

James Apthorpe generously continues to send, as he has for some time, very useful information and photos.

Peter Fritz and the late **Gerritt Beverwyck**, former Editors of the *Marx Toy Collector Newsletter*, kindly allowed the use of the excellent newsletter as a resource and offered many good suggestions.

Lillian B. Gottschalk permitted the use of information from her fine book, *American Toy Cars and Trucks*. **Donald Kaufman** provided useful color slides of Marx toys to be used for this book. **Reverend Carl H. Kruelle, Jr.** contributed intriguing information. **Walt Maeder** contributed information and allowed his toys to be photographed.

Al Marwick, the well-known writer, **Frances** and **James Nichols**, and **Ken Pfirman**, **Larry Jensen**, and **Robert Straub** provided valuable information. **Eric J. Matzke**, always helpful, assisted with detailed toy listings besides being a reader.

Lawrence P. Orr lent a copy of a fascinating catalog. Lloyd W. Ralston granted use of his fine Auction Catalogs as a reference.

Grover Van Dexter from Second Childhood® in New York City reviewed prices and lent invaluable insight from his years of collecting Marx toys. Others who assisted with pricing were **Terry** and **Sandra Bauer**, **John M. Iannuzzi**, **Ivan Kling**, **Anna Manson**, **Aaron Roy**, and **George Wilhelm**.

Lenore Swoiskin, former Chief Archivist at Sears, Roebuck & company, and **Victoria Cwiok**, her assistant, did everything they possible could to be helpful.

PHOTOGRAPHED COLLECTIONS

The following collectors graciously allowed toys from their collections to be photographed:

Brice Allan, **David W. Allen**, **John M. Iannuzzi**, **Dr. Malcolm Kates**, **Walt Maeder**, **John S. Newbraugh**, **Ed Owens**, **Trip Riley**, **John S. Ritter**, **Philip Rolin**, **Elaine** and **Larry Shafle**, and **Cheryl** and **Charles Weber**.

INTERVIEWEES

The following former Marx employees provided valuable information on the history of the company:

Richard Carver, **Cal Cook**, **Edmond Galloway**, **C. Edward Hjelte**, **Kenneth L. Johnson**, **William J. Kalsch**, **Edward L. Kelly**, **Leroy "Chippy" Martin**, and **Lawrence Passick**. **Philip Zacks** also provided essential information.

READERS

The readers made helpful suggestions, checked errors and omissions, and provided prices. In addition, they supplied new information. They took their work seriously, some even passionately. Many times, they were obliged to read large sections under pressing deadlines. Their hard work has been of great value and is much appreciated. They include:

Bert Adair, **Gary Anderson**, **David T. Ashworth**, **Mike Dency**, **Georges Denzene**, **Ron Fink**, **Larry Jensen**, **Erick Matzke**, **John Newbraugh**, **Fred J. Pauling**, **Trip Riley**, **John Ritter**, **I. D. Smith**, **Wayne Smith**, **Len Warner**, **Charles Weber**, **Anne D. Williams**, and **Keith Wills**.

PUBLISHER and STAFF

Grateful thanks to my Publisher, **Linda Greenberg**, for her continued commitment, interest, concern, and problem-solving abilities.

I have been in the unusual position of having not one, but two editors, both of them excellent. **Leslie Greenberg** was the first; when **Marcy Damon** took over, she worked on the unfinished chapters and edited the entire book. Marcy also had the challenging task of designing the layout.

Both editors organized, clarified, asked pertinent questions, and did all the work that editors do, and did it very well. In addition, both brought something of their own qualities to their work. As well as being sensitive to my feelings, Leslie was amazingly observant — she missed nothing. Then there were the searching questions, asked in a unique manner. I would know a Leslie Greenberg question anywhere.

Warm and thoughtful, Marcy improved readability without changing meaning. Extremely hard-working, she once gently complained, during a slow period when she had not received work back from me, that she did not have enough to do. As the final Editor, she pulled the entire manuscript together and made it into a unified, polished work.

Other staff at Greenberg Publishing included **Donna Price** who performed many tasks including proofreading, photograph selection, and layout design; **Wendy Burgio** who helped prepare the Index, edit, and make corrections; **Cyndie Bare** who helped with final proofreading as well as organizing Trip Riley's material on trucks into a chart; **Donna Dove** who computerized the charts in the Tank and Buses chapters; **Terri Glaser** who assisted with typing and corrections; and **Virginia McNicholas** and **Pat Shipley** who organized photographs. **Maureen Crum** designed the front cover, **Dallas Mallerich** the back cover. **Mabel Sager** searched through Marx catalog advertisements and other material to be included in the book. **Sam Baum** gave overall support for the book's production.

Robert B. Grubb photographed many of the striking photos, including the cover photo. Other photographers include **Bruce Greenberg**, **Dick Kaufman**, **Cary Myer**, and **George Stern**. **Bill Wantz**, staff photographer, printed the fine quality black and white photographs for the book.

Maxine Pinsky
April 1990

The pre-1950s toys are covered in Volumes I and II. Volume II contains the vehicular toys. Third and fourth volumes are planned for the Marx post-1950s toys.

CHAPTER ORGANIZATION

Considering the millions of toys that Marx produced in all shapes, sizes and types, it is not surprising that grouping the toys into individual chapters is somewhat difficult and, at times, may seem fairly arbitrary. To illustrate, the Mickey Mouse Disney Dipsy car is found in the Eccentric Cars chapter in this volume, although there are other Mickey Mouse toys in the Walt Disney Toys and Honeymoon Express chapters in Volume I. Thus, although a toy may be categorized any number of ways, we have chosen the grouping of any particular toy so that its most important facets are highlighted. The Mickey Mouse Disney Dipsy car, then, has been placed with other Eccentric cars because its comparison to like cars is significant. Likewise, the Reversible Coupe is grouped under the heading, "Reversible Coupes and Similar Cars," rather than with other coupes in the same chapter. This is to emphasize the Reversible Coupe's design and production similarities to vehicles of the same period, rather than with other coupes, which were made over a number of years.

At the beginning of each chapter is an explanation of how the chapter is organized, whether the toys are listed chronologically, alphabetically, by size, or by group types. For example, trucks are divided into numerous groups, including Army trucks, assorted trucks, dump trucks, Mack trucks, and tow trucks. Again, the reason for the various kinds of organizations is to make significant comparisons between the toys.

CATALOGS

Toy catalogs from the 1920s to 1950 were used as reference material for the toys in the book. The catalogs included Sears, Montgomery Ward, Blackwell Wielandy Company (St. Louis, wholesale), Butler Brothers (St. Louis, wholesale), Decatur Hopkins, Edw. K. Tryon (Philadelphia), N. Shure, and Shure Winner. PB84 is the abbreviation for the modern auction catalog published by Sotheby Parke Bernet, New York (June 1977) from which the toys' auction catalog numbers are taken.

HOW TO USE THE BOOK

DETERMINING VALUES

The author has not provided any of the market values shown in this book. She has provided the detailed descriptions and variations of the Marx toys, highlighting their historical significance and technical development. The toy prices were supplied by the Greenberg Publishing Company staff with the assistance of several Marx Toy collectors.

The toy prices shown in this guide may vary somewhat with the prices at auctions and shows for several reasons. Marx toy prices are sometimes influenced by events completely outside of the toy industry. For example, Cinderella toys sold at higher prices during the 50th anniversary of that film. In addition, prices do not necessarily reflect the availability of a particular toy, and this information has been added to the listings when known. Finally, prices fluctuate between regions, such as the East and West coast, with higher prices usually expected in the West. While we have attempted to compile toy prices from several collectors in different regions, buyers should be aware that the prices in this book serve as a guide only. **It is recommended that the novice consult with experienced collectors for large purchases.**

Condition:

Good — scratches, small dents, dirty.

Excellent — minute scratches or nicks, no dents or rust.

NRS — **N**o **R**eported **S**ales; information is insufficient to determine price.

These standards are descriptive of the condition of the finish, and in no way describe the operation of the toy. Prices will be higher for a toy sold in its original box.

From whimsical Eccentric Cars to beautiful Convertible Coupes to sparking Climbing Tanks, Marx vehicles such as these were sold by the millions. Marx toys offer variety, endless variety in color, special effects, and loads of play action. Tanks, for example, spark, climb, turn over, or have Doughboys pop in and out of their hatches. Tractors push and pull, and one model even pulls an airplane.

Louis Marx had a great intuition for "play appeal" which was well developed. Yet, he considered six practical qualities when judging whether to manufacture a toy: Familiarity, Surprise, Skill, Play Value, Comprehensibility, and Sturdiness, according to a 1959 *LIFE* magazine article. [1] In fact, Marx's slogan was "Mechanical Toys That Are Durable and Mechanically Perfect." [2]

While using this book the reader should bear in mind that this Guide covers most but not all Marx toys. Because Louis Marx & Company made a profusion of toys, it is likely that some have inadvertently been omitted. If you have one that has been omitted, please complete the ADDITION/CORRECTION FORM inside the book and return to Greenberg Publishing, so that it will be included in the next edition.

New information about Marx toys is constantly being discovered. Early Louis Marx & Company catalogs are extremely rare. Therefore the catalogs of Montgomery Ward and Sears are important in the research of Marx toys. The Sears catalog is particularly helpful because Sears was one of the largest outlets for Marx toys. None of the toys mentioned in this book are currently available at Sears.

Although helpful references, catalogs are not without their limitations. Catalogs of the same year sometimes differ slightly from city to city, particularly as to price. Sometimes a toy listed in one city's catalog does not appear in another city's. Sometimes a catalog page is marked with the Marx name, although not all of the toys on that page were manufactured by Marx.

Two logos were used by Marx on toys covered in this volume (the 1920s and 1950). The earliest logo, from the 1920s, consists of the letters "MAR" over a large "X" within a circle. The letter "A" is in the middle part of the "X". At the base of the circle, in small letters, is "TOYS". On February 14, 1939 a new logo was published in the *Official Gazette*. It resembles the earlier one, but has the additional words "Made in United States Of America" around the logo's circle. Another circle surrounds the words. This logo was used until the end of the 1950s. In the 1960s the logo changed again.

When they are known, Marx catalog numbers are listed. Collectors have expressed curiosity over the fact that it is possible to have the same catalog number on different toys. Cal

Cook, a former Marx employee explains that, "Sometimes, a long time ago, let's say they used the number 502 in the late 1930s or early 1940s. Now, all of a sudden, it's 1960. Who knows about that — let's give the number to something else."

Yet, Marx did try to differentiate variations, even minor variations, between items whenever possible. If a toy was made for Sears that was slightly different from the regular production toy, that toy could have a different catalog number. As Cal Cook explains, "Let's say the number was 502. It might say 502-S for Sears, but if it was something they wanted specifically for them, it might be 501 or something like that and nobody else was able to buy it." [3] Apparently this happened frequently.

Of all the items described, probably the least familiar to some collectors are prototypes. Marx collectors are fortunate, indeed, that so many Marx prototypes have survived and are being collected today. A prototype, as defined here, is a "one-of-a-kind" item, or one of an extremely small number of items, made by Marx prior to the time when all of the necessary tools, dies, or equipment were available to commence mass production. Frequently, a prototype was made for the purpose of arriving at production and / or marketing decisions. Consequently, a prototype will have one or more of the following characteristics which readily distinguish it from any similar mass-produced item: numbers, letters, or logos will be hand-painted, hand-applied, or will appear as hand-cut decals rather than as if produced by a mass production technique; not ready for operation, or without wiring or complete assembly; and modified or assembled from a previously mass-produced item. [4]

Considering the number of prototypes that Marx made, relatively few were mass-produced. Collectors sometimes shy away from prototypes for a number of reasons. Prototypes, particularly character toys, are expensive. Some appear less attractive: many are hand-painted, frequently with peeling or dull-appearing paint. Parts may be soldered to the prototype from other toys and some parts may be missing. Other times, a prototype is painted with such skill that it takes scrutiny to determine that the toy is hand-painted.

Prototypes are fascinating and collectable for two reasons. First, if the prototype was mass-produced, it represents the brain-storm, germ of creativity or inspiration, if you will, which subsequently became a child's delightful plaything. Second, if the prototype was not produced, for whatever reason, it represents what could have been, and in many cases collectors feel what should have been!

Beautifully designed and vibrantly colored, Marx toys are ingenious playthings. It is no wonder that Marx toys continue to be as popular today as they were over 60 years ago.

---

[1] "Top Toy Maker's Buying Guide," *LIFE*, Novermber 23, 1959, p. 119.
[2] *Playthings* magazine, March 1932, p. 145.

[3] Interview with Cal Cook, October 29, 1983.
[4] Jim Sattler, *Postwar Lionel Guide*, Volume II. (Sykesville, MD: Greenberg Publishing Company, 1988.)

AIRPLANES AND AIR TOYS

Marx airplanes were made in a variety of ways. Some airplanes have comic figures, several perform stunts, others spark, and one even comes with a parachute. Many of the planes are floor toys, while others are attached to and "fly" around towers. Typical of Marx toys, a standard body is used for numerous lithographed airplanes. Other aeronautical toys, such as Zeppelins and airports, were also produced by Marx.

Except where indicated as a pull toy, friction toy, or actually flying, all are tin lithographed windup floor toys. It was customary for children to pretend metal planes could "fly" by maneuvering them in the air with their hands. *The toys are listed in chronological order (except Zeppelins, which are listed by size) within each of the following categories: Civilian Airplanes, Military Airplanes, Air Toys: Airports and Hangars, Rockets, Tower Flyers, and Zeppelins.*

CIVILIAN AIRPLANES

AIRPLANE 1925 and 1926: 10" long x 2-3/4" high, 9-1/4" wingspread. The first of the Marx airplanes, this high-winged monoplane, priced at 43 cents in a 1925 Sears catalog, features an open cockpit, an adjustable rudder, and a turning propeller. It travels straight or in a circle on the floor.

Good   Exc

The 1926 Sears catalog advertises the plane in two sizes. Priced at 69 cents, the larger plane measures 12-1/2" long with a 10" wingspread and is described as "our largest airplane" and able to travel straight or in a circle, with an adjustable rudder and a turning propeller. The smaller 1926 airplane is similar to the 1925 airplane, but it does not have an adjustable rudder. Excellent price includes original box.   125   275

This 12-3/4" "Airways Express Plane" is a three-propeller monoplane. Although made by the Girard Model Works in 1929, it was advertised with Marx toys. Dr. M. Kates Collection. R. Grubb photograph.

Good   Exc

AIRPLANE 1926: 12-3/4" long, 9-3/4" wingspread. Interestingly, this Mail biplane is a Girard plane with a Marx spring-wound motor. (Louis Marx worked for Girard as a salesman before acquiring the company. When Marx first started to manufacture toys in 1921, he had other companies making toys for him.) The biplane, priced at 95 cents in the 1926 Montgomery Ward catalog, is described in the ad as "Length 12-3/4". Wings 9-3/4" x 2-3/4" are ribbed and curved. Red wings, blue tonneau. Man's head, three wheels. Yellow propeller revolves when biplane runs along the floor."

Advertised at 43 cents in the same 1926 Montgomery Ward catalog is a monoplane version of the plane, 9-1/4" long, with 9-7/8" x 2-3/4" wings. This monoplane had been advertised in catalogs at least a year earlier without mention of the Marx name.

From 1926 on, the wings of Marx airplanes have a circle in each corner. By 1928 illustrations in some ads do not show these circles. Excellent price includes original box.

125   275

AIRPLANE 1927: 12" long x 4-1/3" high, 9-7/8" wingspread. Priced at 83 cents in the 1927 Sears catalog, it is described as an almost identical biplane to the 1926 airplane, but it has two propellers. The Girard name and "Mail" are not mentioned, the entire page being under the heading of Marx Toys. The plane also has "an adjustable rudder so plane can run straight or in a circle. Man driver in cockpit. Just see it whiz along floor. 12" long, a 9-7/8" wingspread and 4-1/3" high." Excellent price includes original box.

140   300

Good   Exc

AIRPLANE 1928: This plane is the 1927 airplane with a third propeller and a new name, the "Overseas Biplane." It is advertised next to the monoplane again, which is now offered in two sizes. The larger monoplane is 12-3/4" long x 3-1/4" high with a 10" wingspread, an adjustable rudder, and priced at 83 cents. The smaller plane, at the bargain price of 21 cents, is advertised as "just right for the little tots" at 9" long x 2-3/4" high and a 7" wingspread. No rudder is mentioned. Both monoplanes are described in the 1928 Sears catalog as making a realistic "exhaust" noise.

In 1928 a small monoplane called a Zip Plane, similar to the early 1926 version, was produced. It is enameled in three colors, has a pointed propeller, and a six-cylinder motor, like the other Marx 1928 monoplanes. The airplane is listed for $2.10 a dozen wholesale in a 1928 Butler Brothers catalog. Excellent price includes original box.

110   250

AIRPLANE 1929: 5-1/2" long, 6" wingspread. Little is known about this airplane, but it has a revolving propeller and a friction motor. [1]

NRS

AIRPLANE with PARACHUTE: 1929. 15-3/4" long, 13" wingspread, 2-1/4" wheels. This high-winged monoplane, priced at 98 cents, is described in the 1929 Fall/Winter Sears catalog: "Just wind the strong spring and let plane proceed as propeller revolves. When plane hits stationary object or a wall,

---

[1] *Dictionary of Toys Sold in America*, 1971, Vol. 1, Earnest A. Long, p. 4.

The colorful four-propeller Airmail Biplane, manufactured around 1936, is 13-1/2" long with a 18" wingspread. Dr. M. Kates Collection. R. Grubb photograph.

Good **Exc**

the front bumper releases a spring and the parachute with man hanging from it shoots up out of the plane cockpit and opens on the downward flight. Airplane is made of aluminum and measures 15-3/4" long. Wingspread 13". Plane is mounted on two 2-1/4" diameter wheels." The patent for this toy, #1,845,613, was applied for on March 15, 1929. The patent drawing resembles the produced toy, except the raised cockpit is not illustrated. Excellent price includes original box. **175** **400**

AIRWAYS EXPRESS PLANE: 1929. 12-3/4" long x 13" wide. Although made by the Girard Model Works, this plane appears in catalogs along with Marx Toys. It has a silver fuselage with dark blue lines and "World Tours" behind the lithographed cockpit and door. The wing is somewhat swept back and has the U.S. Army Air Corps insignia of a circle within a star within a larger circle on a red background. "Air Mail" is printed in the circle. Within these words is a smaller circle with "Making Childhood's Hours Happier — Girard Toys". This insignia is repeated on either end of the wing with "Airways Express" between the insignias. The aluminum tail displays a star within a dark blue circle. The yellow propellers have an unpainted circular center area against a black cowling. When the plane is wound, the middle propeller turns which also causes a clanking sound as the plane moves forward. The rudder and rear wheel are joined so that they pivot together and turn the plane in a circle. Excellent price includes original box. **150** **350**

EAGLE AIR SCOUT: 1929. 26" long x 9" high, 26-1/2" wingspread. This silver high-winged monoplane has blue trim and a 9-1/2" revolving propeller with a ratchet noise-maker. The toy is lithographed with eagles, pilots, and passengers. "Eagle Air Scout" is on the fuselage behind the wings. Excellent price includes original box. **150** **350**

PIONEER EXPRESS PLANE: 1929. 24" long, 25-1/2" wingspread. This pull toy is a red and yellow high-winged monoplane with a movable noise-making propeller. Priced at 69 cents in the 1929 Montgomery Ward Fall/Winter catalog, it has American Indian decals on the wings, lithographed passengers in the windows, and "Pioneer Express" on the side of the fuselage. Excellent price includes original box. **200** **450**

SPIRIT of ST. LOUIS: 1929. 9" long, 9-1/4" wingspread. Two different ads for this plane are shown in Earnest A. Long's helpful book, *Dictionary of Toys Sold In America*. In the first ad, the plane is described as "1929 Marx tin 'Spirit of St. Louis' 9" long, 9-1/4" wingspread. Aluminum finish, gold wheels, printing in red. Movable propeller with motor ratchet noisemaker."

The second ad, dated 1930, is essentially the same but now it lists larger measurements at 9-3/8" long with a 12-7/8" wingspread and a six-cylinder radial motor.

Actually, this airplane was made by Girard but various ads state that it has a Marx spring. The plane shown in the illustrations is a high-winged monoplane with "Spirit of St. Louis" written across the wings and "NX211" in each wing corner.

In 1929 and 1930 the Spirit of St. Louis is listed in catalogs for 25 cents, advertised next to the similar U.S. Marines Plane

(see Military Airplanes on page 13). Excellent price includes original box. **125** **275**

AIRPLANE #90: Circa 1930. 5" long. This plane has a blue fuselage, red wings, and wooden wheels. Each wing corner has a white star in a circle with a black center on a blue background. The plane is thought to come in other colors. **30** **70**

LITTLE LINDY AIRPLANE #160: 1930. 5-1/2" long x 2-1/4" wide x 3-1/2" high. This high-winged one-propeller plane has "N.X.60" on the wings and fuselage. A design on the fuselage consists of squares and rectangles. The plane is friction-powered with a movable propeller. Excellent price includes original box. **65** **150**

SPIRIT of AMERICA: 1930. 17" long, 17-1/2" wingspread. This high-winged monoplane has "Spirit of America" on the nose, "No. 60" on the rear of the fuselage, and stars in circles on the wings. This heavy stock (26 gauge) plane is three-color enameled with a movable propeller and a cord bead grip. It sold for $3.95 a dozen wholesale in 1930. Excellent price includes original box. **275** **600**

INTERNATIONAL AIRLINE EXPRESS: 1931. 17-1/2" long, 17-1/2" wingspread. This high-winged three-propeller monoplane has "International Airline Express" across the wings. In the upper corner of the wing is a feather-like design that resembles the edge of a bird's wing. Priced at 48 cents in the 1931 Sears Fall/Winter catalog, the plane is described as "All metal finished in a beautiful cracked silver finish trimmed in contrasting colors. Exceptionally strong in construction." This airplane, actually made by the Girard Model Works, is driven by the "famous Marx spring motor", according to the ad. The plane also comes in a one-propeller version. Excellent price includes original box. **175** **400**

CRASH-PROOF AIRPLANE: 1933. 9-1/2" long, 11-3/4" wingspread. This unique monoplane with a single propeller, priced at 59 cents, is described in the Sears catalog for Fall/Winter 1933:

"Under proper conditions this little ship will fly a surprising distance. Happy landings every time because when crashing or striking an obstruction the wings and the light weight metal under the carriage detach themselves from the aluminum fuselage. Then you have the fun of putting the ship together again for the plane is not harmed by the crash. Equipped with a strong strand gum rubber motor. Plane is 9-1/2" long, has 11-3/4" wingspread yet weighs only one ounce." **80** **175**

AIRMAIL BIPLANE: 1936. 13-1/2" long, 18" wingspread. One of Marx's most colorful toys is the floor toy, the Airmail Biplane. Lithographed in red with yellow, black, and green trim, it has a center door and an open front window similar to the Marx Bombers and Flying Fortress planes, but unlike those toys, the cockpit shows the pilot directly behind the front window. Passengers appear in the seven windows on each side. A yellow "U. S. Mail" is to the rear of the door and the Marx logo is on top of the plane.

Yellow wings are printed in pale green with "U. S. Mail" on one wing and "990-5" on the other. Four red and black

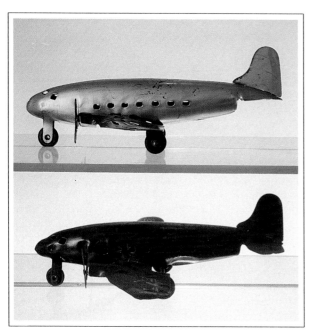

These rather plain DC-3 airplanes, manufactured in the 1930s, measure 7-1/2" long and have a 9-1/2" wingspread. T. Riley Collection. C. Myer photograph.

Good   Exc

motors on the top wing have blue, movable celluloid propellers. The green and yellow tail has "T W A" on each rudder. This plane, which sold originally for 47 cents in 1936, also comes in blue and silver. Excellent price includes original box.

170   375

MAIL PLANE: Circa 1936. 13-1/2" long, 18" wingspread. Made around the same time as the Airmail Biplane is another similar mail plane. This two-motored monoplane is thought to be red, white, yellow, and blue, with markings similar to those on the biplane. (Also see Airplane 1926 on page 10.) Excellent price includes original box.   **170   375**

CHINA CLIPPER: 1938. 13-3/4" long, 18-1/4" wingspread. This passenger plane has four motors, celluloid propellers, and a double rudder. Its shape resembles the Marx bombers which were made in the same size. A 10" China Clipper was also made by the manufacturer Wyandotte.   **80   175**

PIGGY BACK AIRPLANE: 1939. 6-1/2" long, 9" wingspread (larger plane). This unique floor plane consists of a tri-motor biplane with a smaller plane attached to the top — a prediction of things to come. A real airplane of this type was later designed. The smaller all-red 3-1/2" plane is detachable. The larger plane has a red fuselage, silver wings, and a silver rudder. Only the center propeller turns. Both planes have cut-out windows. Some versions of the smaller plane come with a cockpit opening at the front and a tin canopy further back and no windows. These planes are sometimes found with Marx airports. Other versions of the smaller plane come with a cockpit and side window openings but no canopy. Excellent price includes original box.   **70   150**

ROOKIE PILOT: Late 1930s to early 1940s. 7" long, 7" wingspread. This yellow low-winged, one-engine monoplane

Good   Exc

with red and black accents is very similar to the Marx Popeye the Pilot plane (see Volume I). Although the lithography differs, the head of the Rookie Pilot, down to his Adam's apple, is similar to the one used in the Mortimer Snerd eccentric car. The Rookie Pilot wears a blue cap. Large in comparison to the plane, the Pilot's head extends from the cockpit as in the Popeye the Pilot toy. Like one of the variations of the Popeye plane toy, the side of the fuselage is decorated in a stylized bird wing design. The same long, thin metal piece with attached small wheel extends from the tail. The metal piece and wheel create the plane's erratic action. Two larger wheels are under the wings.

In keeping with the plane's erratic action, the wings are lettered "erratically" and read "ROOKIE PILOT" with one "o" in "Rookie" placed right above the other.

The June 1977 PB 84 auction catalog gives this toy the catalog number 77. The toy comes in a plain unillustrated box. Excellent price includes original box.   **200   450**

AUTOGYRO: 1940s. 5-1/2" long. This unusual steel toy, the forerunner of the helicopter, appears in the well-known and beautiful book, *Past Joys*. [2] Ken Botto, the author, states that the toy is not motorized so it does not fly, but "It can BUZZZZ over the backyard patch like some searching mechanical dragonfly." The Autogyro is a low-winged monoplane with a red fuselage, cut-out cabin windows, yellow wings, and a large metal propeller on the top   **80   175**

PASSENGER AIRPLANE: 1940. 21" long, 27" wingspread. Various ads describe this airplane as new in 1940 with a 40-passenger capacity. James Apthorpe states that it has "AA" on the left wing and "NC-2100" on the right wing. It resembles a Douglas DC-4. The silver plane has a door which opens and a wheeled boarding ramp for passengers. In 1942 there was a red version of this plane with the same wing markings, but without the opening door. Similar versions of the plane were made in the 1950s. Excellent price includes original box.

100   250

AIRPLANE 1942: 7" long, 9-1/2" wingspread.
First Version: As described by James Apthorpe, this twin engine airplane has pink wings and landing gear, a cream fuselage, and green tail fin. He remembers receiving a plane like this at Easter in 1942. The airplane also has cut-out windows and, like many Marx airplanes, engine nacelles (which hold the motor) that are formed from part of the wing, rather than being tabbed to it. The plane may have had candy attached to it.   **70   150**

Second Version: This rarer version has one red propeller, red wings, a silver fuselage, and silver tail. A lithographed cockpit with pilots is tabbed to the top of the fuselage. This plane is an adaptation of the stamping of the first version. It has the same wing without the engines and the same fuselage without cut-out windows. The propeller and cowling are fastened to the nose, but the cowling does not fit well. Excellent price includes original box.   **110   250**

---

[2] *Past Joys*, Prism Editors, Chronicle Books, 1978, Ken Botto, p. 95.

Good Exc

AIRPLANE: 6-3/4" long, 9" wingspread. These pressed steel airplanes are similar to the 1942 Airplane, Second Version above. Whether they are actual variations is uncertain.

First Version: This monoplane has one engine, a metal propeller, silver fuselage, red wings, and an open cockpit. Excellent price includes original box.   **80   175**

Second Version: This version has a red fuselage, blue wings, and a separate lithographed tin part that represents a closed cockpit with two figures inside. Excellent price includes original box.   **80   175**

MILITARY AIRPLANES

Louis Marx's experiences in the Army during World War I had a direct influence on his company's design and production of military toys. Many of the military planes bear the insignia of the U. S. Army Air Corps, which became the U. S. Air Force in 1947.

Good Exc

ARMY BOMBER #1120: Circa 1930. 24" long, 25-3/4" wingspread. This biplane pull toy has one revolving propeller which makes "exhaust" noise. No bolts or nuts are required when assembling the wings to the fuselage as they automatically catch when placed in position. The plane has stars in circles on each wing, on the side, and on top of the fuselage, a striped rudder with a star in a circle, and lithographed pilots and cockpit.   **225   475**

ARMY BOMBER #1220: Circa 1930. 24" long, 25-3/4" wingspread. The three propellers of this biplane revolve and produce "exhaust" noise when the plane is pulled. Wings are snapped on without nuts or bolts. On each wing and on top of the fuselage is a star in a circle. Pilots and the cockpit are lithographed.   **225   475**

U. S. MARINES PLANE: 1930. 17-5/8" long, 17-7/8" wingspread. The high-winged monoplane with a single propeller, priced at 48 cents in the 1930 Sears Fall/Winter catalog, is described in the ad: "As propeller revolves, realistic noise is made. Strong Marx spring." The wings read "U. S. Marines" and have a stars-in-circles insignia. The U. S.

Three colorful, little Pursuit Planes with varying lithography, manufactured in the late 1930s, measure about 6-3/4" in length with an 8" wingspread. Dr. M. Kates Collection. R. Grubb photograph.

This Prototype Plane, made March 25, 1939, has a hinged metal wheel which can be pushed up or pulled down. It is possible that the wheel is intended to produce an erratic action. The toy measures 7-1/4" long with a 6-1/2" wingspread. W. Maeder Collection. R. Grubb photograph.

Good   Exc

Marines Plane was advertised with another similar Marx plane, the "Spirit of St. Louis", which came in a different smaller size. Since the "Spirit of St. Louis" was manufactured by the Girard Model Works, but was advertised as having a Marx spring, it is likely that the U. S. Marines plane was also made by Girard.

150   350

ARMY BOMBER: 1935. 25-1/2" long, 25-1/2" wingspread.
First Version: When pulled, this low-winged tri-motor monoplane with three revolving propellers makes a ratchet noise. Markings on the plane include "Army Bomber" on the side of the fuselage, a star-in-a-circle insignia on the top, and "PAE" on the rudder. Crew members are shown in the lithographed cockpit. 250   500

Second Version: This similar one-motor biplane has about the same size wingspread as the first version, but the lithography shows a machine gun and a pilot. The plane has a pyramid-shaped nose, a striped rudder, and wings with stars-in-circles insignia. A variation of this biplane has three motors and a different rudder configuration. 300   400

ARMY BOMBER with BOMBS: 1930s. 12" wingspread. This metal one-propeller plane has a camouflage pattern and lithographed pilots and silver cockpit. The airplane comes with four metal bombs which are released when a lever is pushed. The plane probably came with targets when it was first produced.

In the early 1940s another plane with bombs was sold along with ship targets and a map. The plane has a celluloid propeller. Excellent price includes original box. 75   180

Good   Exc

BOMBER: 14-1/2" wingspread. This four-propeller metal airplane has a red fuselage and yellow wings. The lithographed cockpit with two pilots is a separate piece that is tabbed onto the plane. Each wing has a lever. On the left wing is a decal which appears to read "This Bomber Drops Bombs". The plane does not carry or drop bombs. [3]   75   150

DC-3 AIRPLANE: 1930s. 7-1/2" long, 9-1/2" wingspread. This airplane comes in aluminum with either blue or red wings, or all dark olive drab. The decals on the wings vary; the red-winged version has the most elaborate decal with an outlined design of stars and bars on each wing. The blue-winged version has smaller stars and bars than the red or olive drab versions. Excellent price includes original box. 90   200

PURSUIT PLANES: Late 1930s. 6-3/4" long, 8" wingspread. This toy comes in at least three versions, each with striped wings and one metal propeller. The sides of the fuselage have three bars and "U. S. Army".
First Version: This plane has a cockpit that is tabbed into the top of the fuselage. It is similar to the cockpit on the Flying Fortress and some of the other bombers. It moves and spins around by a windup mechanism under the wing. The wings are lithographed in red, white, and blue, with the U. S. Army Air Corps insignia on either wing and "712" towards the rear. It has a red rudder and balloon wheels that read "Balloon 15 x 9.00". This airplane does not have guns. Excellent price includes original box. 75   200

---

[3] *Collecting Toys*, 5th Edition, by Richard O'Brien. (Books Americana, Florence, Alabama) 1990.

Good Exc

Second Version: Colored like the first version, this plane has a lithographed cockpit and, in addition, two twin red sparking machine guns mounted on the wings. It also comes with red machine guns, lithographed with black and white stripes. The plane goes in a straight line rather than in circles. The black wheels have red hubcaps. Excellent price includes original box.
75   200

Third Version: This plane has a blue fuselage with white and black markings, a lithographed cockpit, and a red rudder. The blue and white tail is lithographed with black markings. The red and yellow wings have two twin sparking machine guns, lithographed in red with black and white stripes, mounted on the top of each wing. The tires are white with blue hubcaps and, like the second version, read "Balloon 15 x 9.00". Excellent price includes original box.
75   200

PROTOTYPE PLANE: 1939.   7-1/4" long, 6-1/2" wingspread. This hand-painted gray metal prototype has a British rondel insignia with a blue circle surrounded by a white and a red circle on the wings. Blue and white stripes are also on the wings, fuselage, and tail. The plane has a movable metal propeller. "41" and the British red, white, and blue stripes are on the rudder. On the side of the fuselage is the Marx logo. Instead of the usual two stylized wings on the edge of the logo, there is only one. The raised and lithographed cockpit resembles the tabbed Marx cockpit in shape. The plane has a sparking mechanism between the cockpit and the nose. Although no machine gun is on this toy, it appears that one would likely have been fitted over the sparker.

The most interesting feature of this prototype is a hinged metal wheel on the middle underside of the plane. It can be

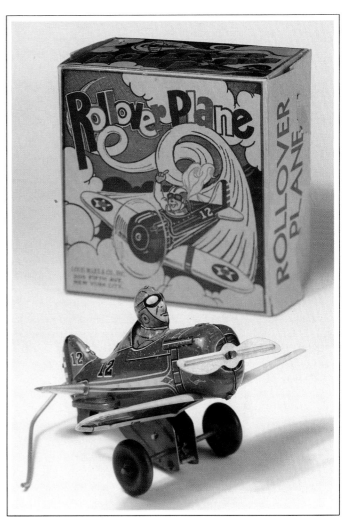

The Rollover Plane, produced circa 1947, measures approximately 4-3/4" in length with a 6" wingspread. Dr. M. Kates Collection. R. Grubb photograph.

Good Exc

pushed up into a recess in the fuselage or pulled down beneath the other wheels of the plane. It may have been used as retractable landing gear or to produce an erratic action since a similar wheel under the tails does just that on the Rookie Pilot and the Popeye planes. The other wheels, two at the front and one at the rear, are wooden. Markings on the underside of the left wing read "Model No. 766 Girard 3-25-39" ("Girard" refers to Marx's Girard branch, not to the Girard Model Works, a company which Louis Marx eventually acquired in the mid-1930s). **NRS**

ARMY AIRPLANE: 1940s, 10" long, 15" wingspread. This is a two-motor bomber, but a shorter size than the bombers described above. Other details about this plane are not known.
NRS

FIGHTER PLANE: Circa 1940s, 5" wingspread. This plane has a stars and bars decal on the wings and fuselage, a short wingspread, two engines, and wooden wheels. **35   80**

AIR SEA POWER BOMBING SET: Early 1940s. 8-1/2" long, 12" wingspread. The convoy bomber airplane in this set

The Looping Plane, manufactured circa 1941, measures approximately 5" in length and 3-1/2" in height. It comes in different versions and runs on the floor, making loops at short intervals. Dr. M. Kates Collection. R. Grubb photograph.

Good   Exc

has a camouflage pattern and a lithographed silver cockpit with pilots. Four bombs drop when a lever is pushed on the side of the plane. The plane comes with an attractively lithographed 42" x 28" target map and four black, white, red, and gray spring-loaded 5-1/2" target ships. The plane is a low-winged monoplane with a celluloid circular propeller. The propeller may also come in tin. The map is lithographed with airports, the sea, roads, and shrubbery. When the plane is held over the targets, the bombs are released, one at a time. When hit, the ships spring into the air. The box reads "Air — Sea Power" and shows airplanes attacking ships. Excellent price includes original box.   **175   400**

SEVERSKY P-35: Early 1940s. 11" long, 16" wingspread. As detailed by James Apthorpe, this is a single-engine airplane with red wings and silver fuselage and tail. The plane has gun fairings used to streamline the aircraft on the nose, but no guns. It also has wire landing gear struts. An earlier version has wire machine guns.

The rudder has the full tent-like appearance common to the P-35. The windows reach far around each side of the cabin, affording good vision for the pilot.   **100   225**

LOOPING PLANE: Circa 1941. 5" long, 7" wingspread. This Looping Plane is the earliest of its type and is very different from the so-called Rollover Plane which followed it. The Looping Plane is an open cockpit, high-winged monoplane with a pilot with the same head that is used in the Marx Jumpin' Jeep.

Good   Exc

It sold for the reasonable price of $3.75 a dozen wholesale in 1941. Ads describe the plane as "Length 5", height 3-1/2". A modern type of stunt plane which moves along the floor and at intervals automatically makes a complete loop .... Furnished in bright copper complete with pilot." The plane in the ad illustration has "Loop-The-Loop" across the wings, "U. S. A.", and the Marx logo.

The Looping Plane also comes in silver or gold with "Looping Plane" and the Marx logo between the two words.

The more common silver version has red and yellow wings with white printing, a red underside, and a blue rudder with red and white stripes. The pilot is dressed in tan and wears a helmet and goggles.

The silver Looping Plane, and possibly the gold one, also come in another version with all-red wings. In addition, the Looping Plane may have military star decals on the wings or a camouflage pattern overall.

In action the plane runs forward, propelled by a clockwork mechanism. The forked flipper underneath may be reversed to make the plane perform back rolls.

The attractive box for the toy shows the plane performing loops. Long before the Marx Looping Plane, there was a German plane made in the late 1920s which had looping action.   **70   150**

This Blue and Silver Bomber, from around 1940, is one of a series of planes with fitted wings and bodies. The plane is 13-1/2" long with an 18" wingspread. Dr. M. Kates Collection. R. Grubb photograph.

The handsome Flying Fortress, manufactured around 1940, is one in a series of planes which are assembled by fastening the wings into slots in the fuselage of the airplane. Others in the series include the 1938 Army Airplane, the Blue and Silver Bomber, the Bomber with Tricycle Landing Gear, the Camouflage Airplane, and the 1951 Army Airplane. Dr. M. Kates Collection. R. Grubb photograph.

ROLLOVER PLANE: Circa 1947. 4-3/4" long, 6" wingspread. This low-winged monoplane has a shorter wingspread than the Looping Plane. The earlier Looping Plane appeared in catalogs up to around 1947, when the Rollover Plane appeared. By 1950, this plane sold for 79 cents.

Its action is to roll over sideways. The plane has a long, bent rod coming from the tail area which changes positions, giving the plane its acrobatic movements. All versions are windups with fixed propellers.

The Rollover Plane is red with black, white, and yellow striping and a "12" directly behind the cockpit and on the rudder. The pilot is lithographed onto the fuselage in one piece and is similar to the drivers in the late Boat-tailed Racers.

The yellow wings have the early insignia of the red circle in a white star within a blue field, indicative of the U. S. Army Air Corps insignia between the two World Wars and in the early part of the Second World War. The silver tail has red outlining. The turnover mechanism protrudes out of the rear of the rudder. The plane has wooden wheels and a metal propeller.

The original box is handsomely lithographed in blue, yellow, and red, but shows the airplane with a blue fuselage and yellow tail and rudder. This color scheme is used on some airplanes.

Good   Exc

The box has multicolored letters with the toy's name, while a swirling design indicates the plane's action.

The red Rollover Plane was also used in the Marx toy called Superman and the Airplane. (See Comic Strip Character Toys in Volume I.) Planes with roll-over action were also made by other manufacturers in countries such as Japan and England.

70   150

The Camouflage Airplane, made in the early 1940s, has a body similar to that of several earlier planes. The bombardier is lithographed horizontally rather than vertically, but without the three bombs on the plane side. The plane is 13-1/2" long with an 18" wingspread. Dr. M. Kates Collection. R. Grubb photograph.

This beautifully lithographed Bomber with Tricycle Landing Gear, made around 1940, is one in a series of planes with similar-shaped bodies but different lithography. The plane is 13-1/2" long with an 18" wingspread. Dr. M. Kates Collection. R. Grubb photograph.

Military Airplane Series with Tabbed Wings / Bodies

Good   Exc

The following six airplanes (Army Airplane 1938, Flying Fortress, Blue and Silver Bomber, Bomber with Tricycle Landing Gear, Camouflage Airplane, and Army Airplane Circa 1951) all have the same basic body shape that was originally used in the mid-1930s (see Mail Plane on page 12). Measuring 13-1/2" long with an 18" wingspread, these planes come from a series in which the plane is assembled by fastening the wings into the body of the airplane. They have either lithographed cockpits or separate tabbed cockpits.

ARMY AIRPLANE: 1938. 13-1/2" long, 18" wingspread. Priced at 49 cents in 1938, this camouflage or Army-colored plane has twin sparking machine guns on each wing, two motors, and a lithographed cockpit. Its lithography is similar to other Marx bombers in the series. The plane may have come in a variation with four motors. **125   250**

FLYING FORTRESS: Circa 1940. 13-1/2" long, 18" wingspread.

First Version: Lithographed primarily in red, silver, and black, this plane has a bombardier's cockpit on the front, just as in a real plane. (Marx, however, put the bombardier in the rear. It must be remembered that these are toys and, as such, are not always realistic.) Below the cockpit are two side turrets containing machine guns. The Marx logo is on top to the front of the fuselage. A turret, lithographed with a pilot and a co-pilot, fits onto the top of the plane. The U. S. Army Air Corps insignia is on the side, behind the center door. Toward the rear of the plane is a lithographed turret with a bombardier on one side and a radio operator on the other. The bombardier is holding the bomb release lever. Beneath this, on each side of the plane, are three bombs. The tail and the double rudder are lithographed in silver and red. The wings are lettered in black "Flying Fortress 2095" on one side and "Army" on the other. The U. S. Army Air Corps insignia is lithographed in black, with the center in black stripes, giving a shaded effect. The two twin sparking machine guns are lithographed in red, black, and white. The four engines are silver with red accents. The white

Good   Exc

balloon wheels with red centers, marked "Balloon 15 x 9.00", were used on other Marx toys such as the Milk Wagon and Horse (see Volume I). Excellent price includes original box.

150   325

Second Version: This version has red celluloid rather than metal propellers. Excellent price includes original box.

150   325

Third Version: A 1984 Phillips Auction catalog describes this version as: "A Marx around 1941 Two Motor Mechanical spring action red and yellow 'Flying Fortress #2095,' an Army bomber with wing sparking machine guns and double disc wheels." Excellent price includes original box.   **150   325**

Fourth Version: There is thought to be another version with a single rudder. Excellent price includes original box.

150   325

BLUE and SILVER BOMBER: Circa 1940. 13-1/2" long, 18" wingspread. This airplane is similar in shape and lithography to the Flying Fortess, but it is blue and silver, rather than red and silver. It has a double rudder and wings which are fitted onto the fuselage. The front top turret with pilots is lithographed, rather than tabbed, onto the fuselage. The bombardier holds a bomb release lever in the bombardier's black cockpit. Two blue engines with black accents are mounted on the wings. The balloon wheels are similar to those of the Flying Fortress, but they have blue, rather than red, centers. This plane does not have guns. Excellent price includes original box.   **150   325**

BOMBER with TRICYCLE LANDING GEAR: Circa 1940. 13-1/2" long, 18" wingspread. This airplane has four motors,

Good   Exc

blue celluloid propellers, and no guns. The lithography of the bomber is similar to that on the Blue and Silver Bomber, but it is copper-colored with black details. The top turret is lithographed. Except for the color, the wing markings are identical to those on the Blue and Silver Bomber. The engines have black and copper cowlings and black propellers. The plane is equipped with tricyle landing gear. The metal balloon tires have no printing. Excellent price includes original box.

200   425

CAMOUFLAGE AIRPLANE: 1942. 13-1/2" long, 18" wingspread. This rust-colored and olive green camouflage plane has a horizontally lithographed bombardier's window and cockpit, rather than vertically lithographed as in the earlier planes in the series. The top turret is inserted into the fuselage and secured with two tabs, like in the Flying Fortress. One gunner is on the side of the turret, in the middle of the fuselage, another is near the rear of the fuselage. The plane has the Marx logo between the top turret and the rear gunner and no bombs on the side of the plane. The camouflaged wings have blue circular decals outlined in red with a white, five-pointed star with a red circle in the center. Each decal is lettered "Made In U. S. of America". The plane has two dark green motors with movable metal propellers and two twin dark green sparking machine guns with black accents. The black balloon wheels have yellow hubcaps and no printing.

First made in 1942, the Camouflage Plane appears to be of a more modern design than the other planes in the series. At this time, khaki or olive green planes were also being made with both two and four motors. The Camouflage Plane also comes with four motors, and with and without the top machine guns. Listed for 65 cents in the 1942 Montgomery Ward Christmas catalog, the plane is shown in the ad as a four-motor

One of several City Airports manufactured in the mid to late 1930s, the base of this version which is 17" long and 11" wide is used on other Marx toys. T. Riley Collection. C. Myer photograph.

Good   Exc

version with disc propellers similar to those of the Marx toy, "Dagwood's Solo Flight". (See Comic Strip Character Toys chapter in Volume I.) The Camouflage Plane may come in a version with a lithographed cockpit. Excellent price includes original box.   **100   225**

ARMY AIRPLANE: Circa 1951. 13-1/2" long, 18" wingspread. The Army Airplane is the last in the series of similarly-shaped bombers, although Marx did make civilian planes with the same design (such as the China Clipper). Priced at 95 cents

Good   Exc

in 1951, it is possible that the plane was produced earlier. It has two motors, no guns, and is lithographed in khaki. "6" appears on the side of the nose and a white star enclosed in a blue circle and red, white, and blue bars is on the side of the fuselage. A white "U. S. Army" and more stars and bars are also on the wings. Directly behind the wings is the gunner and, in the rear, the bombardier. Above the bombardier is the Marx logo. In the 1950s, Marx made a civilian plane of this type which had some plastic parts.

100   200

AIR TOYS

AIRPORTS and HANGARS

Marx made a variety of airports; frequently the base and hangars have the same basic shape, while the colors of the control towers and pylons vary. In at least one variation, Marx used the roof, arm, and two airplanes from the Sky Hawk Tower on top of the airport's control tower. Marx manufactured army as well as civilian airports.

The base of the airport is used for other Marx toys, such as the General Alarm Fire House, the Hollywood Bungalow, and the Greyhound Bus Terminal. The hangars of the airport have the same stamping used in the General Alarm Fire House and the Greyhound Bus Terminal. Hangars with Zeppelins as well as airplanes have been reported.

It has been said that Marx's first airport (which may be the 1929 Municipal Airport Hangar described below) failed because not enough children knew the significance of an airport.[4] However, Marx persevered and children became more knowledgeable. Consequently, Marx airports became successful toys for many years.

MUNICIPAL AIRPORT HANGAR: 1929-35. This rather small hangar sold in 1929 for 50 cents and comes in at least two versions.
First Version: A 1930 Butler Brothers catalog describes the toy as "Hangar with two airplanes, yellow, red and black litho steel hangar, base 5-3/8" by 5-5/8" [actually 5-3/8" wide x 6-1/8" deep]. Airplanes 4-1/2" long, 4-1/2" wingspread, 2-1/2" assorted green and yellow revolving propellers, 1-1/4" red disc wheels. Yellow and orange bodies assorted, aluminum and red trimmed, high speed friction motor that can climb a grade." The planes shown in the ad are high-winged one-propeller monoplanes with "NX60" across their wings. Two gas pumps are also illustrated with the hangar in this ad and in others, but no mention is made of them.

Unlike the catalog description, the hangar has been seen with only one similarly-sized plane but in a different shape, a

low-winged monoplane without markings. This primarily red plane has a celluloid propeller. Whether this particular plane is a replacement or whether the hangar was also produced as described in the catalog is uncertain.

The orange hangar has black accents and orange sides with red stripes. The orange lithographed shingled roof has green-outlined shingles and reads "Municipal Airport Hangar" in a black stand-up sign across the front edge with the Marx logo between "Air" and "Port". There are red windows at the sides of the hangars and two courses of red foundation block. The base of the toy is dark gray with six slots in the front (their use is not known). A Marx service station with a similar shape was made with the same orange and green roof.   **75   175**

Second Version: This version, as described by John Ritter, is similar to the first, but it has a lithographed green roof with black-outlined shingles. In addition to the sign on the front of the roof in the first version is a 4-5/8" x 1-7/8" sign which reads "Municipal Airport" in green on a black background and has an arrow pointing to the right. The hangar has been seen with a 4-1/2" x 4-1/2" high-winged monoplane and 2-3/8" gas pump, both of which are probably original with the hangar. The plane is all silver except for 1-1/4" dark blue disc wheels and has a metal propeller, friction motor, and no markings. The gas

A Municipal Airport Hangar, manufactured in 1929, has a 5-3/8" long x 6-1/8" wide base. Pictured is one of three versions. T. Riley Collection. C. Myer photograph.

---

[4] "Louis Marx: Toy King," *Fortune*, January 1946, p. 124.

The 1928 Lucky Stunt Flyer, measuring 6-1/4" x 4" x 1-1/2", performs somersaults as it flies around the tower. W. Maeder Collection. R. Grubb photograph.

	Good	Exc

pump has a dark blue base with orange and red accents, "Aero Gas" on the top, and "Gasoline" lower down. A similar Marx service station was made with the same "Aero Gas" pump.

75 175

Third Version: This version more closely resembles the catalog ad than the first version. It has sides with two courses of foundation block, yellow-tan sides with orange stripes, orange windows, and a dark blue unpatterned gable roof which, like the first version, slopes to the front end. **75 175**

Marx used the same basic shape of the airplane hangar for another toy, a gas station. However, the front of the gas station, unlike the solid side of the hangar (except for windows), is cut out to accommodate cars and the front of the building roof is supported by pillars at the corners.

BUSY AIRPORT GARAGE: See Automobiles chapter.

CITY AIRPORT: Mid to late 1930s. 17" x 11" base. This well-known City Airport was produced after the Municipal Airport Hangar and comes in several versions. All versions are based on the first one.

First Version: The airport has a large, red steel base with landing strips decorated in a geometric design and outlined in silver. Two battery-powered landing strip lights are on the outer corners of the base. It comes with two or more monoplanes and has two yellow-roofed hangars. On the left hangar is "City Airport" in black, while the right hangar has a black arrow. On the front of each hanger is "Main Street Airport" in

white with a red background. The sides and backs of the hangars, lithographed in green, yellow, white, and black, show pedestrians. Two posters cover the back of the building. The left poster reads "Air Express" and "Sky Queen Sky King"; the right, "Air Mail Plane" and "Sun Racer Sky Chief". A green pylon with a red top is on each hangar roof. One holds a metal windsock, the other holds an American flag made of cloth. Between the two hangars is the control tower. On its red roof are battery-powered landing lights, a beacon, and a hand crank to turn the beacon light housing. Under the beacon is a multicolored brick platform with "Sky Way" and the Marx logo. An on/off switch and room for a "D" cell battery are at the rear of the building. The control tower has yellow walls, red and white lithographed windows, and green balconies. A small lithographed building in red, yellow, and white juts out of the front of the control tower and is lettered "Information and Ticket Office". Excellent price includes original box. **50 125**

Second Version: This airport has red, silver-topped pylons and four small, two-engine silver-toned metal planes with a 2-1/4" wingspread, a windsock, and flag. It is not known whether the planes are original, but the airport may have come with two larger planes. A metal lever in back of the control tower makes a clicking sound when pushed. Excellent price includes original box. **50 125**

Third Version: The silver design on this airport's landing strip makes an approximate "X"-shaped pattern. It also has all-green pylons, a light bulb instead of a rotating beacon, and

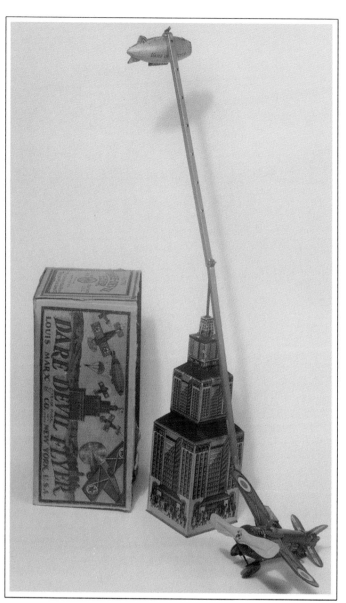

The very attractive Dare Devil Flyer #700, made in 1928, is attached to a 10-1/2" "skyscraper" resembling the Empire State Building. Dr. M. Kates Collection. R. Grubb photograph.

	Good	Exc

two silver-toned, high-winged monoplanes. One plane has a silver-toned, metal propeller, the other a yellow, metal propeller. The 4" planes are larger than those in the second version. There does not appear to be a clicker switch. Excellent price includes original box. **50 125**

Fourth Version: This airport has blue pylons (they also come in blue with silver tops). The control tower has blue balconies, a rotating beacon, and a clicker. Its planes have a 4" wingspread, but they are low-winged monoplanes with double rudders. One plane is silver, the other is red. They are similar to the plane on the Marx Army Train and the planes on the Military Airport (First Version). The landing strip has the same geometric pattern as the first version. Excellent price includes original box. **50 125**

	Good	Exc

Fifth Version: One of the most interesting City Airports, this version has an extra red and white tower with the roof, planes on the base, and planes from the Marx Sky Hawk Flyer on top of the control tower. Unlike the loose planes on the base, the two 4" tower planes with a 3-1/2" wingspread are red with silver trim and blue celluloid propellers. The tower has loudspeakers or sirens lithographed on all of its sides. There are no pylons on this airport to impede the circling planes. Another difference from the other versions is that the platform on top of the central tower roof (now underneath the tower with the planes) is no longer multicolored, but is black and white. Like the fourth version, this airport has blue balconies on the control tower and two similar unattached planes (both red). Catalog illustrations show a third, larger plane as well as the two smaller planes. Unlike the fourth version, the landing strip pattern is an "X". Excellent price includes original box. **80 200**

Sixth Version: This airport has the same red and white tower as the fifth version, but it has no Sky Hawk Flyer roof and attached planes. In place of the planes is a red and gray battery-powered revolving 2-1/4" searchlight which can be tilted in any direction. This airport has a clicker, but no pylons. The airport comes with three loose monoplanes: a larger plane with a wingspread of approximately 7-1/2" and a tail with a conventional single rudder, and two smaller planes with double rudders and a 4" wingspread. All three planes have twin motors. It has an "X"-shaped landing strip. Excellent price includes original box. **80 200**

MILITARY AIRPORTS: Marx manufactured at least two versions of military airports. They have the same basic shape as the City Airports, clickers, and red bases with "X"-shaped silver landing strips. However, the color and the lithography of the hangars and the control towers differ. Some have tin bases with a lip added for strength, while others have pressed steel bases with no lip.

First Version: This airport, lithographed in Army colors, has a clicker and a searchlight with a 1-1/2" reflective lens. (The searchlight, which could be purchased separately, is also used on another Marx toy, the four-unit Military Train.) The platform on which the light sits and the hangar roofs have a camouflage design. The hangar walls show military personnel and lithographed guns on a gray background. The gray control tower walls have dark gray balconies. Underneath the camouflage platform is the red roof of the control tower. A large, silver-barreled cannon at the front of the airport shoots wooden shells. The airport has a thin lightweight red base with lights. A lip has been added to strengthen the base.

The Military Airport comes with three red and olive bomber airplanes which are similar to those included with many of the City Airports and with the Marx Army Train; however, they have raised tin, lithographed cockpits. **80 175**

Second Version: This version has a heavier base but no supporting lip. The control tower roof is dark gray or khaki with only a pole for a windsock or a flag on top. A small building that juts out of the control tower reads "Flight Squadron". A small anti-aircraft gun, similar to one on the Marx Army Train, is in two of the corners. **80 175**

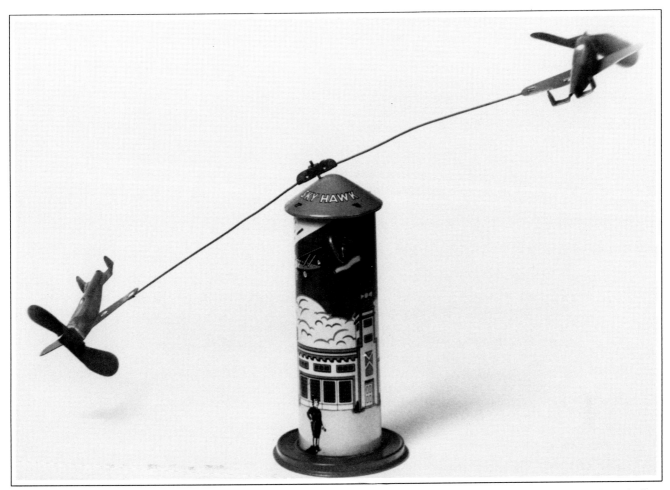

The Sky Hawk Flyer flies for an exceptionally long time. Made in the 1930s, it measures 7-3/4" in height while the bar including the planes measures 19-1/2". W. Maeder Collection. R. Grubb photograph.

Good   Exc

CITY AIRPORT: Circa 1938. This is a new City Airport and very different from the one described on page 21. It is one in a series of toys which include Union Station, the Blue Bird Garage, and a bus terminal. The airport, Union Station, and bus terminal sold together for 89 cents in the 1938 Sears Christmas catalog, but could be bought separately. All of the toys are about 12" long, 6-3/4" wide, and 3-1/4" high. The airport is cut out in front to make two hangars and comes with two small gray planes and a dummy gas pump.

The City Airport is a red, yellow, and white art deco-style building. Various offices are lithographed on the building. The base has arrows enclosed by two black lines pointing left or right. A zigzag pattern is on the left side of the yellow roof, while "City Airport" appears on the right side. To the right of the building is a predominantly blue gas pump. The box for the toy reads "Universal Airport".   **70   150**

HANGAR with ONE PLANE: 1940s. 5-3/4" long x 7" wide x 3" high. This small hangar is brightly lithographed mostly in red with yellow, blue, and white. It has yellow hangar sides with blue windows and an unlithographed yellow hangar back wall. On the illustrated hangar sides in the foreground, a lithographed, low-winged monoplane is being worked on by workmen, while another plane can be glimpsed in the background. The other side of the hangar shows a similar scene.

Good   Exc

The blue hangar base has a yellow bottom and back. Except for the Marx logo towards the rear of the roof, no wording is on the hangar. The red roof slopes slightly and has lithographed blue windows, lights, and a loudspeaker. A thin and a thick white band stretch across the roof top.

Accompanying the hangar is a 5" long high-winged monoplane with a 6" wingspread, wooden wheels, and a metal propeller. The plane has a blue fuselage and red wings which are decorated with white stars in blue circles and the Marx logo. The plane also comes with a yellow fuselage. Excellent price includes original box.   **100   250**

ROCKETS

Marx produced rockets that are among its most desirable and creative toys. For information about the Buck Rogers Rocket Ship, the Buck Rogers Police Patrol, and the Flash Gordon Rocket Fighter, see the Comic Strip Character Toys chapter in Volume I. (The Tom Corbett Space Ship will be covered in a future volume.) Marx also manufactured the "Rocket Racer" car that resembles a rocket (see Automobiles chapter).

Good Exc

MOON-RIDER SPACE SHIP: This rocket is not as well known as other Marx rockets, probably because it was produced in England. Authorities disagree on the date of the ship's manufacture, with estimates ranging from the 1930s to the 1950s. But, physically, the ship most resembles the Tom Corbett Space Ship, manufactured around 1952. Both have similar bubbles on their tops, and neither has the large wing-like fins of the other ships.

What makes this rocket so charming and unique is its unsophisticated lithographed subject matter. A stewardess, for example, serves passengers, who are comfortably seated as if in an airliner. The rocket sides read "745" and "Moon-Rider Space Ship" and the ship's nose shows two uniformed astronauts. Like the other rockets, the Moon-Rider is 12" long and shoots sparks as it moves across the floor.[5]   **100   225**

TOWER FLYERS

These fun toys consist basically of a control tower with a pivoting rod or beam attached to its top, and an airplane and Zeppelin, or two airplanes, suspended at each end of the rod. The flyers work in two different ways. In one method, the motor is located in the tower, while in the other method, it is inside the fuselage. The flyers are balanced by a weighted Zeppelin, or in some cases, by an actual weight. Marx made these toys in a series of interesting versions.

TOWER FLYERS: 1926. The earliest date found for these toys is 1926 when catalog illustrations show two different versions. In one version, on a globe-topped tower lithographed with a flying airplane, the rod suspended from the globe has an airplane on one end and a Zeppelin on the other. In the second version, the Zeppelin is replaced by a weight. Although very different, both versions each sold for 89 cents. A 1926 Fall/Winter Montgomery Ward catalog describes the toy: "Wind up the guaranteed unbreakable spring and the airplane taxis a short distance, lifts and swings around and around. When running down it settles gradually, taxis along and stops. Made of metal, lithographed in colors. Tower 8" high. Length of balance arm 24". Fitted with Marx's guaranteed spring."

A year earlier in 1925, the German manufacturer Bing sold a similar toy, but the tower was made of scaffolding with a house on top instead of a globe. It is possible, indeed likely, that Marx was influenced by this toy.   **125   300**

SKY FLYER: 1927.
First Version: Advertised most often, this flyer has a 8-1/2" high tower, lithographed in a red brick pattern with soldiers near an arched entrance and a cannon, a biplane about 7" in length, and a weighted 4-1/2" Zeppelin suspended from a 24" beam. The Zeppelin is red, yellow, white, and black with "Sky Flyer" in red and has a movable red celluloid propeller. Porthole windows and a gondola provide a lot of detail, even in this

The Cross Country Flyer, produced in 1929, measures about 19" high. It is the only one of the flyers with a hangar. The Zeppelin and airplane can be detached and stored in the hangar. Crossbar shown may be a replacement part. W. Maeder Collection. R. Grubb photograph.

Good Exc

small-sized toy. The colors of the biplane are not known. The toy sold originally for 89 cents.

The patent for this flyer, #1,853,567 filed December 23, 1926, resembles the actual toy except that the drawing shows two open cockpit monoplanes with pilots instead of a biplane and a Zeppelin. Excellent price includes original box.

175   400

Second Version: The illustration of this version shows a monoplane, instead of a biplane, and a Zeppelin. The brick building has the arched entrance like the first version, but no soldiers and cannon. It is described as having a "10" tower representing a lighthouse in red, white, and blue enameled finishes, 24" metal crossbeam with 6" red, yellow and blue enameled airplane on one end and a 4-1/2" dirigible in gilt, yellow and red on the other."

In the 1930s Marx sold a similar tower. Other manufacturers also made similar brick tower-design airplane toys. Excellent price includes original box.   **175   400**

DARE DEVIL FLYER #700: 1928. One of the most attractive of the flyers, the Dare Devil Flyer, priced at 98 cents in the 1928 Montgomery Ward Fall/Winter catalog, is described: "Plane rises from the ground. Like a wild man the pilot drives

---

[5] A photograph of the Moon-Rider can be seen in David Presland's, *The Art of the Tin Toy* (New York: Crown Publishers, Inc., 1976).

The Prototype Bombing toy measures 8-3/4" in height with a 12" diameter base. Markings on the base indicate it was made on "12-26-40". When wound, the top of the tower with the hollow tube revolves. W. Maeder Collection. R. Grubb photograph.

at full speed through dangerous loops. Zeppelin-shaped weight to balance. Skyscraper 10-1/2" by 3-1/2". Airplane 6-3/4" by 6-3/4"."

The control tower is a multicolored lithographed building which resembles the Empire State Building. Although the Empire State Building in New York City was built during 1930 to 1931, plans for it could have been published much earlier. Whether the Dare Devil Flyer is supposed to be this building is not known for sure. The control tower is built in four

Good   Exc

block-like shapes which decrease in size up from the base where people are shown walking around the building.

As described by Dr. Malcolm Kates, the tomato-red high-winged monoplane with green edgings and markings has a central door and shows passengers looking out of several windows. The two-dimensional flat pilot is mounted on top of the plane. The green, yellow, and red tail and rudder has the Marx logo on each rudder. The plane has a movable propeller and flies under its own power. There is a red "Dare Devil Flyer" on the silver dirigible and red markings on the gondola.

The flyer has a bent crossarm, but it may have been made with a straight arm, since photos of this toy with straight arms and a biplane have been seen. Whether the toy came this way originally or the parts were replaced is not known.

The patent for the Dare Devil Flyer, #1,804,737 filed September 17, 1928, basically resembles the actual toy. The patent was submitted by Samuel Berger, the head of Unique Art. Price for toy in Excellent condition without box is $450. Excellent price includes original box.   **200   650**

LUCKY STUNT FLYER: 1928. This Lucky Stunt Flyer differs in size and appearance from the earlier flyers. An ad of the time describes the toy as: "New! Stunt Flyer 6-1/4" x 4" x 1-1/2" litho base, a 2-1/2" tower airship attached, fast revolving airship makes complete somersault." The toy sold for $2.15 a dozen wholesale. Although the ad text mentions an airship, the illustration shows an airplane. Other ads also show the airplane.

Unlike earlier flyers, the red tower in the Lucky Stunt Flyer is situated at the side of a rectangular rather than circular base. The top of the base is lithographed with a scene of parked cars while people wend their way up to see the flyer. "Lucky Stunt Flyer Louis Marx & Co. New York U. S. A" is on the side of the base in red. A red monoplane in the sky is

The New Sky Bird Flyer, manufactured in 1947 and probably one of the latest flyers, has a 24" crossbar with an airplane attached at each end. T. Riley Collection. C. Myer photograph.

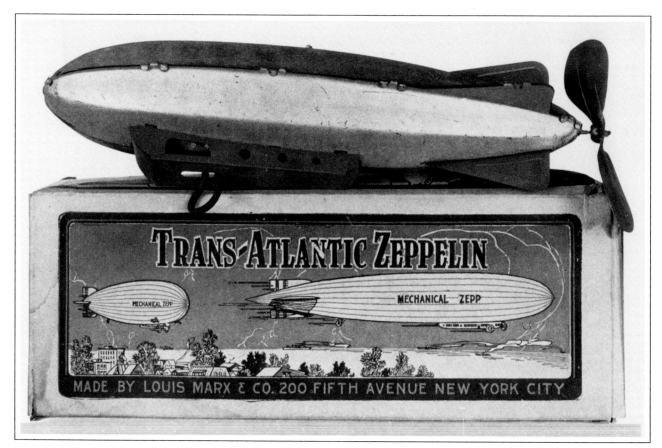

The 10" Trans-Atlantic Zeppelin, manufactured around 1930, has either a striped or a plain rudder. C. Holley Collection.
B. Greenberg photograph.

	Good	Exc

depicted while two ships float in the water. At one side are skyscrapers and the Statue of Liberty, while the Eiffel Tower is shown on the other. The lithography is blue-green, red, yellow, white, and salmon.

The yellow, red, and green monoplane has a fixed propeller and two stars in circles on each wing. Red and green stripes edge the fuselage, rudder, and wings. When the key under the base is wound, the plane performs somersaults as it flies around the tower. Excellent price includes original box.

200   **450**

CROSS COUNTRY FLYER: 1929. 19" high. This handsome flyer, which sold for $1.00 in 1929, consists of a tower, airplane, and Zeppelin. What makes this toy different from previous flyers, however, is the addition of a hangar at the base of the tower where the Zeppelin and airplane can be disconnected and stored. While these detachable toys are an extra plus for children and collectors alike, their detachability contributes many times to the toys being lost and incomplete.

This large toy measures approximately 19" high, the hangar 6-1/2" square, and the arm 38" long. The 4-1/2" weighted Zeppelin is the same one used in the Sky Flyer, but it reads "Cross Country Flyer". It has a movable celluloid propeller.

The good-looking biplane is approximately 6" in length with a 7" wingspread. It is similar in shape, color, and markings to the monoplane in the Dare Devil Flyer, except that the Cross Country Flyer has a silver fuselage and no windows. The

	Good	Exc

airplane operates on its own power when a key in the rear of the tail is wound. The metal propeller revolves and the plane and Zeppelin fly around the tower.

The yellow tower has lithographed black scaffolding and sits on a dark orange hangar with "Airmail Hangar" in black with two arrows on each side of the name and "41" in back of the hangar. The hangar, lithographed with four windows each on three sides, opens up in the front for storing the detachable pieces. When the front doors are closed, the lithography shows one man holding the hangar door while another man moves an airplane.

The entire toy gives an appearance of sturdiness which is enhanced by the addition of the hangar. Marx may have been trying to compete with such manufacturers as Bing by making a stronger toy. (In 1925 Bing made a similar flyer toy with actual, as opposed to lithographed, scaffolding, but no hangar.) Excellent price includes original box.

300   **700**

POPEYE FLYER: 1936. The Popeye Flyer is the only comic character flyer that Marx made.

First Version: In this red, white, blue, yellow, and black flyer, Popeye and Olive Oyl each fly airplanes. The toy, listed for $8.00 a dozen wholesale in the 1936 Blackwell Wielandy catalog, is described as "Measuring 7-3/4" high to top of tower, length of cross-bar with two planes 17", attractively lithographed, whirling celluloid propellers, has a very strong motor."

Good Exc

The Popeye figures waving from the airplane and the base are the same ones used on the Honeymoon-type Popeye Express toy (see Volume I) made at the same time. The base shows Olive Oyl in a field and has many illustrations of Popeye's head, both with and without his sailor's cap, that alternate with stylized anchors on the edge. The red airplanes have blue propellers. On the control tower is the same lithography used on the Sky Hawk Flyer (see below). On the top of the tower is "Popeye Flyer", but the top may also have been made with "Sky Hawk", like in the Sky Hawk Flyer. This version may have come with a smaller base. Excellent price includes original box.   **450   950**

Second Version: This red, yellow, green, blue, and white version has characters associated with Popeye, such as Wimpy and Swee' Pea (sic) lithographed on the tower, but Popeye and Olive Oyl are not in the airplanes. It has a small un-lithographed base and blue planes with silver trim. Although the Popeye Flyer and the Sky Hawk planes both have turning celluloid propellers, the Popeye Flyer planes have a cockpit canopy while the Sky Hawk planes have an indentation. Catalogs illustrate the flyer with characters associated with Popeye lithographed on the control tower, Popeye and Olive Oyl in the airplanes, and a wide base, but examples of this version have not yet been reported. Excellent price includes original box.   **475   1000**

SKY HAWK FLYER: 1930s. Like the Popeye Flyer, the Sky Hawk Flyer has similar lithography on its tower, though without any reference to Popeye. The Sky Hawk measures 7-3/4" high and the bar including the two planes measures 19-1/2". Both of these planes are red low-winged monoplanes, with silver accents and movable green or red celluloid propellers.

The tower is lithographed in red, white, blue, yellow, and black and shows an airport building with a searchlight and windsock at the top. A plane flies overhead, while in front of the building stand three uniformed men, two holding flags. The third man is most probably a pilot since he wears a helmet and goggles. "18" and an arrow, both in red, are on a pillar in front of the building. It has a blue base and a red roof with the Marx logo and "Sky Hawk".

What makes this flyer stand out is the unusual length of time the planes fly after the key in the tower side is wound. (One plane has been timed as flying over six minutes.)

The toy's box is unillustrated and simply marked "Tower Aeroplane". Excellent price includes original box. (Price for toy in Excellent condition without box is $200.)   **100   300**

SKY FLYER: 1937. 9" high tower, 23" long crossbar, 4-1/2" long dirigible, 7" plane wingspread.

This Sky Flyer was the first new Sky Flyer to appear in catalog pages since 1927. Listed at 97 cents in the 1937 Sears Christmas catalog, the flyer is actually very similar to the 1927 Sky Flyer, second version (see page 24). As in the 1927 Sky Flyer, the high-winged monoplane and Zeppelin revolve around a lighthouse, but a 1938 Sears Christmas catalog states that the detachable plane also runs on the floor.   **110   250**

Good Exc

PROTOTYPE BOMBING AIRPLANE TOY: 1941. The patent for this toy, #2,298,951, was filed on April 4, 1941. Marx employee, Richard Carver, who worked on the patent, explains that:

"This was originally a tower airplane, then just a tower with a windup motor, a wire going across and a plane. It was a bombing version, different from some other tower airplanes in that it had a bigger base. The airplane was on a hollow steel tube and you loaded BB shot into the airplane. I think we had a lever some place which would trip the airplane. Each time the airplane was tripped, it dropped one BB down on the base, on the target."

The prototype seen has a large base which measures approximately 12" in diameter, bigger than the Honeymoon Express' 9-1/2" base, while the tower measures 8-3/4" high. Unlike the patent drawing, the prototype does not have a plane attached to the hollow steel tube. Either the plane was lost from this prototype or one was planned to be added later.

The hand-painted illustrations on the prototype are peeling somewhat but there is enough paint left to see that the design is very colorful and interesting. The scene on the base consists of different numbered targets, such as an anti-aircraft gun, a railroad junction, a bridge, and gun factories. The building also has numbered targets. The tower sits on top of a platform labeled "Munitions Plant". Levers on this building are marked "Bomb Release" and "Stop and Go". The platform, in turn, sits on the base, which is marked "Erie X-13? (third number either 4 or 6), 12-26-40 RE 1-21-41". When a key on the building roof is turned, the top of the tower with the hollow steel tube revolves. The tower top is labeled "Sky Raider". It is not known if this toy was ever produced, but such a quality toy would seem to have merited production.   **NRS**

NEW SKY BIRD FLYER: 1947. This is one of the most popular of the flyers. It sold originally for $1.89. As described by Dr. Malcom Kates, the toy consists of two planes on either end of a 24" blue crossbar which fly around the 9-1/2" high tower. One of the planes has a motor, while the other acts as a balance.

The control tower is lithographed in yellow, red, blue, white, and black with "Control Tower" in red above a pair of blue Air Force insignia wings. The tower shows people entering a door with personnel around the base of the control tower and people in the top of the tower directing traffic and taking radio messages. Searchlights are pictured around the middle of the tower. The base reads "Sky Bird Flyer" in yellow.

Both planes are basically the same and are lithographed in yellow with red accents, and "Sky Bird Flyer" above the windows. "39" is on the front of the fuselages. On one plane, the silver wings are printed in dark red with a circle in a star within a circle insignia and "712". The same pattern is repeated on the other plane, but it has blue and white wings with a blue center circle and white five-pointed star on a red, larger circle background insignia.

The original box is beautifully lithographed in blue, red, yellow, and shades of green showing a dirigible lettered "Rocket Liner" and an airplane circling around a control tower. The artwork is in art deco style. The top of the box also shows the

Good   Exc

plane and dirigible circling the control tower. The side of the box says "New Sky Bird Flyer", but "New" is omitted from the title on the box front. Excellent price includes original box.

125   450

ZEPPELINS

Marx Zeppelins are not very well known to collectors. Most Zeppelins were manufactured around 1930 and have little lithography. Usually found in an aluminum finish or painted silver, the Marx Zeppelins range from 6" to 28" in length. Small Zeppelins are used in many of the Marx flyer toys and in the Coast Defense toy (see Volume 1). Zeppelins come as pull toys, friction toys, or windups. The location of wheels varies, but normally the flying Zeppelins do not have wheels. Zeppelins on cords have spring-wound motors so that they can "fly" in circles. *The following Zeppelins are listed by size.*

6" ZEPPELIN: This steel friction pull toy has two big metal wheels in front, one small metal wheel in rear. It has stabilizers but no rudder, is marked "Zepp" on the side, and has a movable propeller on the gondola front. Another version comes in a set with four other toys: an airplane, a bus, a racer, and a tank. It has stabilizers, but no propeller.   **80   175**

10" TRANS-ATLANTIC ZEPPELIN: Circa 1930. This windup model has a key protruding from the gondola. It comes either with a striped or a plain rudder, and with two stars in blue circles on top of the fuselage. The toy's box is beautifully illustrated and shows two Zeppelins marked "Mechanical Zepp" floating in the sky above buildings and shrubbery. The striped-rudder Zeppelin, and perhaps the plain Zeppelin, is marked "Trans-Atlantic". The Trans-Atlantic also comes as a 9-1/2" floor toy, and possibly in a larger size, with two large front wheels and one small back wheel. It has "Trans-Atlantic" on the side, two stars in circles on the body, and a striped rudder. Excellent price includes original box.   **175   400**

9" and 17" FLYING ZEPPELINS: 1930. Similar to the Trans-Atlantic Zeppelin, this toy first appeared in advertisements in 1930. In a later 1931 ad, the Zeppelin has no wording and is referred to as a "Flying Zeppelin" with a "strong cord, flys (sic) in circles when suspended in air." The smaller 9" version sold for $1.95 a dozen wholesale; the larger 17" version sold for $3.75 a dozen wholesale. Excellent price includes original box.

	Good	Exc
9" Zeppelin:	175	400
17" Zeppelin:	300	650

9-1/2" and 16-1/2" FLOOR ZEPPELINS: 1931. Advertised with the Flying Zeppelin in a 1931 Butler Brothers catalog is a floor Zeppelin with a small revolving propeller and smaller disc wheels. This toy has stabilizers, a rounded rudder, and a third wheel near the tail to give extra balance. The smaller 9-1/2" version sold for $1.85 a dozen wholesale; the larger 16-1/2" version for $3.75 a dozen wholesale. Excellent price includes original box.

	Good	Exc
9-1/2" Zeppelin:	175	400
16-1/2" Zeppelin:	300	650

Good   Exc

10" FLYING ZEPPELIN: This Zeppelin has a large silver propeller at the front, two smaller blue propellers on the sides of the fuselage, and a red gondola. The rudder of this Zeppelin is more curved than that of the Trans-Atlantic Zeppelin, the key protrudes from the rear, and there is an embossed line on both the propeller and rudder. The toy comes with directions in a plain box marked "Zeppelin". The Zeppelin is held by a string and will "fly" in a circle. When the key is wound, the propeller turns for an extended period of time. Excellent price includes original box.   **275   500**

17" ZEPPELIN: 1930. Priced at 49 cents in 1930, this Zeppelin is unlike the Zeppelins described above. When hung up or held by its string, this Zeppelin flies in circles. The key is located between the gondola and the tail. Behind the slightly curved rudder is a movable propeller. Excellent price includes original box.   **300   650**

28" ZEPPELIN (First, Mammoth): Circa 1930. As shown in the *Marx Toy Collector Newsletter,* [6] this pull toy has "Mammoth Zeppelin" on the side with the Marx logo. The toy has stabilizers and a rudder, but it does not appear to have a propeller. The front wheels are located near the back of the gondola while the back wheel is close to the rudder. Stars in circles appear on the top of the fuselage.   **350   750**

28" ZEPPELIN (Second): Although similar to the Mammoth Zeppelin, this toy has large back wheels, one wheel closer to the front of the gondola, stars in circles on top of the Zeppelin fuselage, and no name on its side. There are stabilizers, but no rudders for some reason. The toy makes a ratchet noise when moved. The fuselage has more ridges than most of the Zeppelins.   **300   700**

28" ZEPPELIN (Third): In this friction Zeppelin, the position of the wheels is the opposite of the Second 28" Zeppelin with two large wheels near the gondola and one small support wheel in the back. The Zeppelin has stars in circles on the top of the fuselage, stabilizers, and a rudder. This Zeppelin may come in a pull toy version and in a version without the stabilizers.   **300   700**

28" ZEPPELIN (Fourth): 1929. This Zeppelin, which sold for $1.00 in 1929, is described in an ad as "All metal, lithographed silver and bright red. Two gondolas on sides and propeller that is operated through connection with the three 3-1/2" steel wheels. Famous Marx construction. No spring motor, but loop in front for attaching string and pulling." The wheels are near the rear of the gondola, and the rudder has curved edges. A small support wheel is in an unusual location near the rear tip of the fuselage behind the rudder.   **300   750**

28" ZEPPELIN (Fifth): Little is known about this Zeppelin. It is believed to be a floor toy called "Akron".   **300   700**

---

[6] *Marx Toy Collector Newsletter*, Vol. 3, No. 2, p. 2.

AUTOMOBILES

Automobiles are among the most popular of all Marx toys. Made in a range of sizes and shapes, they frequently spark and have sirens. *All of the automobiles are lithographed tin windups unless otherwise specified.*

Due to the complexity of material in this chapter, items are organized alphabetically under the following groupings: ambulances; assorted cars; coupes; fire chief cars; public service vehicles and similar cars; racers — miniature and large; reversible coupe and similar cars; special coupes, racers, and roadsters; station wagons; and automobile-related toys — buildings and track, highways, and speedways.

AMBULANCES

ARMY AMBULANCE: Late 1930s. 13-1/2" long x 5" wide x 5" high. This ambulance has a siren, a brake for stopping the car in the middle of a run, an olive green body with white and red stripes, and Red Cross insignia on the sides and roof of the

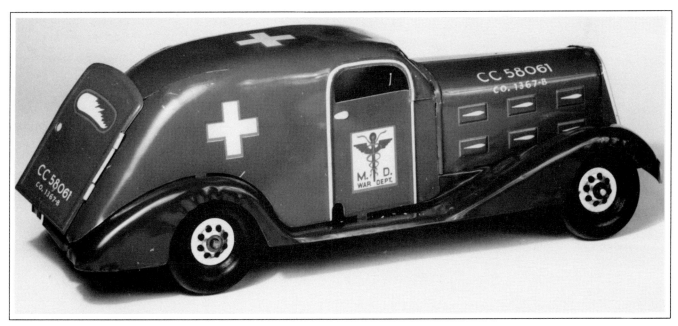

13-1/2" Army Ambulance was manufactured in the late 1930s. It has a brake, siren, and opening rear door. Dr. M. Kates Collection. R. Grubb photograph.

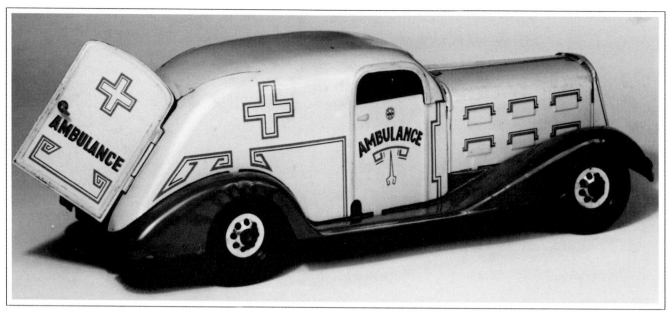

The Civilian Ambulance has a similar body, but is lithographed and colored differently from the Army Ambulance. Dr. M. Kates Collection. R. Grubb photograph.

The 7" Bouncing Benny Car was manufactured in 1939. The upper and lower sides of the toy are the same. The metal body cannot touch the floor since its over-sized rubber wheels absorb the impact first. Dr. M. Kates Collection. R. Grubb photograph.

The Careful Johnnie (right) and Dottie the Driver cars were manufactured in the 1950s and each measure 6-1/2" long. It was claimed that these cars would not run over a table edge. W. Maeder Collection. R. Grubb photograph.

Good   Exc

body. "CC 58061 Co. 1367-B" is on the side of the hood with a design made up of six rectangles. The physicians' shield and "M. D. War Department" are on the side door. "CC 58061 Co. 1367-B" is on the opening back door with a red and white rectangle above it. The front grille is lithographed in olive, green and white, while the front bumper is unpainted, stamped metal. There is no rear bumper. The wheels are black with silver centers.   **200   450**

CIVILIAN AMBULANCE: 1937. 13-1/2" long x 5" high x 5" wide. This ambulance has a brake, a siren, and a lithographed off-white body with red and black stripes. On the side and rear doors are the Red Cross insignia and "Ambulance". The latter is in red with black accents and is below the Marx logo on the side door. The front grille is lithographed in off-white with black trim. Although this ambulance has red fenders, other versions have white fenders. An art deco design appears on the rear fender.

This ambulance has different lithography and colors than the Army Ambulance, but is similar in all other ways. It sold for $1.00 when it was new in 1937. The ambulance is also similar to the Marx G-Man Pursuit Car and other Public Service Vehicles (see page 39), but has a flatter roof.

200   450

ASSORTED CARS

BOUNCING BENNY CAR: 1939. 7" long. The most striking aspect of this pull toy is the large rubber wheels measuring approximately 2-1/2" in diameter, which dwarf the racing-style car. Since rubber has the unfortunate tendency to harden with age, it is very difficult, perhaps impossible, to find the Bouncing Benny with the wheels in their original soft rubber. An interesting feature of the toy is that both the upper and lower sides of the body are the same. The driver is made in two halves and is identical on both. The metal body of the car cannot be dropped on the floor because of the over-sized wheels which absorb the impact before the body does. The body of the toy is primarily red with yellow and black outlining, and "Bouncing Benny The Safety Car" and the Marx logo in front of the open cockpit. A large "1" and "Made in U. S. A." in tiny letters are behind the driver. The sides of the car are lithographed with simulated exhausts. The small driver is a yellow figure without any lithographed details. The car makes a clicking sound when moved and comes with a beaded pull cord.

The original box is lithographed in orange, black, and white; shows a child pulling, pushing, and dropping the Bouncing Benny toy; and reads "The New Safety Car / The Car With Nine Lives, Louis Marx & Co., 200 Fifth Ave., N. Y. C. / U. S. A." "The New Safety Car / The Car With The Sponge Rubber Balloon Wheels / It Will Bounce Around Like A Rubber

Good **Exc**

Ball And Will Not Scratch Or Mar Furniture Or Floors. The Driver Is Always Upright When The Four Wheels Are On The Floor" is on the side of the box and "One Of The Many Marx Toys. Have You All Of Them?" is on the end. This car sold originally for 53 cents.

The patent for the toy is #2,064,309, filed February 1936. The patent drawing resembles the actual toy except the drawing shows a flat radiator (the toy has a round radiator) and no markings. Excellent price includes original box. (Price for toy in Excellent Condition without box is $475.) **225** **600**

Prototype: The larger 8-1/4" prototype is made of plastic, but the yellow body is designed in the same way and has the same over-sized rubber wheels, a large hand-painted "5" on the hood, and an external turbo on each side. The driver, who is all red and wearing goggles, is molded as part of the car. Hand-painted prototype markings on the car rear are "3215 Erie 8/18/50". This prototype was not produced. **NRS**

CAMERA CAR: 1939. 9-1/2" long. This intriguing toy, which sold for 25 cents, consists of a newsreel camera attached to the roof of a heavy gauge steel car. The camera makes a clicking noise when cranked. The car has "Pathé News" on the door and a one-piece tin grille with dummy headlights. The black- and white-lithographed camera has "Pathé" on one side with the Marx logo below. On the other side, "Pathé" is repeated with "Marx" in small letters above. The camera tripod is red.

Since the camera is detachable from the car, many collectors have the camera without the car. Occasionally, the camera turns up at toy shows, the car much less frequently. At Lloyd Ralston's November 1986 auction, this toy in complete condition sold for $1,300. **700** **1700**

CANNON BALL KELLER: See Roadster and Cannon Ball Keller on page 35.

CAREFUL JOHNNIE and DOTTIE the DRIVER: 1950s. 6-1/2" long x 4-1/4" high. Although the names are not similar, the two toys are a matching pair (and originally could be bought separately). The identical red and yellow cars have black and white stripes, a black- and white-checked pattern door on each side, and a small Marx logo in front of each door on the left side. The grille and headlights are lithographed and the license number for both cars is "520". The cars travel in a circular pattern. Like the Mickey the Driver and Donald the Driver cars (see Volume I), both cars have the under-carriage lithographed onto the bottom of the cars.

The Johnnie and Dottie figures are plastic and are identical to those used in the Dan and Dora eccentric cars (see the Eccentric Cars chapter). The heads of the figures are mounted on springs and shake as the cars move. The little boy is dressed in a red sweater and cap. The little girl wears a blue and white dress with a white collar. She has reddish-brown hair with two pigtails. It is likely that her hair may have come in other shades, such as a darker brown, as it did with the figure in the Dora Eccentric car.

The art style on the red, white, and blue boxes for both toys is similar, although small details differ in the illustrations. The front view of Johnnie's box shows Johnnie driving, with both hands gripping the steering wheel, a puff of steam or smoke at the back of the car, while in the distance are silhouetted trees and a house. Lettering includes "Careful Johnnie", "Watch Him Drive", "His Head Moves", and "Powerful Spring Motor" plus the Marx logo along with an abbreviated version of the Marx slogan "One of the Many Marx Toys". (Usually the slogan has the added sentence, "Have You All of Them?".)

The other side of the box reads "Careful Johnnie", "He Is a Careful Driver", "Watch His Head Move", "He Won't Run Over a Table Edge", along with the Marx logo. The illustration for this side of the box shows a little boy watching the car as it performs on a table. Actually, cars with this type of action such as the Tricky Taxi (see page 36) and the Mickey the Driver car

11" Convertible was manufactured in the 1930s to 1940. Car also came in a nickel-plated version. C. and C. Weber Collection.

Good   Exc

(see Walt Disney Toys chapter in Volume I) have to be watched since they do occasionally run off a table's edge.

The illustration on the box is similar to the actual toy except that Johnnie's sweater has short rather than long sleeves and both his cap and sweater are red- and white-striped instead of solid red.

The box illustration for Dottie also shows her in her car, but unlike Johnnie, she is waving. There is no puff of smoke from her car and the background shows a tree, fence, and building (which are not illustrated on Johnnie's box). The Marx logo is larger. The title on this box is "Dottie the Driver". Other wording is similar to Careful Johnnie's. However, there is a typical touch of Marx whimsy in the bow tied around the letter "D" in Dottie's name.

Like Johnnie, the box details of Dottie's clothes differ from the actual toy. Dottie is shown on the box with short, not long sleeves, and with bows in her hair.

The same two cars came as part of a set with a tin lithographed base marked "Dipsy-Doodle Bug Dodg' Em". The name is repeated on the single box for the toys, with the added words "Mysterious Action". The illustration on this box differs from the two boxes described above and shows both Johnnie and Dottie driving in their cars on the base. Excellent price includes original box.

	Good	Exc
Set:	150	350
Each:	75	175

CONVERTIBLE: 1930s. 11" long. This car has balloon tires with two embossed lines behind both the front and rear tires. The car also came in an all nickel-plated version. Eric Matzke describes a second version as "A non-powered push toy with a red body, blue top, silver trim, and steel construction. The lithographed balloon tires are white with red tread and black hubcaps, and the vintage is 1940." This version also has embossed lines and balloon wheels with red and black hubcaps.

Another car of the same size with very similar lines has been seen with the top down and with a driver. Whether this car is otherwise identical is not known for certain, but the appearance is close. And yet another car with the top up has been seen pulling a two-wheel trailer marked "Lonesome Pine". This car has the same features as the nickel-plated and red and blue versions. An entirely different car, a coupe, also pulls the trailer. (See the Reversible Coupe and Similar Cars section.) Excellent price includes original box.   **175   350**

JEEP: 1946-50. 11" long. A 1946 Sears Christmas catalog, which listed the price at $1.98, describes the Jeep: " . . . look how the windshield folds back and how the hood lifts up, just like a real jeep! Dummy headlights, spare wheel and bumper." The ad illustration shows "Jeep" on the windshield and a vertical pattern on the radiator. (Actual examples of the Jeep have also been seen with "Willy's", instead of "Jeep".) The Jeep is described a year later in 1947 ads as having a red baked-on enamel finish in bright colors.

By 1948 the same Jeep is described in the Sears Fall/Winter catalog as "This tough little army-cousin in 'civilian' colors will be a hit with your youngster. It's an authentic copy of the real thing right down to details like these electric headlights

The 7" "Old Jalopy" was manufactured in 1950, but is frequently mistaken for being manufactured earlier. The driver is missing from example shown. W. Maeder Collection.

Good   Exc

operated by standard flashlight battery-on-off switch . . . ." The price was now up to $2.39.

Around 1949 "Jeep" on the windshield disappears from some ads.

By 1950 the Jeep has acquired a 10-3/4" blue trailer. Although the Jeep has been advertised since 1946, it has now become a "Replica of famous Willy's Jeep. With electric headlights and horn. Horn is operated by depressing steering wheel. Headlights can be turned on and off by switch in driver's compartment, operated by standard flashlight battery . . . Detachable two-wheel Trailer of heavy gauge steel, finished in bright enamel." The toy sold for $2.79.

The Jeep is red with a yellow steering wheel, blue seats, and red and black wheels. The toy comes in a plain, unillustrated box.

Also in 1950 the Jeep with dummy headlights and without the trailer was sold for $1.29 in the 1950 Montgomery Ward Christmas catalog.[1]

The Jeep also comes in dark green with "Jeep" embossed on the side and a canvas top. None of the ads show this top, but not all Marx toys and versions appear in catalog pages. Excellent price includes original box.   **70   150**

LEAPING LIZZIE and OLD JALOPY: Circa 1927. 7" long.

First Version: The Leaping Lizzie was first advertised in 1927 although it may have been produced earlier. This amusing little car is "Lots of fun to see it wobble and shiver as it runs along the floor while driver in front seat holds on for dear life." Such sayings as "Mrs. Often", "99 44/100% Pure Tin", "Thanks for the Buggy Ride", "Four Wheels, No Brakes", and many other funny popular remarks are printed all over the car. The toy sold for 25 cents in the 1927 Sears Fall/Winter catalog. The sayings on the car are reminiscent of those on some of the Marx eccentric cars.

---

[1] In later years, Marx made many jeeps with trailers, including both Army and Navy versions with searchlight trailers.

Manufactured in 1950, the 11-1/4" Roadster tows a 5" plastic racing car. J. Iannuzzi Collection.

Good   Exc

The car is primarily black with a white radiator and a small "4D" and "Pray As You Enter", both in black. The embossed wheels come in black or white and have cut-out spokes. The wheels may have come in additional colors. The bent axle of the rear wheels contributes to the comic action. The driver is black and red, a color scheme Marx used with drivers in other cars. He sits on a red seat. The car comes with a rear spare tire although ads for some reason do not show this feature. There are no markings to indicate that Marx manufactured the car. Excellent price includes original box.

225   500

Second Version: No advertisements could be found for this version, but as the *Marx Toy Collector Newsletter* describes it, the toy is quite similar to the first version.[2] The wheels are black and white with cut-out spokes and the car has similar lithography. The radiator reads "4 Everything Breaks" with a much larger "4" than in the first version. There are other sayings such as "Rolls Nice", "Baby Here's Your Rattle", and "Leaping Lena". The last saying was also on the roof of a similar car manufactured by Strauss. Some of the sayings from the first version are repeated.

The cream, blue, and orange driver, who was used in other Marx vehicles, sits on a brown seat. There is no Marx identification on this car either. Excellent price includes original box.

225   500

---

[2] Gerritt Beverwyk (no title), *Marx Toy Collector Newsletter*, Vol. 3, No. 1, p. 2. Strauss also made a similar car called "Dizzie Dan."

Good   Exc

Third Version: 1950. Ads were common for this Old Jalopy version which sold for 85 cents. Since this toy has a similar appearance to the earlier versions, the date of manufacture is frequently mistaken for the 1920s. However, this car does have the Marx logo near the front of the roof and near the top of the radiator. There is no longer a "4" on the radiator. Instead, a lithographed sign reading "Do Not Disturb" is hung around the Marx name. The company frequently came up with delightful touches such as this one.

There is a similar graffiti design with different sayings all over the black car, such as "Luke the Spook", "Kilroy Wasn't Here", and "Blonde Local". The black and white wheels have lithographed spokes. These same wheels were also used on the 8" 1930s Coupes described on page 37. (Marx made efficient use of material by letting nothing go to waste.)

The driver of the car is blue, white, red, and tan and sits on a red seat. The back seat is slotted the same as the front seat, but there is no passenger.   **80   175**

The title of the toy "Old Jalopy" was used on the box of a Marx eccentric car which came out in 1950. This car also has sayings, plus the initials of actual Marx personnel. (For more information on Marx personnel, see the Old Jalopy in the Eccentric Car chapter.) The Old Jalopy came in an additional version consisting of four students in a small convertible with Old Jalopy markings.

In the 1960s the rarest version of this car was made by Marx's Mexican subsidiary, Plastimarx, and featured the characters from the comic strip "Archie."

Prototype: There is no prototype coding on this car and it has no markings or lithography on the grille, headlights, or license

TOP SHELF: Three 6-1/2" Tricky Safety Cars, circa 1950, come with blue, red, or yellow tops and are marked "Car No. 1 Safe Driving School". They are shown with an original box. Like the Tricky Taxi, they are designed to not fall off a table. BOTTOM SHELF: The Tricky Taxis are also shown with an original box. The car on the left has a checkered pattern. J. Iannuzzi Collection.

	Good	Exc

plate as in the production cars. The driver is the same one who is dressed in red and black from the first version, and the black rubber wheels have cut-out spokes.

Similar in color to the other cars, the prototype is black with hand-painted white markings. The sayings are those used on both cars, such as "Mrs. Often", "My Lizzie of the Valley", "Baby Here's Your Rattle", and "Leaping Lena".

NRS

MYSTERY CAR: 1936. 9" long. This car has been seen in red and blue. A 1936 Sears Christmas advertisement states that mere hand pressure will make the car go and any child can work it. The car is made of colored steel with a separate tin radiator. The ad does not show this car with a rear spare tire. The car sold for 25 cents.

In 1938 this car was advertised in catalogs as "Mystery Taxi." The car appears to be the same except for the addition of a rear spare tire and a "taxi" decal on the trunk. The taxi has been seen in red or yellow. "Taxi" is rubber-stamped in black on the door. "Taxi" is also found near the front of the roof, along with "Made by Louis Marx & Co., N. Y., U. S. A.".

The Mystery Car bears a strong resemblance to the Camera Car described earlier and probably comes from the same die as that car. The manufacturer Wyandotte made similar cars. Once Marx had this design, it was used with many different toys such as Mystery Speeding Bus (see the Buses and Trucks chapter), Cat, Sandy, and Pluto (see Volume I). Excellent price includes original box.

	Good	Exc
Mystery Car:	75	175
Mystery Taxi:	125	275

ROADSTER: 1949. 11-1/2" long. New in 1949, this toy sold for 87 cents in the 1949 Sears Christmas catalog. The open car has a transparent windshield, a dummy steering wheel, and rubber wheels. The car, which originally came with a plastic driver, has been seen in blue, red, and yellow. **60 150**

By 1950 the same car was still being advertised along with another version called the "Mechanical Convertible with Trailer and Racer". (This was also known as the Cannon Ball Keller set, named for William Keller, former general manager of the Marx Erie plant.) The set is described as "Sleek 11-1/4" metal convertible tows plastic trailer which carries 5" plastic racing car. Strong clockwork motor on both racer and convertible. Rubber wheels on all three vehicles." The roadster in the set also comes with a top. A 5" plastic racer similar to the one in the set was sold by itself in 1948. The set is listed for $1.49 in the 1950 Sears Christmas catalog. Excellent price includes original box. **100 225**

ROADSTER and CANNON BALL KELLER: The yellow roadster has black trim, a blue-green top, and comes with a red trailer and an ivory racer. The driver of the racer has a blue helmet or head and an ivory body. Both the trailer and racer have black wheels. **150 325**

SEDAN: 9-1/2" long. This red four-door open sedan has off-white trim, "103" on the front, the older Marx logo on the left rear door, and a driver. It is possible that this toy came from a Strauss die. **125 275**

SUPER HOT ROD: Late 1940s-early 1950s. 11" long. The shape of this rather flat car somewhat resembles the 1949 Roadster described above. The Hot Rod has an open cockpit, windshield, a plastic driver, and a lithographed grille and headlights. "Super" is on the hood in large letters and "Motor Oil" underneath in much smaller letters. "Hot Rod" is on the door and "777" to the rear of the door. The illustrated box for the toy has more wording than most boxes. As well as the name "Super Hot Rod", there are instructions for working the toy: "To operate, set toy on floor. Give a firm push — and release. Also operates in reverse." In addition, there is the Marx slogan, "One of the many Marx toys. Have you all of them?" "Electric

Three versions of the 8" Coupe manufactured in 1933. T. Riley Collection.

Good   Exc

Flashing Motor Block" and the Marx name and address are on the bottom of the box. Excellent price includes original box.

175   350

TRICKY FIRE CHIEF CAR: See page 39.

TRICKY SAFETY CAR: Circa 1950. 6-1/2" long. Like the Tricky Taxi, the Tricky Safety Car supposedly will not run off a table. However, this car is bigger than the Tricky Taxi and has a different appearance. The pale bluish-gray Tricky Safety Car has black trim and lithographed grille, bumpers, and lights. "Learn To Drive" is on the hood in black and "Car No. 1 Safe Driving School" and the Marx logo are on the side. The car has the type of body that covers much of the wheels. The plastic roof of the car has ridges and, typical of Marx, it comes in various colors of red, yellow, or blue. The body may have come in different colors, too. The roof is often missing, which substantially reduces its current value.   **70   150**

TRICKY TAXI: 1935. 4-1/2" long. The ingenious little Tricky Taxi was new in 1935 and was priced in the Sears Fall/Winter catalog, along with a lithographed base, at only 39 cents. The car is described as, "Daredevil 4-1/2" metal taxi with sturdy clockwork motor, whirls and dashes about on the 10" colorful metal platform map of city streets which is included — it goes right to the edges but seldom off . . ." In the same year, it was sold without the base for 25 cents. The Reverend Carl H. Kruelle, Jr., provides the interesting information that "This

idea originated with Louis Marx one night when he was riding in a yellow taxi on the streets of New York City. It was a rainy night and the cab skidded around almost in a circle and ended up against a railing — no one got hurt. He ordered the Tricky Taxi into production and it was made so that if it were played with on a kitchen table, it would not drop off the edge of the table, but would turn around and come back." Most of the time the car works as intended, but once in a while it goes off the table, so it is best to be ready to rescue the taxi before it falls to the floor.

Eric Matzke describes the car as having a lithographed steel body with two drive wheels at the rear and one pivoting wheel under the front to perform 180-degree turns. The car has dummy front wheels and tin-plated bumpers and grille. It comes in green with black and white trim, red with black and white trim, orange with black and white trim, red with black and yellow trim, red and white, black and white, yellow and black, and, less commonly, purple. On the door is "Tricky Taxi".

By 1948 the taxi had a slightly varied design on the side with a line of checkers extending from the rear to the windshield and "Taxi" above the windshield. The checkered version was still being advertised in 1950.

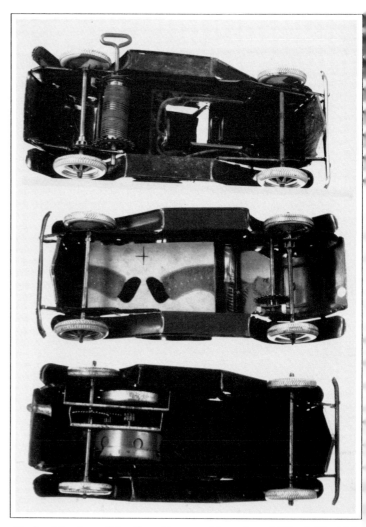

Underside view of the three Coupes. Note the middle shelf which shows Marx's use of scrap material. The farmer shown was usually sold with a tractor. T. Riley Collection.

The Tricky Fire Chief car and base were manufactured in the 1930s. This commonly-found car measures 4-1/2" while the hard-to-find base measures 6" x 10". J. Iannuzzi Collection.

Prior to 1948 the toy came in a plain, unillustrated box. From 1948 on, the toy's box in orange, green, white, and black reads "TRICKY TAXI" in large letters. The taxi is poised at the table edge. Other lettering reads "What..keeps it from running off edge of table". In a circle is "Fun Mystery Novelty". An illustration on another side of the box shows a cartoon-like figure made of gears, cogs, and other parts holding the Marx logo. The front, back, and side of the taxi are illustrated.

The Tricky Taxi is easily available, but unfortunately this is not true for the base. The 10" x 6" lithographed rectanglar base was not seen advertised after 1935. The base has very attractive illustrations, which show a busy street scene with traffic coming from all directions, a horse and cart, an ambulance, a police car, and a fire engine all on the street, but no taxi. As well as these vehicles, there are crowds of people with some even on the building's roof. "Tricky Taxi On Busy Street" is on the upper right-hand corner with the Marx logo and "Trade Mark Pat. Pend'g. Louis Marx & Co. N. Y. U. S. A." underneath. A Tricky Fire Chief was also made with a finely illustrated base. (See Tricky Fire Chief Car on page 39.)

There appear to be two patents for the toy. The earliest one, #2,001,625, applied for in February 1935, was by Heinrich Muller of Nuremberg, Germany. Marx either copied or acquired this patent from Muller. It is known that Louis Marx often made trips to Germany. Later in June 1935 Marx put out a similar patent, #2,096,333, under his own name. Both the drawing and text for this patent are more complicated than the

earlier Muller patent. The bases are not shown in either of the patent illustrations.

	Good	Exc
Without base:	40	75
With base:	175	300

YELLOW TAXI: Circa 1927. 7" long. This car is similar in shape to the Leaping Lizzie described earlier and was probably made around the same time. The car has wheels with embossed spokes, embossing on the side of the hood, "Yellow Taxi" on the side, and no Marx identification.[3] Excellent price includes original box.   **225**   **500**

COUPES

COUPE: 1933. 8" long.

First Version: This coupe was advertised with battery-operated headlights. It has a windup motor with the key on the right side, a battery holder on the underside, a cream body, and red top. The wheels have lithographed spokes. On the hood are three patches with a red- and black-striped design, which is continued on the radiator. Markings on the car include the Marx logo and "American Made / Patent Applied For". The illustrated box for the toy reads "Speeding Coupe" and "Electrically Lighted". The cream body version is rarer and has a slightly higher price.

The most often seen of the Speedway Coupes has a black frame, red body, brown roof, with or without headlights. No battery box or rivet holes are in the version without lights. Excellent price includes original box.   **150**   **350**

Second Version: This dark red and dark tan coupe has a black frame. The toy may have had a windup motor or may have come with just a few gears. The car has the same three patches on the hood as the first version, but they are dark tan with black stripes. It also comes with or without battery-operated headlights (the latter has no battery box or rivet holes). A few years after 1933, the same coupe in a lighter red came with "Fire Chief" on the door. (See the Fire Chief Cars section.) Excellent price includes original box.   **150**   **350**

---

[3] "Yellow Cab" by Gerritt Beverwyk, *Marx Toy Collector Newsletter*, Vol. 2, No. 2, p. 7. Strauss and Chein both manufactured similar Yellow Taxis.

The 11" Fire Chief Car was manufactured in 1950. The car has a flashing roof light and a siren. E. Owens Collection.

The G-Man Pursuit Car #7000 was manufactured in 1935 and is about 14-1/2" long. The G-Man in the car shoots a sparking gun which also makes a noise. Dr. M. Kates Collection. R. Grubb photograph.

	Good	Exc

Third Version: This Police Car was sold at the same time as the first version. This toy is friction driven and has a siren. The green car has black trim and black stripes on the side of the hood. The car may also have come with dark tan trim. It is marked with "Police" on the hood, "Dept. of Police" on both doors, the Marx logo, and "American Made, Patent Applied For, Dept. of Police". Excellent price includes original box.

150 350

DAN and DORA DIPSY CARS: See Eccentric Cars chapter.

FIRE CHIEF CARS

FIRE CHIEF CAR: 1949. 6-1/2" long. The Fire Chief Car is the usual red and has a rather cartoon-like appearance. The lithographed headlights and grille help to give this effect. On the hood is a somewhat triangular black and yellow shield with "Chief" inside in yellow above "F. D." and "Official Fire Chief" on the door. Although this Fire Chief Car is a windup, it is very similar to a Marx friction-driven Dick Tracy Car and probably also came in a friction version. It is known that a Marx friction-driven Fire Chief Car with a slightly different lithographed design was manufactured around the same time. Although the size is not known for certain, it was probably 6-1/2" long as in the windup version.

45 100

FIRE CHIEF CAR: 1950. 11" long. This car is similar to the Dick Tracy Car that also came out in 1950. (See page 68 in Volume I.) "Fire Chief" appears on the front, with "Chief" and "Car #1" on the side. On the door is an emblem with banners that are lettered "Fire Dept." and "Chief". Pictures of fire

fighters are lithographed on all the windows; one of them is shown talking through a loudspeaker. The license number is "FD3EM26". Above the rear window is "1 Chief 1". The car is red with white from under the window through the hood. The front wheels of the car are adjustable. When the car moves, the battery-powered light on the roof flashes red and the siren wails. (See also Siren Police Car in the Public Service Vehicles section.)

80 200

FIRE CHIEF (Friction Auto): 1936. 8" x 3". This car sold for $2.00 a dozen wholesale in a 1936 Butler Brothers catalog and is described as "Steel, bright red with black fenders and bumper, sloping radiator, black and white metal wheels. Momentum of heavy flywheel friction motor propels toy, loud siren." "Fire Chief" is on the door and embossing is on the side of the hood. This car, minus the wording, comes in at least three different car versions. (See Coupes section.) Excellent price includes original box.

130 275

FIRE CHIEF CAR with BELL: Circa 1940. 10-1/2" long. This is a larger Fire Chief Car with a bell, covered fenders (unlike the Friction Fire Chief Car), and "Fire Chief" on the door. Although not known for certain, it is strongly suggested that Marx made this car.

125 300

SIREN FIRE CHIEF CAR: 1934. This red car comes in four versions, all of which have sirens.
First Version: This car, which sold for 89 cents in the 1934 Sears catalog, has a friction motor and a lever to start and stop the siren, plus a 23" detachable wood handle which can push or pull the toy. The car without the handle was probably produced a year earlier. "Siren Fire Chief" is on the door and "Fire Dept." on the hood. Excellent price includes original box.

175 400

TOP SHELF: 4" *racers manufactured in 1942.* ***BOTTOM SHELF:*** 6-1/4" *Mechanical Speed Racer manufactured in 1950. B. Allan Collection.*

	Good	Exc

Second Version: This version has electric lights and is a windup. The car has the standard six rectangles on the hood plus "Fire Dept. 1". The black wheels do not have the same holes in the silver centers as does the G-Man Car. "Siren Fire Chief" and a fireman's hat are on the door. "1st Batt." is in front of the door. Close to the rear fender is "F. D." Advertisements state that this car could run either in a circle or straight ahead. Excellent price includes original box. **175 400**

Third Version: The car only has "Siren Fire Chief" and not the firemen's helmet on the door. This car is a windup, but does not have electric lights. The wheels are similar to those on the G-Man Pursuit Car. This version has a different design of embossed stripes on the hood. Excellent price includes original box. **175 400**

Fourth Version: This car is like the third version, but with electric lights. Excellent price includes original box.
175 400

In 1933 a very similar car was sold by Girard although it was advertised under the Marx name. Possibly, this car was sold under the Girard name as well. This car has "Fire Chief Siren Coupe" on the door and a similar fireman's hat. The Girard car has battery-powered head and taillights, a siren, and the same wheels as the G-Man Pursuit Car. The slanting narrow shapes on the hood are different from the other cars.

TRICKY FIRE CHIEF CAR: 1930s. This Tricky Fire Chief Car resembles the 4-1/2" Tricky Taxi which also has the feature of seldom falling off the edge of a table. It is red and has black trim and wheels, "TRICKY FIRE CHIEF" on both doors, and "3rd V. F. D." on the hood sides.

As with the Tricky Taxi, the Tricky Fire Chief Car comes with a 6" x 10" metal base. The multicolored base is lithographed to show a wonderfully animated scene with "Tricky

	Good	Exc

Fire Chief . . . Where's The Fire?" on the upper right in red on a yellow background. Fire trucks seem to be coming from all directions, frightening a horse which rears up. People are gathered on the roof and looking out of windows to see all the activity.[4] Unfortunately, these bases are difficult to find. (See Tricky Taxi on page 36.) Excellent price includes base and original box. **225 450**

PUBLIC SERVICE VEHICLES and SIMILAR CARS

There are a number of these good-looking heavy gauge steel vehicles, all measuring approximately 15" in length.

ELECTRIC AUTO: 1933.

First Version: This car was advertised in Sears' first Christmas catalog in 1933. The Marx name is not used in the ad, but the illustration closely resembles the actual toy except the toy has a small oblong shape near the rear fenders.

The car is described as "The first of its kind! A toy auto that runs by its own electric power. No springs to wind, just throw the switch, and away it goes! Real electric headlights and tail light. Dual switch operates motor and lights independently." The car and four flashlight batteries sold for $1.89.

The car that the ad resembles has a red top, red fenders, and red trim, a front bumper, a separate tin grille, a cream-colored body with six rectangular shapes on the hood, and black wheels with silver centers.

---

[4] "Tricky Toys" by Peter Fritz, *Marx Toy Collector Newletter*, Vol. 4, No. 1, p. 10.

The 4-3/4" Midget Special #2 Racer, manufactured around 1950, has a spring motor. Dr. M. Kates Collection. R. Grubb photograph.

Racer #5 was manufactured in the 1940s. This 5" racer is a windup and has balloon tires. Dr. M. Kates Collection. R. Grubb photograph.

The 5" Racer #7 was made in the late 1940s. E. Owens Collection.

Good **Exc**

The car has a rumble seat, license "#A7132", two headlights, and one taillight, and "Louis Marx & Co., Patent Pending".   **175** **400**

Second Version: Advertised in the 1933 Montgomery Ward catalog is this very similar version, identified as Marx, but it is a windup. The selling price was considerably less, only 89 cents. One reason for the lower price is that batteries were not included as they were with the first version. However, since batteries were inexpensive, their absence did not completely explain the lower price of the Montgomery Ward car. Apparently the windup car was less expensive to make than the first version which runs by its own electric power.

The design on the hood has six slanting narrow shapes instead of the six rectangular shapes of the first version. These shapes are the same as in the Fire Chief Car made by Girard. In fact, there is a possibility that Marx had Girard manufacture both cars and merely added the Marx name. It is known that in the earliest days of the business, Marx did have this type of arrangement with other manufacturers.

A couple of years earlier another manufacturer, Kingsbury, also made a strikingly similar car with electric lights and a rumble seat. The Kingsbury car has some differences in color, a slightly smaller size, and other shapes on the hood. Nevertheless, the similarity is obvious and Marx was no doubt influenced by this earlier car.   **150** **325**

G-MAN PURSUIT CAR #7000: 1935. 14-1/2" long. The G-Man Pursuit Car is described as "Hear the rat-a-tat of machine gun! Look at those quick turns! The first combination of a shooting gun with sparks and a moving car. Colored metal, decorated with G-Man colors and insignia. Long running clockspring motor. Speeds along straight or in a circle. Brake to stop or start car." New in 1935, the toy sold for $1.39 in the 1935 Sears Christmas catalog. (The Marx G-Man Gun is also shown on the same page.) Two extra refill flints could be bought for 10 cents.

The car has a red top, fenders, and running boards; a navy blue body with cream trim; and "G-Man". A shield bearing the word "Justice" and an eagle are under the front window. A similar shield appears on the rear of the car. "Pursuit Car" is along the hood. The aluminum rear bumper has a taillight and

Good **Exc**

a license plate that reads "G-511". "Louis Marx & Co., Made in America" appears on the rear.

The car has a blue and yellow grille, an unpainted stamped metal front bumper, and a police officer with a gun pointing out of the front window. The windup mechanism protrudes out of the side on the left immediately behind the door. The six rectangles on the hood of the earlier Electric Auto is retained, but now there is a striped design on them. The black wheels have holes in the silver centers. This toy has the catalog number 7000 in the June 1977 PB 84 auction catalog.

The "G-Man" trademark was patented in 1935, to be used for pistols and revolvers, but it could apply to the car, too. The patent for the G-Man Pursuit Car itself, applied for in 1935 and reissued in 1937, is clearly #2,055,848. Excellent price includes original box.   **225** **500**

GANG BUSTERS CAR: This car is very similar to the G-Man Pursuit Car. (For further information, see the Film, Radio, and Television Toys chapter in Volume I.)

H. Q. — STAFF CAR: 1930s. Similar to the G-Man Pursuit Car, this car has a gunner that shoots a sparking machine gun.

On the door of the khaki-colored car are three stars, "H. Q. — Staff", and an eagle insignia. The eagle is repeated on the hood, along with "U. S. A. — 7". There are simulated rivets on the car to give the appearance of an armor-plated car. The wheels are similar to those on the G-Man Pursuit Car. Excellent price includes original box.   **275** **600**

SIREN POLICE CAR: 15" long. This green car with yellow trim is similar to the Siren Fire Chief cars. There is a siren and "Siren Police Car Patrol" on the door, "1st Pct." to the left of the door, and "P. D." to the right near the rear fender. It has a rectangular hood design, similar to the other cars, and the wheels, like the battery-powered Siren Fire Chief Car, have no holes in the center. The Police Car also comes in a windup version with and without headlights. The version without headlights just has "Siren Police Car" on the door, the same horizontal lines on the hood, and the same wheels as the third

The Racer #61 is only 4-3/4" long and was made in 1930. The racer is friction-powered. Dr. M. Kates Collection. R. Grubb photograph.

The prototype of the Racer #61 with an over-sized driver. The wheels are marked "Wyandotte Toys". Dr. M. Kates Collection. R. Grubb photograph.

Note how large the key is in this version of a miniature racer with a lithographed driver. B. Allan Collection.

Good   Exc

version of the Siren Fire Chief Car. It also has the catalog number 8300 from the June 1977 PB 84 auction catalog.

A patent for a similar car was applied for in 1933. This patent (#1,962,870) is interesting in that Marx shared half of it with Hoge Manufacturing Company. It is the only instance found of the two companies sharing a patent. The name Girard is not mentioned in the patent. Although similar, the car illustrated in the patent drawing differs in its window arrangement, a rear tire, and a varying hood pattern. The Hoge Fire Chief Car is closest in appearance to the patent drawing. Excellent price includes original box.   **275   600**

The 13" Boat Tail Racer #2 was made around 1948. It has a heart-shaped radiator and the same wheels as some of the Marx Eccentric Cars. Dr. M. Kates Collection. R. Grubb photograph.

RACERS

Racers are among the most popular Marx toys for collectors. They were made in both miniature and large sizes, and were shown in catalogs for many years.

MINIATURE RACERS

Good   Exc

CHROME RACER: 1937. 5" long. This chrome-finished racer is similar in shape to the 61 Racer, but the back is pointed, not boat-tailed. Also the Chrome Racer is a windup with balloon wheels. **75   100**

MIDGET SPECIAL #2 and OTHER RACERS: 1950. The Midget Special #2 was advertised along with two other racers as selling for 94 cents for the group. However, it is possible that the Midget Special #2 was available earlier than 1950, although no ads have been seen for it before that time.

The Midget Special #2 is similar to Racer #61 except that the earlier racer has thin tinplate wheels measuring 1-1/4" in diameter, whereas the Midget Special #2 has thick balloon-type wheels 1-1/2" in diameter. Markings on the tires are "Balloon 15 x 9.00". The wheels are off-white with black-lithographed tire treads and red hubcaps. Another difference between the two cars is that Racer #61 is friction-powered while the Midget Special #2 is clockwork-powered. The two cars have the same driver. The Midget Special #2 has a similar shape and the identical tires as Racer #5.

The body of the Midget Special #2 is lithographed primarily in red and yellow with "Midget Racer" beneath the open cockpit containing the driver and "2" on the rear of the body, which is boat-tailed in shape. These racers also come with "7" and possibly other numbers.

The racer is primarily yellow with black and red accents and has black and red tin wheels. The toy comes in a plain unillustrated box lettered "Mechanical Speed Racer".

Advertised in the same set as the Midget Special #2 Racer is another racer in yellow, also with "2" in black on the rear and on the hood. However, this racer is not lettered "Midget Special" and is larger at 6-1/4" in length. The driver is also different, resembling the drivers used in the Marx Eccentric Car "Jumpin' Jeep". The radiator of the car is rounded instead of pointed. The car is lithographed with a red lightning pattern, exhausts on the side, and a checkered pattern on the rear. Its tin wheels are black and red. Similar racers also come with "1". The toy comes in a plain unillustrated box lettered "Mechanical Speed Racer". **30   70**

PLASTIC RACER: 1948. 6" long. Although not known for certain, it is strongly suspected that this racer is a Marx toy. A similar racer appeared as part of the Marx toy, Cannon Ball Keller. This plastic racer has dummy exhaust pipes extending from the motor to the rear, a "7" on the rear, and front wheels

Good   Exc

that can be set to go either straight or in a circle. The toy sold for 77 cents in the 1950 Montgomery Ward Christmas catalog.

In 1950 a similar appearing car, now 8" long, shot sparks from the exhaust as the car moved. This car had adjustable rubber wheels, an exhaust pipe, and a pressure pump. This toy sold for 92 cents in the 1949 Sears Christmas catalog.
35   60

RACER #5: 1948. 5" long. By the late 1940s, racers with actual, three-dimensional (rather than lithographed) drivers were being copiously advertised. The numbers seen most often are "3", "4", "5", and "7". These racers come with both black and white wheels.

The primary colors of Racer #5 are yellow, red, and black. "5" is on the top of the hood, on the rear, and beneath the open cockpit. There is a raised exhaust design in red on the side. The driver is similar to the others of this series. The thick, balloon-type tires are marked "15 x 9.00". The off-white wheels have black-lithographed tire treads and red hubcaps. The Marx logo is on the back of the car. **50   100**

RACER #7: Racer #7 is another racer in the same series as Racer #5. The lithography, however, more closely resembles the earlier Racer #61. Racer #7 is also red with lithographed exhausts in yellow, but it has a diamond pattern around the number as in the earlier car. **50   100**

RACER #61: 1930. 4-3/4" long x 2" wide x 2-1/4" high. This little racer first appeared as part of sets with other toys in 1929. At that time, a friction orange and red racer, whose number could not be distinguished, was produced along with a bus as part of a Marx Gas Station Set. [5] Oddly, the earliest racer to appear with a number is Racer 61, which has the highest number. (In 1927 a Racer #1 appeared with a gas station, but the toy is thought to have been made by Lehmann.) No other racers have been seen with numbers above 7, although it is possible they were made. The Racer #61 appeared as part of a set, along with an unusual large-wheeled Zeppelin and a small Mack truck. The Racer #61 was a very popular car. William Kalsch, former production superintendent of the Marx Erie plant, said that, in one year, four million of them were sold.

The friction-powered racer has a lithographed red and orange body with "61" in a diamond beneath the open cockpit, blue metal wheels, a green front, a pointed radiator, and a boat-tailed back. The Marx logo is on the back of the car. Only the head of the racing driver who is wearing a helmet and goggles can be seen. **50   100**

Prototype: This fascinating prototype has a red body and is identical to the production toy, but the prototype appears to have white rubber wheels and "Wyandotte Toys" on the tires.

---

[5] Small racing-type cars were frequently used as part of larger toys. The small Mack Auto Transport is an example.

The Giant King Racer was manufactured in 1928 and is 12-1/4" long. A later version of the racer was manufactured in the 1940s. The driver is missing from the example shown. Dr. M. Kates Collection. R. Grubb photograph.

The 1941 Giant King Racer is 13" long and differs in many ways from the earlier 1928 Giant King Racer. Dr. M. Kates Collection. R. Grubb photograph.

The Rocket Racer was produced in 1935 and is 16" long. It is similar in shape to the Speed King Racer. Dr. M. Kates Collection. R. Grubb photograph.

Good **Exc**

An over-sized figure with a funny face and a blue- and yellow-striped shirt is holding the steering wheel. The figure is so tall that the height of the toy increases from 2-1/4" to 4-3/4". "1171 Erie" is marked on the inside of the toy. The date is almost illegible, but appears to be "Nov. 8, 1936". The toy was never put into production. [6] **NRS**

RACERS with LITHOGRAPHED DRIVERS: As well as having various numbers, the miniature racers come with different lithography on the cars and with lithographed instead of separate three-dimensional drivers.

In 1942 a 4" racer of this type was sold for 36 cents. The racer has a key-wind clockwork motor and a brake. "Blue Streak" is on the roof, a large "3" is on the hood and rear, and the Marx logo is on the side.

This same style racer also comes with "1", is lithographed primarily in red with cream and blue with "Ace" on the roof, and has silver wheels which are smaller than on the other racers, measuring approximately 1/2" in diameter.

An additional version of this racer is mustard, black, red, and white with a lithographed black cat. Like some racers, this car comes with a speedway, but it may well have been sold in a set. **50** **100**

Another racer has similar coloring but different lithography, blue "Racer" on the roof, and a blue "4" on the hood and the rear. Other versions may also come in yellow with "2" and in light blue with "5". [7]

---

[6] In the 1950s Wyandotte Toys was acquired by Marx.

[7] It is known that a Racer #4 with a lithographed driver was sold with some track.

Good **Exc**

Around the 1940s to 1950, another windup racing car in yellow, red, and green was sold. The black-lithographed tires have red treads and "Balloon 15 x 9.00". The racer is 6-1/4" long. Cars of this slightly larger size were not noted in catalogs until 1950, but it is possible that they were sold earlier.

LARGE RACERS

BOAT TAIL RACER #2: Circa 1948. 13" long. This racer has six lightly embossed exhausts in a "V" shape, a heart-shaped radiator in a red- and yellow-checked design, and a boat-tailed back. The car is lithographed primarily in yellow and red with black outlining and with "2" on the top of the hood and on the side at the rear of the racer. The same racer was also made with a "3" (and probably with other numbers) and comes in a plain box marked "MECHANICAL SPEED RACER". A small Marx logo appears above the rear wheels. The driver fits directly into a lithographed cockpit and is similar to the driver in the depressed cockpits of the late Giant King Racer and Speed Racer previously described. The 2-1/2" diameter fixed wheels are black and red with simulated tire treads. The same wheels are found on some of the Marx Eccentric Cars.

Similar to this racer is one marked with a "1" which appeared in catalogs around 1948. Excellent price includes original box. **75** **225**

GIANT KING RACER: 1928. 12-1/4" long x 3-1/2" wide x 3" high. The earliest of the large racers, the Giant King Racer first appeared in catalogs in 1928. (This racer should not be confused with a different car, the Marx 8-1/2" King Racer, which came out in 1925.) The Giant King Racers have various types of lithography.

The 1937 Speed Racer is 13" long. There are no numbers on the car. Dr. M. Kates Collection. R. Grubb photograph.

Good   Exc

First Version: Appearing in the early ads, this racer has a dark blue body with embossed red exhaust pipes, a blue radiator, and a red "7-11" in a white circle with a red rim on the side. The white and red Marx logo is on the boat-tailed rear. The 1-3/4" diameter green wheels with embossed spokes are similar to those in the early Marx trucks; the front wheels can be set in three different positions. Excellent price includes original box.   **225   500**

Second Version: This later version is pale yellow with black trim, exhaust pipes, and wheels. "7-11" is on the side and the driver is dressed in black. The 12-1/4" car is the same length

Good   Exc

as the First Version. The black and yellow grille is bent over with "7" on one side and "11" on the other. Ads have been seen which show both numbers together on each side of the radiator. Excellent price includes original box.   **175   400**

GIANT KING RACER: 1941. This racer is very similar to the Speed Racer described on page 48, but it is primarily red, yellow, and black with green and black tin 2-1/8" wheels, without simulated tire treads, and a driver wearing a red cap. The front axle has three positions.

The later 1941 Giant King Racer is made from a different die than the earlier 1928 Giant King Racer. The wheels vary

Racer #12 is the same shape as the Speed King Racer and Rocket Racer, and was probably manufactured around the same time. Dr. M. Kates Collection. R. Grubb photograph.

Good Exc

also. The numbers "711" are not separated by a hyphen and are no longer in a circle. "711" appears beneath the driver and cockpit and on the front of the grille. There is some lithography on the front and rear of the later car that is absent on the earlier car. The later racer is 13" long x 4" wide x 3-1/4" high (not including driver) while the earlier racer is 12-1/4" long x 3-1/2" wide x 3" high. The back of the later racer is broader than the earlier one. The later racer comes in a plain, unillustrated box. Excellent price includes original box. **175 400**

GIANT MECHANICAL RACER: 1948. 12-3/4" long. This racer is much more simply lithographed than previous racers, having just a long stripe with four exhausts on it and a "6" or "7" on the rear of the racer. The toy comes with two different types of wheels. Similar to the wheels on the Marx Jumpin' Jeep, the first type has centers lithographed with a design and embossed treads; the second type, like the Speed King Racer, has plain centers and rims. **60 150**

MECHANICAL SPEED RACER: 1948. 12" long x 4" wide. This bullet-shaped Indianapolis 500 racer is described by William A. Allen, Jr. in the *Marx Toy Collector Newsletter* as red and yellow with black tin wheels with red and yellow inserts. It has a beautifully lithographed grille, exhaust system, and louvers on the hood, a large white "27" on the rear of the car, and a red "27" on the front. Lithographed on the side and under the white plastic driver are two insignia: "Grand National 500-Mile Champ" and "Indianapolis Champ — 1948". The red and cream box for the toy has the later Marx logo and "Mechanical Speed Racer" across the front. The car is shown against a checkered-flag background. [8] **70 175**

---

[8] William A. Allen, Jr. (no title), *Marx Toy Collector Newsletter*, Vol. 1, No. 6, pp. 16-17. Strangely, this toy was not seen in any catalogs.

Good Exc

RACER #12: 1942. 16" long. Compared with the earlier rocket-shaped Racer #12, it has a flatter front and no fishtail back. Marx tried something a bit different in this car which now has two drivers, like the type used in the Marx Rollover Plane and the Jumpin' Jeep. Racer #12 has six lithographed pipe-like exhausts and a large "#12" on the rear of the car. The wheels are the same type as the Speed Racer described earlier. The racer also comes with a single plastic driver and the same wheels as the Milton Berle Eccentric Car. The date of this later version was probably from the late 1940s and early 1950s. Excellent price includes original box. **175 400**

RACER with PLASTIC DRIVER: 1950. 16" long. Another nicely lithographed racer, this car is similar in shape to the later Racer #12 from 1942. The lithography on the body and wheels, however, differs from the Racer #12 although the grille design is similar. The racer has lithographed exhausts, a wing-like design towards the rear, a brake lever, and a plastic driver, as shown in the 1950 Montgomery Ward Christmas catalog. Excellent price includes original box. **100 250**

ROCKET RACER: 1935. New this year, the racer is actually the same shape as the Speed King but the lithography is exceptionally well done and has an art deco appearance.

The racer has a lithographed body primarily in red with green, blue, black, and yellow accents; a black and yellow grille; a white "Rocket Racer" on the side; a rubber nose bumper on the front; exhausts on the racer's side at the rear; green and black wheels; yellow, white, and green fins; a red windshield; and a blue backrest. The driver, who wears a red cap and dark green coat, is the same driver as in the Speed King Racer. The car originally sold for 25 cents.

The unillustrated box reads "Marx New Rocket Racer. Fast as Lightning / THE CAR OF THE FUTURE". Excellent price includes original box. **225 500**

The Speed King Racer is 16" long and was manufactured in 1932. There are two different-colored Marx logos on the tail fins. Dr. M. Kates Collection. R. Grubb photograph.

The Reversible Coupe is about 16" long and was made in 1936. When the bumpers hit an object, the car reverses itself. Dr. M. Kates Collection. R. Grubb photograph.

	Good	Exc

Prototype: 16" long. As described by John Ritter, the Rocket Racer Prototype is red, white, and black. The large solid wooden wheels are painted the same color as the car and are 3-1/4" in diameter. The car has a white top and red sides outlined in yellow.

The three-dimensional driver is painted in olive green, has a pink face, and wears a red cap. There is a counterweight attached to the driver so that when the car is turned over, the driver faces the rear of the car. **NRS**

ROCKET-SHAPED RACER #12: 1930s. Although not seen in catalogs, this racer was probably made in the 1930s, the same time as the other rocket-shaped racers, the Speed King and the Rocket Racer. While similar to those cars, Racer #12 is lithographed primarily in red and white with black and yellow outlining. It has "12" in silver in the mid-portion of the racer, silver exhausts, black wheels, and a blue headrest. On the front of the car is a rubber nose bumper and a small Marx logo. There is a later Racer #12 with a flatter front and without a fishtail-shaped back. Excellent price includes original box. **225 500**

SPEED KING RACER: 1932. 16" long x 4" wide x 3-1/4" high. Unlike the Giant King Racer, this car has a bullet-shaped front and fishtail back.

This yellow racer has red exhausts, "Speed King" in large black letters above the exhausts, a long red arrow on the hood, a red headrest, and yellow tail fins. The Marx logo is red on one tail fin and black on the other. The racer has a driver dressed in blue with an orange cap, a blue windshield, black and off-white or orange and black wheels 2-1/8" in diameter. Excellent price includes original box. **250 600**

SPEED RACER: 1937. 13" long x 4" wide x 3-1/4" high (not including driver). Different from the earlier Speed King Racer, this racer has a bent-over type radiator and a boat-tailed back. Colored blue, silver, and black, the car has an exhaust in a black and silver raised design, a small Marx logo on the radiator, and no numbers on the body. The black, blue, and cream 2-1/2" diameter wheels are in a fixed position and are the simulated balloon-type. The driver is similar to the airplane pilot in the Rollover Airplane and the drivers in the Jumpin' Jeep. Excellent price includes original box. **200 450**

Prototype Coupe features an open rumble seat, open sun roof, and adjustable front wheels. There are no bumpers on the car. Dr. M. Kates Collection. R. Grubb photograph.

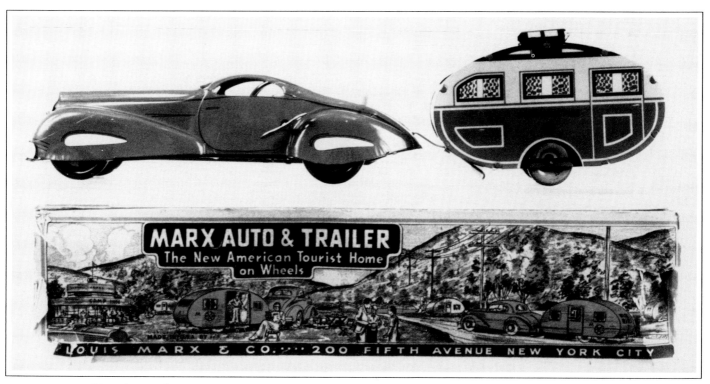

Manufactured in 1936, the Marx Auto and Trailer together measure 22" long. T. Riley Collection.

REVERSIBLE COUPE and SIMILAR CARS

These beautiful streamlined cars with art deco styling are among the most handsome cars that Marx made. Of the group, the best known is the Reversible Coupe.

REVERSIBLE COUPE: 1936. 16" long. This car has dark red lithography with aluminum trim and black striping, a stamped metal grille, a brake, metal wheels, and front and rear bumpers that protrude noticeably outward. If either the front or rear bumper hits an object, the car reverses itself, hence the name of the toy. By 1937 the car was being advertised with rubber pieces on the bumpers so furniture would not be marred. Also by this time, ads mentioned that the coupe could be run either straight or in a circle. The car has the license "OT711", a lithographed taillight only on the left rear, and the Marx logo on the right door. It sold for 94 cents in 1936.

The car also comes in a blue version. Al Marwick has said "... some had bright metal decor flanges that were fitted over the enclosed fender panels, front and rear. Some were painted on to simulate the dimensional type." The latter was thought to be done as a cost-cutting measure. [9]

The peach and black box for the toy has "Reversible Coupe" in large letters, "The Marvel Car" in smaller letters, and the Louis Marx name and address are at the bottom. The exceptionally fine box illustration shows several children playing

---

[9] "Louis Marx Streamline Coupe, Historical Time It Represented" by Al Marwick, *Antique Toy World*, February 1987, Vol. 17, No. 2, p. 51.

Good   Exc

with the cars in a large, mansion-like living room. Directions for operating the toy are on the side of the box. Excellent price includes original box.   **300   700**

In the late 1930s and early 1940s two other versions were made of this car, the comic Blondie's Jalopy and the Charlie McCarthy Mortimer Snerd Private Car (called Coupe on the box). These are the same as the Reversible Coupe except for different lithography and the fact that the heads of the characters stick out through the roofs. (For more information on Blondie's Jalopy, see the Comic Strip Character Toys chapter in Volume I. For more information on Charlie McCarthy Mortimer Snerd Private Car, see the Film, Radio and Television Toys chapter in Volume I.) The patent for the car, #2,146,021, was applied for in 1936. Former Marx employee Richard Carver is one of those whose name is on the patent. (See Volume I.)

Prototype: This electroplated prototype has fenders without flanges and a closed rumble seat in the back of the car.

NRS

COUPE PROTOTYPE: The body of this prototype is similar to the Reversible Coupe and Marx Auto (and Trailer), but there is no room or provision for the bumpers. It has an open tan rumble seat, open sun roof, and adjustable front axle which allows the wheels to be set to run straight or in a circle. The same license number "OT711" is on the rear of the car, but unlike the Reversible Coupe, the prototype has both left and right lithographed taillights. On the right door is the Marx logo. Prototype markings on the base are "Erie 11 / 6 / 37".

300   700

This 11" Cadillac Coupe was manufactured in 1931. The car has bumpers and side-mounted spare tire. Dr. M. Kates Collection. R. Grubb photograph.

Good   Exc

DRIVE-UR-SELF CAR: 1940. New this year, the car sold for 89 cents in the 1940 Sears Christmas catalog. The great new feature of this car was that it could be turned left, right, or straight ahead simply by tightening or lessening tension on the cord attached through the roof of the car down to a small additional wheel on the base.

Like the Reversible Coupe, the car is predominantly red, but the roof is blue. This car also came in solid blue. [10] "DRIVE-UR-SELF" is on the door along with the Marx logo. Two patents for the toy, both filed the same day, January 3, 1938, are #2,167,245 and #2,167,246. Marx employee Richard Carver (see Volume I) was involved in the first patent. Neither drawing of the cars in the two patent illustrations really resemble the Marx coupe. But it is apparently the idea, not the form, that is important, as evidenced by the fact that both a dog and a car are illustrated in the first patent. (For information on the dog, see Running Scottie in the Animal Toys chapter in Volume I.)   **100   175**

MARX AUTO and TRAILER: 1936. 13-1/2" long (excluding reversible bumpers); 22" long (with trailer). The same Reversible Coupe was produced this year with a more standard bumper that was closer to the body. It pulls a rounded trailer marked "Lonesome Pine". The car has been seen in a red version, and a blue version that has a small hole in the trunk to receive the trailer hitch. The two-wheeled trailer is predominantly red and yellow with black and white accents, and has a lithographed door and windows. The end of the trailer has a decal marked "Caravan / Trailer / Louis Marx & Co., New York, N. Y.". The body of the trailer, which was also used for tank bodies, was also sold in a version pulled by an 11" long convertible instead of a coupe. (See Convertible on page 33.) The green and black box is lettered with "Marx Auto & Trailer / The New American Tourist Home / On Wheels" and the Marx name and address. The box has a very elaborate drawing of the car and trailer both parked and on the road. Excellent price includes original box.   **250   600**

SPECIAL COUPES, RACERS, and ROADSTERS

Good   Exc

This group of distinctive cars is designated as "special" because the cars bear a resemblance and relationship to one another. These attractive and desirable cars all have similar bodies. (Marx also made different coupes and racers. See Racers — Miniature and Large, and Reversible Coupe sections.)

CADDY PROTOTYPE: The property of Rick Rubis, this prototype appeared in the *Marx Toy Collector Newsletter* and is described as: "The chrome Caddy was plated chrome over a green plastic car 6-1/4" long, 2" high, painted on underside of toy 'Erie x-1604-A 6/6/49' also 'Sample Louis Marx & Co.'" [11]   **NRS**

CADILLAC COUPE (Large): 1931. 11" long x 4" wide x 4-1/2" high. (Also see Cadillac Coupe (Small) below.) Ads from 1931 describe the car as having a trunk rack, but some variations lack this feature. The toy sold for 25 cents at the time.

The car has a body lithographed in orange with black striping and edging, the Marx logo on the rear, black fenders and top, and orange running boards. The top may also have come in blue or yellow. Some tops have landau bars lithographed on them. The driver, from the very early series, sits upright and is not a racing driver as in the other cars. The tin orange and black wheels come with both embossed or lithographed spokes, lettered "Balloon Cord 28 x 4.75". There is a side-mounted spare tire similar to the other tires. Stamped metal bumpers are found in both the front and rear of the car. The orange-lithographed grille has dummy headlights with black striping. Excellent price includes original box.   **175   400**

[10] "Louis Marx Streamline Coupe, Historical Time It Represented" by Al Marwick, *Antique Toy World*, February 1987, Vol. 17, No. 2, p. 51.

[11] "Prototypes" by Rick Rubis, *Marx Toy Collector Newsletter*, Vol. I No. 4, p. 14.

The Second Version of the King Racer. Dr. M. Kates Collection. R. Grubb photograph.

Good   Exc

CADILLAC COUPE (Small): 1931. 8-1/2" long x 3" wide x 3-3/4" high. (Also see Cadillac Coupe (Large) above.) This yellow car is trimmed in red and has red running boards and fenders, a green top, and blue disc wheels. The top also comes in blue. In place of the Marx logo on the Large Cadillac Coupe is a rumble seat with a spare tire behind it, a front hood, and front and rear bumpers. The driver hunches forward, similar to the drivers of the other racers. Except for the rumble seat, the car is similar in construction to the King Racer. It comes in a handsomely illustrated box marked "Royal Coupe".

The Coupe may have come in a larger size since one was advertised in 1931 that resembled the Large Cadillac Coupe in size and price. Excellent price includes original box.

125   300

KING RACER: 1925. 8-1/2" long.
First Version: The car has a yellow body with red trim, a green top with a sun visor, blue disc wheels, a hood ornament, black running boards and fenders, and dummy lights on the radiator. The front license number is "50-50", the same for all the racers except the Sparks Racer. On the trunk is the Marx logo in red and a spare tire. The radiator has horizontal stripes. The hunched-over driver is dressed all in black. Excellent price includes original box.

350   750

Second Version: The car is bright yellow with black outlines and running boards, green wheels, and a blue top. As in the first version, the Marx logo appears on the trunk. The driver

The 8-1/2" Cadillac Coupe has a rumble seat and spare tire in back. It was manufactured in 1931. D. Morrison Collection and photograph.

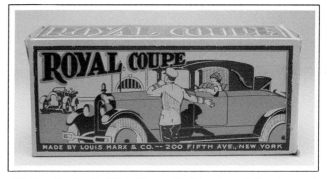

The box for the Cadillac Coupe. D. Morrison Collection and photograph.

The 8-1/4" long Rex Racer was sold as early as 1923. The car also comes with blue wheels. Dr. M. Kates Collection. R. Grubb photograph.

	Good	**Exc**

is similar to the one in the first version, and the car body is similar to the Sparks and Rex Racers. The car also comes with a light orange body with green trim.

Further color variations include a yellow body with green trim and wheels, and a yellow and red body and red or blue wheels with a green top. It is not known how many other color combinations exist. The King Racer should not be confused with the larger Giant King Racer, which is an entirely different car. The box for the toy reads "King Racer" and in smaller words "The Monarch of All". The car is illustrated going downhill. Excellent price includes original box.   **250   550**

REX RACER: 1923. 8-1/4" long. This Marx toy was advertised along with Strauss toys in *Playthings* magazine in 1923 (one of the earliest dates in which a Marx toy appears), all

under the name of Louis Marx & Co. The driver in the ad is shown sitting erect instead of hunched over as in the actual car; however, this may be just the artist's conception. [12]

This racer, unlike those described previously, has an open cockpit. The body is similar in construction to the Sparks Racer as is the driver. However, the floorboard is separate instead of being a continuation of the back of the racer. The black fenders are larger than the fenders on the Sparks Racer. The dark red car has black trim, yellow disc wheels and rear spare tire (the wheels also come in blue), the license plate "50-50", and the Marx logo on the rear of the car.   **135   300**

[12] *Playthings* magazine, February 1923, p. 79, advertisement.

The 15" long Stutz Racer was manufactured in 1928. It comes with or without a top. The front bumper is missing from the example shown. Dr. M. Kates Collection. R. Grubb photograph.

Good   Exc

SPARKS RACER: 1928. 8-1/4" long. This car is similar to the Rex Racer, but there is no floorboard or rear spare tire.

The most striking feature of this yellow car is the lithography. Red stars, lightning streaks, and zig-zags abound all over the car, even on the yellow wheels. As the car's name implies, there is a sparkler mechanism in the rear. The car has "Sparks" on the side, the Marx logo and "Sparks" immediately behind the driver, and black fenders. Priced at $2.10 a dozen wholesale in 1930, the car is described as running either straight or in a circle.   **135   300**

STUTZ ROADSTER: 1928. 15" long x 4" wide x 5-1/2" high. Although larger than the other cars, the body is similar. Ads call the car by an assortment of names, such as "Stutz Flyer", "Stutz Racer", or "Stutz Roadster". It was sold both with and without a top.

The pale yellow car has red accents. Some ads mention that the car came in yellow with green trim. The car has a dark red top, metal wheels with red centers and gray rims, red fenders, red running boards with a step, a pale yellow grille with green accents, and stamped metal dummy headlights. The Marx logo appears on the rear along with a spare tire. The driver is of the early series and sits upright instead of being hunched over. "Stutz" in green letters is on the upper part of the grille. [13]   **275   600**

---

[13] A Marx Stutz Pedal Car was made in the 1960s.

STATION WAGONS

The following station wagons are listed by size.

Good   Exc

6-3/4" STATION WAGON: This car was probably sold in a set with other small cars. In 1950 this station wagon and a similar roadster came with a 9", two-door metal garage lithographed with a tile roof and shrubbery. When either car hits the garage, the doors automatically open. (Marx used the same idea of a garage that opens when touched, with other cars and even a tractor.) The set sold for $1.69 in the 1950 Montgomery Ward Christmas catalog.

The color of the roadster is not known, but the station wagon is green with a wood-grained pattern. The car is lithographed with a man and a woman in the front seat and a child in the back seat   **40   90**

6-3/4" STATION WAGON: This blue and white car has a wood-grained pattern on the body and a light on top, similar to the Dick Tracy Car. A family of four people with dogs is lithographed on the back window.   **45   100**

7" STATION WAGON: This green windup station wagon, marked "Marx" on the front left fender, has a wood-grained pattern. No people are lithographed on the silver windows. The rear license plate reads "75A2".   **40   90**

7-1/2" STATION WAGON: This light purple car has a wood-grained pattern on the body. No people are lithographed on the windows. The rear license number reads "7JA2".   **45   100**

The 8-1/4" long Sparks Racer was manufactured in 1928. The lithography on this car is particularly vibrant. Dr. M. Kates Collection. R. Grubb photograph.

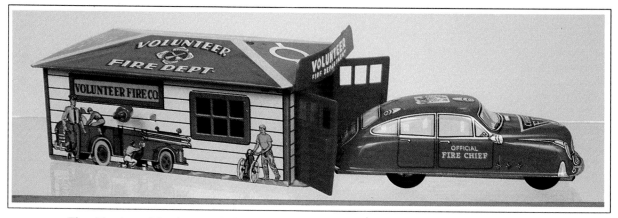

The side view of the Automatic Fire House #3234 with Fire Chief Car. B. Allan Collection.

Good   Exc

11" STATION WAGON: Circa 1950. Marx made a friction station wagon, with a wood-patterned design and lithographed occupants, grille, and lights. Except for the addition of the roof, the car is similar to the 1949 Roadster described on page 35. Former Marx employee, Richard Carver, had a part in designing the patent, #2,590,508, which was filed March 1949.

The drawing in the patent varies somewhat from the actual toy in that the roof is a slightly different shape and there is an approach ramp in front of the garage door. However, the patent states that the automatic door mechanism will open when a toy touches it and does not require an approach ramp. The patent drawing shows a truck rather than a car.   **75   200**

Box and base view of the Automatic Fire House #3234 and overhead view of the Fire Chief Car. B. Allan Collection.

The Blue Bird Garage, measuring 11-3/4" long x 6-1/2" wide, was manufactured circa 1937 and is one of a series of similar buildings. Dr. M. Kates Collection. R. Grubb photograph.

AUTOMOBILE-RELATED TOYS

BUILDINGS

AUTOMATIC FIRE HOUSE #3234 with FIRE CHIEF CAR: 1940s. This is very similar to the Dick Tracy Police Station. (See Dick Tracy Police Station and Riot Car in the Comic Strip Character Toys chapter in Volume I.)

The 9" deep fire house is tin with plastic doors. When the crank on the building is wound, the doors open and a 7-1/2" friction-powered Fire Chief Car is ejected. The car is also similar to the Dick Tracy Riot Car but, of course, is lithographed differently.

The Fire House has a red and yellow roof. On each side of the roof is a sign in yellow lettering which reads "Volunteer Fire Dept." Between the words is an emblem with the initials "F D" on either side. "Volunteer Fire Department" in white letters is repeated above the red doors except that "Department" is spelled out instead of being abbreviated. There is also what appears to be a white directional arrow on the roof.

The side of the house shows a lithographed scene of firemen cleaning a fire engine while a boy with a bicycle looks on. Beside a sign reading "Volunteer Fire Co." is a green window. Another side shows two green windows and three men working

*The Brightelite Filling Station (**right**) with a later version (**left**). The left one has differently-shaped pumps. P. Rolin Collection.*

The Brightelite Filling Station was manufactured in the 1930s and measures 9-1/4" x 3-1/4" x 6-1/4". The light bulbs on the pumps are battery-powered. Dr. M. Kates Collection. R. Grubb photograph.

1940s Gull Service Station base measures 16" x 11". The pump lights are battery-powered. The small sign is missing from the example shown. W. Maeder Collection. R. Grubb photograph.

Good   **Exc**

with fire equipment. One of these men is bald, a typically realistic Marx touch.

The back of the house shows a dramatic lithographed scene of three firemen giving first aid to a victim who lies on his stomach. One of the firemen appears to be pressing his back. Above the firemen is a blackboard with a heading in yellow "Daily Orders". Under this in white is "First Aid Training All Men". On the left side are four names, "O'Reilly, Malone, Dillon and Smith". These may well have been the names of real people. Marx was known to have used the names of real people on at least two other toys. (See the Eccentric Car chapter.) The red base of the house has instructions for the toy along with the Marx logo.

The 7-1/2" red car has "Official Fire Chief" on the door and lithographed lights on the side of the hood and roof. Also on the roof is a paper label with directions for working the car. The hood has "F. D." in a black triangle with yellow edging, and a lithographed grille and lights. The back of the car has "Fire Chief" and the license number "14C77".

The red, yellow, black, and white box is illustrated with a scene of the car emerging from the fire house. Markings on the box are the toy's name "Automatic Fire House" and the Marx logo, name, and address. A red sign on the lower left front flap emphasizes that the toy is complete with "Friction Fire Chief Car".

The patent for the Automatic Fire House may be #2,050,892 applied for in 1935. The drawing differs somewhat from the actual toy as it shows a chimney that the toy does not have. In addition, the drawing shows double garage doors with "Engine Co." above the doors, and a truck as well as a car. Of these features, only the car comes with the fire house. (Patent drawings sometimes differ in small details from the actual toys.)   **110**   **250**

This variation of the Magic Garage was manufactured from about the 1940s to the 1950s. When the car touches the garage door, it opens automatically. J. Iannuzzi Collection.

BLUE BIRD GARAGE: Circa 1937. 11-3/4" long x 6-1/2" wide x 2-3/4" high.

First Version: The Blue Bird Garage is part of a series of similar buildings manufactured by Marx, including a Union Station, a bus terminal, and an airport. It may have been sold by itself, as well as in a set.

As described by Dr. Malcolm Kates, the walls of the Blue Bird Garage are off-white with gray, blue, and black outlining and lithography. The front of the garage shows several doors which are closed, as though there were entrances into the auto bays. Several doors are open, showing workmen fixing tires and standing at a work bench. "Cars Greased" appears over the pair of open doors on the right. "Blue Bird Garage" and a bluebird are between "Blue" and "Bird". To the right of the office door is another open window below "Parts for all cars". A man behind the counter sells stored parts, and an oil can and dispenser. Immediately to the right is an open door.

The roof is medium blue, similar in color to the blue outlining and lithography on the walls. The base is primarily red with an orange-yellow track. To the left is a gasoline pump which is mostly blue with white outlining. A glass light bulb on the top of the pump works electrically with a wire running underneath to battery terminal posts at the rear of the base. An air pump to the right is lithographed in red and orange-yellow with "Free Air" beneath a dial and the Marx logo at the base. "In" and "Out" are on the pale orange-yellow track and

Good   Exc

"Day and Night Service", enclosed in a rectangle, is in front while "Danger Gasoline" is to the rear. Excellent price includes original box.   **110   225**

Second Version: Trip Riley describes this Blue Bird Garage as having the same colors and inwardly-embossed windows and doors as the first version, but it has an extra art deco-style sign unit lettered "Gas" on the center of the building at the roof. "Blue Bird" near the roof is missing from this version. In contrast to the first version, this one has three unlighted pumps, two on the left side and one on the right side. The garage is the same building as the Marx small Grand Central Station. Excellent price includes original box.   **110   225**

Prototype: In the April 1989 issue of *Antique Toy World* magazine, Continental Hobby House[14] was selling a Marx prototype. The prototype had been made into a bank and was hand-painted to resemble a variety store. "Drugs" could be distinguished on the front and "Bank" was on either side of the roof. The base resembled the Roadside Rest Service Station, instead of the Blue Bird Garage. The asking price was $1250.   **NRS**

BRIGHTELITE FILLING STATION: 1930s. 9-1/4" long x 3-1/4" wide x 6-1/4" high.

First Version: Marx used this item in combination with other pieces to make several additional toys.

Dr. Malcolm Kates describes this toy as being mounted on an off-white base with red edging. There are two battery-powered gas pumps which have a bottle-shaped outline, white gas pumps lights with "Gas" rubber-stamped in black, and a blue pump with yellow and white outlining to the left. In the middle of the gas pump is "Motor Gas" with the Marx logo beneath it lower down. "American made" is on the very bottom of the gas pump. The pump to the right has "Ethyl Gas" in the middle over the Marx logo with "American Made" immediately underneath.

An oil and grease rack in the center has an opening door which holds a battery. The rack has lithographed oil bottles and cans, with "Oil — Grease" on top, and "Anti-Freeze Compound" underneath. Below these words, on two separate shelves, are lithographed bottles and cans.

To the far left of the base is an "OUT" sign and to the far right is an "IN" sign. The signs are mostly orange with black lettering.

Many Brightelite Filling Stations come with embossed bulbs.

The original box has "Brightelite Filling Station" (with the unusual spelling) and an accurate illustration of the toy except that the gas pump light bulbs read "Motor" and "Ethyl" rather than "Gas". On the box cars are lined up next to the filling station and attendants are filling the cars with gas. The

---

[14] Addresses: *Antique Toy World*, P. O. Box 34509, Chicago, Illinois 60634 and the Continental Hobby House, P. O. Box 1933, Sheboygan, Wisconsin 53082

The 1935 Roadside Rest Service Station base measures 13-1/2" wide x 10" deep. Attendants are thought by some to resemble film comics Laurel and Hardy. J. Iannuzzi Collection.

	Good	Exc

primary colors of the box are similar to the red and blue colors of the toy itself. Excellent price includes original box.

200 350

Second Version: A German version of the toy was manufactured which is noticeably similar to the first version except that it has a third pump. Excellent price includes original box.

200 350

Third Version: This later version has pumps which are more rectangularly shaped almost to the top and lack the protuberances of the earlier pumps. Some of these later pumps have lithography on them while others are plain. Excellent price includes original box. **175 300**

Instead of one of the gas pumps in the first version, there is a red air pump with white and black accents. It has a lithographed dial at the rounded top and "Free Air" on its mid-section.

Fourth Version: This version has the gas pump on the left, the oil-grease structure in the center, and a pump with a rounded top which says "Free Air". The "In" and "Out" signs of the first version are retained. This piece was thought to come with both an oil wagon and a watering can. Excellent price includes original box. **175 350**

BUSY AIRPORT GARAGE: 1936. This imaginative toy consists of the Brightelite Filling Station with the air pump previously described and, in addition, several 6" cars: an ambulance, tank truck, dump truck, bus, roadster, and racer. The cars were also sold by themselves. An airplane with a 9-3/8" wingspread completes the toy.

The cardboard box for the toy can be set up as a lithographed garage measuring 10-1/2" x 8" x 10". The toy sold for

	Good	Exc

$1.00 in the 1936 Sears Christmas catalog. Excellent price includes original box. **175 400**

BUSY PARKING LOT: 1937. With this toy, Marx, ever alert to the outside environment, attempted to copy a real parking lot. The 1937 Montgomery Ward Christmas catalog, which sold the toy for 94 cents, describes it: "What fun you'll have parking the five heavy gauge streamline autos in the spaces marked off just as in real Parking Lots! Keep traffic going on the plainly marked in and out runways — or for emergencies, pull up to the building in the corner where there are gas pumps and a tool box. Neat little fence encloses lot which is set on brightly decorated steel base 16-1/2" long by 11" wide. The average size car is 4-1/2 x 1-1/2 x 1-1/2"." On the roof of the building to the left are the words "24 Hour Service". On the right is a large sign which reads "Park Here".

The parking lot has a blue base with white or silver markings, a lithographed fence, and the same garage found with the Marx Hollywood Bungalow. The building has both solid lithographed and red celluloid windows, a terminal clip, but no place for a battery. Marx used the base with several other toys, including the Gull Service Station described below. Excellent price includes original box. **175 400**

BUSY STREET: 1935. In this toy, the Brightelite Filling Station is featured again. Although the toy is called "Busy Street", there is no actual street, just six vehicles waiting to get gas. The 6" vehicles consist of a dump truck with a real dumping body, a tank truck, a bus, a Chrysler car, a sport coupe, and a roadster. The toy sold for $1.00 in the 1935 Sears Christmas catalog. The vehicles in this toy are similar to the Busy Airport Garage. **175 300**

GULL SERVICE STATION: 1940s. 16" long x 11" wide base. This base is the same one that came with the Busy

Good   Exc

Parking Lot described on page 59. The building was also used on other Marx toys such as the Greyhound Bus Terminal and General Alarm Fire House. (See the Buses and Trucks chapter.)

The station is lithographed predominantly in red, white, and blue with touches of yellow. The building consists of a center structure and two garages or bays. The center structure has a brick design on its walls and two skylights on the red roof. Between the skylights is the Marx logo. "Parking" in red lettering is on both sides and "Gull Service", a clock above the door, and a window displaying tires are on the front. A sign that reads "Deluxe" is on the tires. (Marx frequently used the word "Deluxe" on its toys.)

The two red-roofed garages each have a lithographed seagull flying above water with the scene enclosed in a circle. On the front of the garage is "Washing" to the left and "Greasing" to the right.

In the front of the Station are two battery-powered pumps with hoses, one blue and white and marked "Motor", the other red and white and marked "Ethyl". Both show numbers plus "Amount Of The Sale" and "Cents Per Gallon".

In front of the pumps are three little signs of the type Marx often used. They read "Oil", "Marx Tires", and "Gas Special 5 Gal. $1.00". On the right of the Station is a 6" yellow vehicle lift which can be raised and lowered by a lever. On the lift is a 4" tow truck with a blue chassis and yellow towing equipment. There are no Marx markings on the truck, only "Made In U. S. A." embossed on the door. The truck has a separately attached tin grille, dummy lights, and wooden wheels.

Near the grease rack is a red and yellow "Free Air" pump. All around the sides and back of the building are lithographed windows through which men can be seen working on cars. The back of the building shows a seagull on each side, plus "Soaring Power", "Gulloil", "More Mileage", and "Gasoline".

The unillustrated box for the toy has "Electric Lighted Service Station With Accessories" in red. On the side of the box is the Marx slogan "One of the many Marx toys. Have you all of them?" and "World's Largest Manufacturer of Toys" with a Marx logo on each side.   **150   325**

HONEYMOON GARAGE: 1935. 7-1/4" x 6-3/8" x 4-3/8". This garage is heavy gauge lithographed steel with a lithographed multicolored tile roof, light blue walls, lithographed red windows, and red door handles. The doors can actually be locked. The roof has a sign on the front that is lettered "Honeymoon Garage" under the Marx logo. The garage comes with two 6" streamlined cars with wooden wheels. These cars, which come in blue and green and possibly other colors, were also sold in a set by themselves. The toy sold for 59 cents in the 1935 Sears Fall/Winter catalog. The June 1977 PB 84 auction catalog gives this set the catalogue number 894. Excellent price includes original box.   **140   300**

LINCOLN HIGHWAY SET: 1933. This toy sold for 98 cents when it was new in 1933. It has the same pumps and oil-grease rack as the Brightelite Filling Station. However, there is an additional traffic light and car, both battery-pow-

The base of 1929 Service Station measures approximately 5-1/2" x 6". Marx made a very similar airport hangar. T. Riley Collection. C. Myer photograph.

Good   Exc

ered. The traffic light measures 7" high. A lever changes the light from green to red. The 8" coupe has battery-powered headlights, and either a cream body and red top or red body with dark tan and blue trim. The car was also sold without the pumps. This car comes in additional versions. (See Coupes, also Fire Chief Cars.) Excellent price includes original box.   **300   650**

MAGIC GARAGE: 1934.

First Version: This toy is described in a 1934 Butler Brothers catalog as a "6 x 7" litho garage with 5 x 11" runway, gyro friction action town car, red and black enameled finish, bumper, rubber tires, spring action opens garage doors as a car goes up runway." The garage is shown as having a wood beamed door with a window above the beams and another window on the side. The runway has a striped design.

In later years, additional toys were designed without the runway, whereby the car touches the garage door which opens automatically. (See the 6-3/4" Station Wagon for information on a similar garage.)

The actual toy is lithographed to appear as if it has a shingled roof, primarily red, with white frame wooden walls. An adult and a child shown working in the garden amongst the shrubbery are lithographed on the walls.

The overhead door of the garage is yellow with red and yellow windows and functions just like a real overhead garage door. Underneath the windows is a white sign with "Automatic Door" in red. Above the door, in a charming Marx touch, lithographed birds are shown near their "nest," a circular hole. There are even "shadows" cast by the birds.

When the door opens, the tan interior of the garage reveals various details, such as a can of motor oil, a bag of lawn fertilizer, a barrel with miscellaneous equipment, and a fire extinguisher. On a shelf are paint brushes and jars of paint and on the wall a dart board. Excellent price includes original box.   **100   200**

The box for the toy has a red line drawing of the garage, a few trees outlined in blue in the background, and "The Magic Garage and Car" in dark blue letters. On another side is a red Marx logo and the slogan "World's Largest Manufacturer of

The 1934 Sunnyside Service Station is similar to the Roadside Rest Service Station, but has no figures of attendants. The base of the toy measures 13-1/2" wide x 10" deep. T. Riley Collection. C. Myer photograph.

Good   Exc

Toys". The illustration on the box does not show a runway for this particular version of the toy.

The patent for the toy is #2,036,802 applied for in April 1934. The patent drawing is basically the same as the actual toy except there are no wooden beams on the door and a truck is shown instead of a car.

Second Version: This toy comes with a windup car and a plain unstriped runway. The garage has a slightly different lithographed pattern. Excellent price includes original box.

125   300

MAIN STREET GARAGE: 1935. 7-5/8" x 4-3/4" x 5-1/8" (box). Manufactured at the same time as the Honeymoon Garage, this garage is actually made out of the lithographed box for the toy. It has a lithographed tile roof. "Main Street Garage" is on the roof and two gas pumps are lithographed on either side of the doors.

The 4" steel vehicles are smaller than those in the Honeymoon Garage. They consist of a wrecking truck to tow a motorless Chrysler car, a dump truck, a stake truck, and another Chrysler car. All have windup motors except the car being towed. The tow truck was also used with the Gull Service Station. The toy sold for 49 cents in the 1935 Sears Christmas catalog. In later years, the garage came with two motorless cars instead of one.

90   200

METAL SERVICE STATION: 1949-50. 26" x 14-3/4" x 11". As described by knowledgeable collector Jim Radican in the *Marx Toy Collector Newsletter,* the toy is a 1940s-style building lithographed in a striking brownstone finish with red and yellow trim. There is a manually-operated elevator to roof parking, an office with an acetate window, and a repair bay. The building is mounted on a 26" green base. Mr. Radican states "Typically, these early sets came equipped with red,

Good   Exc

yellow, and blue polystyrene plastic accessories including a toilet and a sink for the restroom. Plastic vehicles were 3-1/4" in length with black snap-on wheels. They appeared late-forties in style and came in a wide variety: 4 different coupes, stake, cargo, van, milk and soda trucks." It generally sold for between $2.98 and $3.29. [15]

It is easy to tell that Marx manufactured this piece since the name "Marx" is perched on the top of the building. Underneath the sign is the top of the elevator with the words "Service Center". To the left of the elevator is a sign that says "Down", to mark the beginning of the vehicle down ramp. Surrounding the elevator top is a flat area for parking cars with "Sky-view Parking" on the area's edge and "Lubrication" around the side.

The first floor is made up of three sections: "Parts" on the left, the elevator in the center, and a repair bay to the right. The base has a windowpane design on it. Lettering around the edge says "Drive In" on the front and "Exit" on the side.

As well as the accessories mentioned above, the Metal Service Station also comes with others including the following plastic items: two gas pumps, an air pump, a grease and wash rack, and a display counter. Excellent price includes original box. (Price for toy in Excellent condition without box is $275.)

125   500

ROADSIDE REST SERVICE STATION: 1935. 13-1/2" wide x 10" long base. This very popular service station is sometimes referred to as the Laurel and Hardy Service Station because of the two attendants' supposed resemblance to the famous film comics. There is a difference of opinion as to whether the two actually represent Laurel and Hardy. The

---

[15] "Service Stations" by Jim Radican, *Marx Toy Collector Newsletter,* Vol. 3, No. 1, p. 4.

resemblance may have been intentional, but it was not close enough to cause Marx any copyright problems.

First Version: As described by Trip Riley, the station has pumps with electrically-lighted bulbs marked "Gas", a light under the vehicle lift, a rear battery box marked "Capacity / 200 / Gallons", and a red box on the side of the lift marked "Motor Oil" that contains ten dummy cans.

Behind the pumps is a refreshment stand with the two smiling flat metal attendants. "Laurel" wears a red- and white-striped shirt while "Hardy" wears a blue shirt with white dots; both wear white aprons and caps.

The building measures 5-3/4" long x 2-1/4" wide x 5-3/4" high. The top of the stand is lithographed with a red, green, and yellow tiled roof. In front of the roof is a sign reading "Roadside Rest Service Station" with the Marx logo between "Rest" and "Service". In front of the three-dimensional counter are two seats and, in a nice touch, two lithographed places set at the counter. The flat metal cash register shows the amount of $1.25. The front of the blue or green base is curved, similar to that of the Glendale Station, possibly to allow placement alongside of a curved section of toy train track.

In front of the refreshment stand are a red "Ethyl" pump and a green or blue "Motor" pump, some with an attractive yellow and black art deco design which other versions lack. The art deco pumps have the amount of the sale and the number of gallons lithographed on the pumps, while the other pumps have less detailed lithography. All versions have the Marx logo on the lower part of the pump. The plainer pumps were also used

in some versions of the Brightelite Filling Station, Lincoln Highway, and other toys.

In the early years, a 6" streamlined coupe was advertised with the station. The Roadside Rest Service Station has also been seen with the 8" red or cream coupe with battery-powered lights. Whether the station came with this car is not known for certain, but ads show the 6" coupe without the electric lights. By 1937 the station was being advertised with a stake truck filled with brand name boxes instead of the car.

The Roadside Rest Service Station also comes with an oil trolley marked "Motor Oil". Even this little item was produced in different colors, including a blue body with yellow and white accents, and blue with an orange top. Both versions have a lithographed yellow eagle on a white circle. Below the eagle is "Motor Oil" and the Marx logo is on the side of the trolley. The toy also comes with a red and yellow water can.

The plain unillustrated box for the toy merely says "One Filling Station" and has the Marx name and address. Price for oil trolley alone is $75; price for complete toy without box in Excellent condition is $400. Excellent price includes original box.   **175   500**

Second Version: Circa 1938. William Smith describes this garage as having the same base, Laurel and Hardy, and building as the first version. However, it has no stools or tab slots for them. Its two gas pumps are 3" tall The free air pump is only about 1-1/2" tall. This toy does not have an oil car or the indentations in the toy base where the oil car wheels sit. (Price

The Loop-the-Loop Auto Racer is approximately 8" high and was manufactured in 1931. J. Iannuzzi Collection.

The 1949 Mot-O-Run 4 Lane Hi-Way has an electric track which moves small vehicles by rapid vibration. The track measures 27" long. E. Owens Collection.

	Good	Exc

for oil trolley alone is $75; price for complete toy without box in Excellent condition is $400.) Excellent price includes original box. **175 500**

SERVICE STATION: 1929. 5-1/2" x 6" base. This small Service Station is one of the earliest that Marx made. Louis Marx may have been influenced by a similar penny toy when he made many trips to Germany. As described by Trip Riley, the base has black walls, two courses of yellow block, a yellow-and green-lithographed roof, and "Tires / Tubes / Accessories / Repairs" on the side walls.

The Service Station is similar to the Marx Municipal Airport Hangar. Both items were advertised on the same page in the 1929 Sears Fall/Winter catalog, although they were sold separately. The Municipal Airport Hangar has larger walls and no space in front for vehicles as in the Service Station. In the airport hangar, the walls run the length of the building so there is no need for the two roof support posts of the Service Station. The unusually-shaped Service Station roof has a long slope towards the front of the building. At the edge of the roof is a sign with the simple title "Service Station". The Marx logo is between the two words.

The Service Station comes with two friction-powered vehicles measuring approximately 4-3/4" each. One car is shaped like the miniature Racer #61 described on page 43, although the number cannot be distinguished in ads. The Racer #61 was being sold at this time. The other vehicle is the Liberty Bus (see the Buses and Trucks chapter) although some ads do not show the striped roof of the bus. It is probably not a coincidence that the Liberty Bus has the number "62" which is very close to the number of the Racer #61.

The Service Station has open grille windows on the front and sides. Two pumps with revolving handles are at the front of the building. The toy also comes in a color variation of red, green, and yellow. Excellent price includes original box. **225 500**

SPIC and SPAN GARAGE: 11-1/2" x 7". This garage was shown in Lloyd Ralston's *Antique Toy Auction Catalog*, October 1982. The garage is lithographed cardboard with a tile roof and

	Good	Exc

is actually the packing box for the five vehicles which comprise the set. These painted, pressed steel vehicles include: three dump trucks, a tank truck, and a streamlined car, all with separately attached tin grilles. This toy is similar to the Sunnyside Garage. Excellent price includes original box. **175 500**

SUNNYSIDE GARAGE: 1935. Like the Spic and Span Garage, this toy has an 11" lithographed cardboard garage which is the packing box for the ten 6" vehicles that make up the set. Some of the vehicles are a tank truck, dump truck, stake truck, coupe, and Chrysler auto. Excellent price includes original box. (Price for toy in Excellent condition without box is $700.) **300 750**

SUNNYSIDE SERVICE STATION: 1934. 13-1/2" long x 10" wide. The Sunnyside Service Station bears a strong similarity to the Roadside Rest Service Station.

As described by Trip Riley, the station has two gas pumps of the type without the art deco design. The blue "Motor" pump and the red "Ethyl" pump come with black rubber hoses and metal nozzles. The toy also has an air pump.

The toy's accessories include an oil wagon and a water can. The oil wagon is orange with a blue top and has different lithography from the one used with the Roadside Rest Service Station, but the shape is the same. Markings on the wagon are "100% Penna. Oil" below which is the Marx logo.

Although advertisements do not show it, the toy has a battery-operated light on a pole at the right rear of the base. (The toy has also been seen with a free air pump instead of a light on a pole.) Ads do mention the light in the base under the vehicle service lift. They also show that the toy comes with a 6" coupe with a luggage rack. The battery box in the rear is marked "Capacity 1200 / Gallons".

The service station has a similar sign to the Roadside Rest Service Station, marked "Sunnyside Service Station". As in the other building, the Marx logo is in the middle of the toy's name. However, unlike the Roadside Rest Service Station, there are no figures of attendants or the three-dimensional counter with

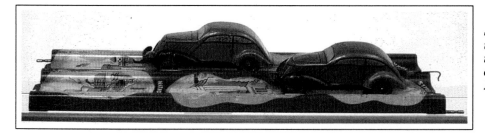

Section of track and two cars from a Speedway manufactured circa 1939-40. The track is lithographed with scenes of various places including the New York World's Fair. C. and C. Weber Collection.

Good   Exc

stools. Instead, the front of the building has a lithographed brick design, a door, and two signs: "Tires" and "Rest Room". Lithographed tires are shown through a window and another window is on the building side. The toy is mounted on the same type base as the Roadside Rest Service Station, but unlike that station, the front doors on this building can be opened.

The patent for the toy, #2,040,521, applied for January 1934, shows the open doors. The patent substantially resembles the toy as it was produced except that it has no cars (the lift is shown) and has two, rather than one, water cans. Excellent price includes original box.   **175   400**

UNIVERSAL MOTOR REPAIR SHOP: 1938. New in 1938, this attractive art deco building has an arched center section and two outer sections, curved at the sides, which extend above the center section. "Universal Motor Repair" is on the roof of the center section and a windowpane pattern on the roofs of the two outer sections. Below the center section

roof is a sign which reads "Machine Shop". On each side of the entrance, or bay, are signs in a vertical lettering style: "Towing" and "Greasing". The toy comes with a 5" wrecker, a 4" sedan, and a rack with four dummy wheels. Two dummy pumps are near the edge of the base.

This toy is pictured in the *Marx Toy Collector Newsletter*, where publisher Peter Fritz describes it as one of a series of toys that share a 16" x 11" metal base first produced in the 1930s. Others are the Gull Service Station, Military Airport, American Airlines Airport, General Alarm Fire House, and Busy Parking Lot.

Mr. Fritz states that the art deco building is bright yellow, red, black, and white and originally came with five die-cast tools that fit into the swing-out tool counter in front of the machine shop. A close-up view of the tool counter shows lithographed sponges, gears, wax, tubing, voltage meter, oil can, air filters, and even a can of Marx Oil. The reverse side of the machine shop has the sign "Super Service" near the roof.

The Stunt Auto Racer was manufactured circa 1931. Cars run down an incline, and jump up and out onto the table or floor. C. Holly Collection. B. Greenberg photograph.

Good Exc

Various bays reveal lithographed attendants working. Markings on the building are in the same vertical style lettering as on the front and say "Oil", "Tires", and "Gas."

The toy also comes with two small signs of the type used so often on other Marx toys. The signs, which resemble open paper match covers standing up (or sandwich boards), read "Marx Tires — Let Us Check Your Car" and "Expert Auto Repairing — All Work Guaranteed".[16] Excellent price includes original box. **225 500**

USED CAR MARKET: 1939. 16" x 11" base. This toy consists primarily of a base, several cars, and signs. The base is the same size used on the Universal Motor Repair Shop and many other toys. This toy comes with five cars and trucks with wooden wheels, each about 4-1/2" long. There is a platform marked "Today's Special" for that special bargain car. Small signs of the type found in the Universal Motor Repair Shop and other toys are also included.

Two sides of the lot have fences and the third side has various billboards with a "Used Car Market" sign over the entrance between the billboards. An added attraction is the inclusion of price tags and play money, as shown in the 1939 Sears Christmas catalog. Excellent price includes original box. **135 500**

TRACKS, HIGHWAYS, and SPEEDWAYS

The company designed at least two patents and a trade mark for speedways. Patent #2,161,314 filed in 1936 consisted of a long, narrow, parallel track with a mechanism designed to direct a vehicle from the inside track to the outside track, or vice versa.

In 1937 Marx applied for the trade mark "Soap Box", with Serial No. 397,263. The name "Soap Box" was intended for toy speedways, race tracks, and miniature toy vehicles. Use was claimed for the name dating from August 26, 1937.

In 1939 the company filed patent #2,248,473 for a sound-producing track and wheeled toy.

CROSSOVER SPEEDWAY: 1938. This speedway is similar to the Streamline Speedway described on page 66, but it has lithographed buildings on the bridge instead of a pattern. The two little cars are now the racers with lithographed drivers, described earlier in the Miniature Racers section. Excellent price includes original box. **135 300**

CROSSOVER SPEEDWAY: 1941. In 1941 the Crossover Speedway was still selling but the size was increased from 144" to 150". The price also increased from $1.89 to $1.98. Ads such as those in the 1941 Sears Christmas catalog now mention that the set has 16 sections of track.[17]

---

[16] "Auto Repair Shop" by Peter Fritz, *Marx Toy Collector Newsletter*, Vol. 4, No. 1, p. 3.
[17] Speedways were also made by Marx's English branch in the 1940s.

Good Exc

In 1949 ads state that the same Speedway comes with instructions.

By 1950 the same toy is still being sold and with interlocking metal track. Now, however, the price has been cut, possibly indicating that interest in this particular Speedway has begun to taper off or that the item was being closed out. Excellent price includes original box. **135 300**

LOOP-THE-LOOP AUTO RACER: 1931. 10-1/4" long x 3" wide x 6-1/2" high. 1-3/4" long car. Apparently this toy appeared in a Sears ad only in 1931, with no description whatsoever. The yellow-tan and blue toy consists of a vertical support that holds up an incline with a loop at the bottom. A blue-green small racing-type car with silver wheels and a driver goes down the slide, around the loop, and out at the end.

The ad shows the Loop-the-Loop Racer along with a group of other toys and selling as a group for $1.00. The toys were made by Marx, Girard, and possibly other manufacturers. The Looping toy is shown near the Marx Hometown Movie Theatre.

The box reads "Loop-the-Loop" and shows the loop with a trestle that is not on the toy.

The patent for the toy #1,725,536 filed in 1928 shows a different drawing for the end piece that protrudes after the loop. In the ad, this piece is straight, but in the patent there are triangular shapes on each side holding a handle-like device across the runway. When the car hits this device, it jumps in the air. Excellent price includes original box. **135 300**

MOT-O-RUN 4 LANE HI-WAY: 1949 (copyright). This intriguing toy has little cars, trucks, and buses that move by the rapid vibration of an electric track. Detour arms cause traffic problems and crashes. The toy operates on 110-120 volts AC. The tiny vehicles measure under 2" long, yet each is lithographed differently. Apparently these vehicles were made separately from the set because their own red box says "Five Mot-O-Run Cars for Use on Magic Motion Sets".

The track measures 27" long. Various outdoor scenes, including a train, are lithographed on the metal auto base.

The multicolored box for the toy has "Deluxe Mot-O-Run Model 1000 4 Lane H-Way with Tunnel and Toll House" with the Louis Marx name and address underneath, and a handsome illustration of the toy itself with "Magic Motion" beneath. **80 200**

NEW YORK WORLD'S FAIR SPEEDWAY: Circa 1939. This speedway has track lithographed predominantly in blue and red with scenes of various American places: Niagara Falls with a waterfall; West Point with cadets; a water scene in Brooklyn; buildings in Albany; New York with the New York World's Fair, which would date the toy around 1939-40.

The two red little cars are similar in shape and size to those with the Streamline Speedway and have silver and black accents.

Earlier, in 1937, a Speedway of the Future was advertised which had lithographed track. Whether this earlier set was the same as the New York World's Fair Speedway without the

The Whee-Whiz Auto Racer was manufactured in 1925 and measures 13" in diameter. The rocking motion of the track makes it uncertain which of the four racers will win. W. Maeder Collection. R. Grubb photograph.

	Good	Exc
World's Fair scene is not known for certain. Excellent price includes original box.	225	450

SPEEDWAY of the FUTURE: See New York World's Fair Speedway.

STREAMLINE SPEEDWAY: 1936. New this year, the toy consists of a 144" figure eight two-lane speedway with a bridge intersecting the center. The cars can drive over or under the bridge. The track is lithographed with scenes from various cities. For some reason, the box for the toy shows only a plain track.

The Speedway comes with two windup cars, each measuring approximately 3-3/4" long, which resemble the Marx Tricky Taxi in shape although, of course, their wheels are different than those on the taxi. Extra cars could be purchased in addition to those which came with the set, according to the 1936 Sears Christmas catalog. In 1937 this set was also advertised with 160" of track. [18] Excellent price includes original box.

	Good	Exc
	135	300

STUNT AUTO RACER: 11" long x 1-1/2" wide x 2-1/2" high. This auto racer appears in the same 1931 Sears catalog ad as the Auto Racer. The ad states that the "Auto runs down an incline and leaps up and over, out onto the table or floor."

The Stunt Auto Racer is much lower than the Loop-the-Loop Auto Racer and the incline much less steep.

The Stunt Auto Racer resembles its patent, #1,703,117, which shows the same kind of loop end of the slide as in the Loop-the-Loop . The only major difference between the patent drawing and the actual toy is that the patent drawing illustrates two slides and cars together.

The red Stunt Auto Racer, unlike the ad, has two blue racers with silver wheels instead of one. The drivers do not have lithographed features.

The navy and red box for this unusual toy has "No. 16 Stunt Auto Racers", "Made by Louis Marx & Co., 200 Fifth Ave., New York City" on the bottom, and the Marx logo with some decorative curlicues attached to the outside of the logo on the end flap. As in the patent, the box shows two Stunt Racers together. In addition, there are two other cars without the

[18] Marx also used the figure eight track for certain train items.

Good Exc

inclines in an outdoor setting. Excellent price includes original box. **135 300**

WHEE-WHIZ AUTO RACER: 1925. In 1926 the toy is accurately described as follows: "After motor is wound, the cars whirl around in their individual courses by the peculiar up and down rocking motion of the track which makes it very uncertain as to the progress of the racers, anyone being likely to win." The toy sold for 89 cents in the 1926 Sears Fall/Winter catalog.

The toy consists of a large circular dish-shaped piece, 13" in diameter, on top of a smaller circular base measuring approximately 7" in diameter. The dish is attached to the base by a small projection in the revolving activating arm on the base. With the dish held evenly, the height measures 4".

This very vivid toy has four differently-colored race lanes in yellow, green, red, and blue. Each of these lanes is edged with yet another contrasting rim. In the center of the dish, a

Good Exc

lithographed house is shown, with several parked cars and a Zeppelin in the sky.

The base is lettered "Whee-Whiz Auto Racer, Louis Marx & Co., N. Y., U. S. A." in red and "Trade Mark / Patents Pending" in black. The side of the base shows a lithographed scene of the race cars driving around the track. The tip of the base is yellow and the bottom is open so that the mechanism of the toy can be seen. On the side is a start/stop lever and a long key.

The four little multicolored race cars each measure 2" in length. The lithographed driver and the wheels are silver.

The patent for the toy is #1,701,503, filed in December 1924. The patent differs slightly from the actual toy in that it shows only two racers and the activating arm in the base has a slightly different shape. Except for these differences, the patent is basically the same as the production item.

200 450

YOUR CHOICE—ANY 4 for Only $1.00

The Ten Most Outstanding Low Priced Mechanical Toys of the Year

All metal toys, prettily lithographed. Sturdily constructed and equipped with superior long lasting spring motors.

1—10-In. Dump Truck With Real Dumping Feature.
2—8-In. Climbing Popeye.
Stand on one end of the string, pull the upper end, and Popeye will climb up.
3—Bucking Broncho with Cowboy.
Clever action imitating a bucking broncho. Size, 6¼x2¼x5¼ in.
4—Mechanical Road Roller.
Has slow motion like the big road rollers. Size, 8¼x4¼x4 in.
5—Kitty Cat Playing Ball.
New easy winding toy. Just push lever (tail) down, release and toy is in motion. Size, 8x3¾x4½ in.
Give Numbers and names of the four toys you select.

6—16-In. Speedy King Racer.
Painted exhaust pipes on sides.
7—Krazy Kat Scooter.
Watch him race around in circles. Size, 8x6½x3⅛ in.
8—12-Inch Cadillac Coupe.
Has bumper in front, bumperettes and trunk rack in rear.
9—10-In. Delivery Motorcycle.
A snappy toy with big play value.
10—Horse Pulling Lumber Wagon.
Front wheels turn to run wagon straight or in circles. Size overall, 13x 4¾x4 inches.

Any 4 for $1.00

49K5791—Average shpg. wt. of 4 toys, 3 lbs. 8 oz.....

③ Buses and Trucks

The chapter is divided into three sections: Buses, Trucks, and Vehicle Sets and Groups. *Toys are listed alphabetically within each of these sections.* Major groups in the Bus section include Buses and Bus-Related Toys. Major groups in the Trucks section include Army Trucks, Assorted Trucks, Auto Transports, Dump Trucks (listed by size), Emergency Service Trucks, Fire Trucks, Mack Trucks (listed by size), Stake Trucks, Tow Trucks, Tractor Trailers: Sets and Groups, and Tractor Trailers: Single.

BUSES

Although Marx made fewer buses than trucks, many of the buses are very attractive. *Buses are lithographed tin windups unless otherwise specified.*

BLUE LINE TOURS BUS: 1930s. 9-1/2" long. This English Marx toy has the same basic body as the American Marx

This 6" Greyhound Bus, probably made in the 1930s, has an attached tin grille and a side luggage compartment. T. Riley Collection.

The tiny Liberty Bus is about 5" long and was made around 1931. It has blue or green wheels. T. Riley Collection.

                                          Good   Exc

Royal Bus. The Blue Line Tours Bus has different lithography, fewer windows, and no rear luggage rack. It has been said about the Blue Line Tours Bus that " 'Bee-Line Tours' might have been a more fitting title for this 1930s, English-made, Louis Marx bus, length 24 cm [roughly 9-1/2"] with the crouched driver wearing a helmet and goggles." (It is known that there was a commuter Bee-Lines Bus Company on Long Island during World War II.) "Blue Line Tours" is on the upper side of the bus, "Seats 29" on the front side of the bus, [1] and "London, Birmingham, and Manchester" near the rear of the bus. The incongruous racing figure who drives the bus is from a Marx racer.   **100   250**

---

[1] A photograph of the Blue Line Tours Bus can be seen in David Pressland's *The Art of the Tin Toy* (New York: Crown Publishers, Inc., 1976), p. 175.

The boldly striped 10-1/4" long Royal Bus Lines toy, made in 1928, has both a rear luggage box and a roof luggage rack. Dr. M. Kates Collection. R. Grubb photograph.

Good   Exc

COAST TO COAST BUS: 1930s. About 10" long. This double-decker bus is similar in its basic shape and size to the Blue Line Tours Bus and the Royal Bus. In 1932 it sold for 25 cents. "Coast to Coast" is above the lower windows, and various cities are listed toward the rear of the bus. "Atlantic" and a greyhound dog are on the lower side. The Coast to Coast Bus has a striped hood and a spare tire, both of which also appear on the Royal Bus. The bus has a bumper, a driver, and head-

lights that do not operate. A photograph of this toy can be seen in an April 1984 Lloyd Ralston Auction catalog. **100   225**

GREYHOUND BUS: Circa 1930s. 6" long. This silver-colored bus has a stamped-steel front and rear bumpers, and a side luggage compartment embossed with a greyhound dog. The door is also embossed. The grille is a separate piece of

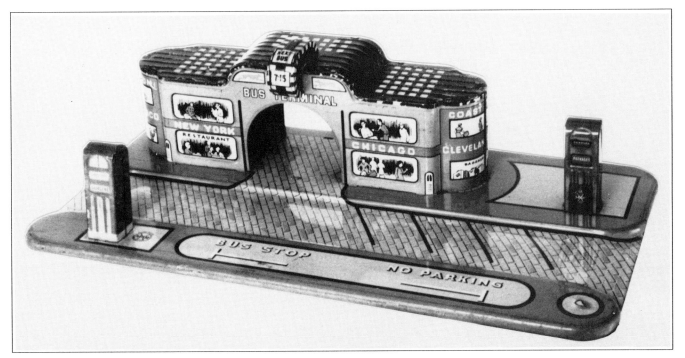

The Bus Terminal, made around 1937, has a 12" long x 6-1/2" high base and an unusual central arch. The "Stop" and "Go" sign is missing from this example. T. Riley Collection.

Good Exc

metal that is attached to the front of the toy. The bus is similar to a Greyhound Bus which comes in the Miniature Pull Toy Assortment (see page 109), but has fewer windows, a side luggage compartment, and an embossed door. This bus may have been sold as part of a set, as well as individually.

75 150

LIBERTY BUS: 1931. 5" long x 2" high. This charming little red bus has a black roof with red stripes, black running boards and fenders, and large, 1-1/4" diameter green or blue wheels. The driver and his seat are made out of one piece of metal (the outline of the driver is punched out of the seat, then bent up). The windshield overhang reads "Limited". "Liberty Bus Co." and "62" are on the side of the bus, and the Marx logo is on the back of the bus. The toy may have been sold individually or as part of a set.

50 125

MYSTERY SPEEDWAY BUS: 1938. 14" long. It is strongly suspected that this bus was made by Marx. Marx made a number of other similar "mystery" toys that moved after being pressed, including the Mystery Taxi, Mystery Cat, and Mystery Sandy, all made around the same time. Priced at 42 cents, the bus is described in the 1938 Sears Christmas catalog as a "New Mystery Bus. Smart streamlined bus. Easy to operate. Simply press down on back of roof — bus speeds away for long distance." It is pictured next to the Marx Mystery Sandy Dog. People are lithographed onto the windows and "Speedway Bus" is on the side.

160 350

ROYAL BUS LINES BUS: 1928. 10-1/4" long x 3-1/4" wide x 3-1/4" high. This bus is similar to the Blue Line Tours Bus and the Coast to Coast Bus. According to Dr. Malcolm Kates, the body of the bus is lithographed in red and pale yellow horizontal bands. A red "Royal Bus Lines" is above the windows. It has blue wheels, green fenders, a blue rear luggage box, and unpainted, stamped metal front bumpers, rear bumpers, and roof luggage rack. The driver is similar to those used in the racers, and there are several cut-out passengers mounted on the frame that runs along the sides and rear of the bus. Two braces run across the bus, one for the driver and one for the

Good Exc

four passengers. The bus has a spare tire on its side and headlights that do not operate. Excellent price includes original box.

175 400

SCHOOL BUS: 11-1/2" long x 4-1/2" high. According to Eric Matzke, this orange pull toy bus has a steel body, wooden wheels, and a ding-dong bell. It has black, rubber-stamped lettering and a "Liberty Bell" decal on the top front. In 1940 another longer pull toy bus was advertised next to several other Marx toys.

160 225

BUS-RELATED TOYS

BUS TERMINAL: Circa 1937. 12" long x 6-1/2" wide. Trip Riley describes this terminal as gray with light blue and black trim and a black roof. The cream, red, and black base reads "Bus Stop" and "No Parking" on its front edge. Directional arrows under these words point to the corners of the base. An art deco sign on the roof, "Next Bus 7:15", is fastened so that it is parallel to the roof line, unlike the sign on the Blue Bird Garage (see page 58). There is a light blue gasoline pump in front of the terminal on the left and a stop-and-go sign on the right. Behind the building, on the right, is a U. S. Mailbox. The same stamping is used on the gasoline pump and on the mailbox. The blue center strip between the upper and lower windows of the terminal is outwardly embossed. The names of various cities are embossed onto the walls of the building, and people are lithographed onto the windows. A central arch lettered "Bus Terminal" extends across the building which is similar in shape to the Marx Union Station and the Blue Bird Garage, minus the arch.

The Bus Terminal was sold individually, but it also came as part of a set that included Union Station and a City Airport. The three sold for the bargain price of 89 cents.

Although this building has a central archway, a 1937 advertisement shows the building with an entranceway instead of an arch and two windows instead of four. The city

The Greyhound Bus Terminal, made around 1938, has a 16" long x 11" wide base with access ramps on each end. T. Riley Collection.

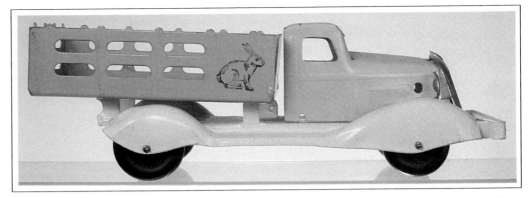

This pastel-colored Type 1 Stake Truck is rubber-stamped with a bunny on one side and a chick on the other. It was probably made for the Easter season. T. Riley Collection.

                              Good   **Exc**

names have been moved from the center to the top of the building. The advertisement states that the toy comes with two buses and a: "House 3-1/4" high, on base representing ticket office and terminal in appropriate design. Furnished with two miniature pull buses. Has dummy gasoline pump and 'stop' and 'go' sign which is operated by means of wire handle."

    The toy, listed for 50 cents in the 1934 Butler Brothers catalog, provides an illustration which is detailed enough to suggest that a version of the Bus Terminal was made without an arch. Also, both Union Station and Blue Bird Garage are made in this shape. To make the Bus Terminal without an arch, the lithography is the only thing that needed to be changed. Excellent price includes original box. **160   350**

GREYHOUND BUS TERMINAL: Circa 1938. 16" long x 11" wide. According to Trip Riley, this art deco terminal has two light blue gasoline pumps, two blue sign boards, and two garage entrances with the Greyhound motif and "Greyhound" repeated near the top of each. The light blue drug store at the center of the terminal shows lithographed people and "Sodas",

                              Good   **Exc**

"Drugs", and, next to the clock, "Next Bus East 10 Min." To the right of the drug store and garages is a light blue waiting room (this wing was also used on both ends of the Marx Grand Central Station). A black "Buses" sign with jagged yellow-outlined red letters is on top of the waiting room; the sign extends down the side of the room and reads "Greyhound". A "Greyhound" sign is above the waiting room window and below three lithographed greyhounds. The back of the terminal consists of a Greyhound waiting room, a telegraph office, a gift shop, and a "Men's Furnishings" store. People are lithographed onto these buildings, and a half-moon design is lithographed over the doors. The Greyhound Bus Terminal originally came with vehicles, but there is no information on them. "Greyhound Bus Terminal" is inside a red rectangle on the front edge of the 16" x 11" base, which is similar to the base used on the General Alarm Fire House. The center sections of the Greyhound Bus Terminal and the Marx General Alarm Fire House use the same stamping. In addition, the Bus Terminal, the Fire House, and the City Airport have the same garage stamping and small parts. Excellent price includes original box. **150   325**

TRUCKS

    Trucks are among the most popular toys with Marx collectors. Like other Marx toys, trucks were made in great variety. They are powered in different ways: windup trucks have a spring-wound motor, electrically-powered trucks have batteries, friction non-windup trucks are pushed by hand to activate a flywheel, and non-powered trucks have no motor. Trip Riley has comprehensively outlined the main types of trucks in the chart on pages 72 and 73.

The 10" Deluxe Delivery Truck is an example of a Type 2 truck. Made in the 1940s, the truck has a hole on each of its sides, but none on the hood or doors. T. Riley Collection. (For a description, see page 81.)

Truck, Cab, and Chassis Types

Compiled by Trip Riley
With the assistance of Cyndie Bare

TYPE	BODY CONSTRUCTION	HOOD	WINDSHIELD
1	Chassis has cab not part of frame (later trucks have one-piece frame and cab). Also "D" notch at base of cab door on each side. See photos on page 71.	Two teardrop embossed vents. 7/32" diameter hole each side behind headlight for electric bus bar.	One-piece windshield with straight top edge.
2	Truck, cab, chassis made from one piece of stamped steel. Separate bumper tabbed onto chassis. Some cabs may have holes for door handles or steel rod that keeps a battery in place. Door handle holes are for battery clamp. Observe green auto carrier cab with headlights which has a formed door lever. See photos on page 71.	Some cabs have two holes on each side of hood (one hole is caused by punching a tab). Front holes on each side of hood are to hold the electric light terminal bar. Hood bends down at windshield.	Divided.
3	Truck, cab, chassis made from one piece of metal. Bumper, grille, headlight are one piece of metal, tabbed onto chassis. No holes in door handle area or in hood. Two holes above running board on both sides of body. Same basic cab as Type 2. See photos on page 74.	Tin center strip. Hood bends down at windshield.	Divided. Upper corners squared by pillar.
4	Truck, cab, chassis made from one piece of metal. Bumper, grille, headlight are one piece of metal tabbed onto chassis. Same grille as Type 3. No holes in door handle area or in hood. Two holes above running board on both sides of body. See photos on page 74.	Tin center strip.	Divided. Upper corners rounded.
5	Truck, cab, chassis made from one piece of metal. Bumper, grille, headlight are one piece of metal tabbed onto chassis. No holes in door handle area or in hood. Two holes above running board on both sides of body. See photos on page 75.	Tin center strip.	Not divided.
6	Truck, cab, chassis made from one piece of metal. Bumper, grille, headlight are one piece of metal tabbed onto chassis. No holes in door handle area or in hood. Two holes above running board on both sides of body. Cab is flatter and has longer windows than Types 1-5. See photos on page 75.	Tin center strip. Larger hood than Types 1-5.	Divided by thick pillar.

WHEELS	EMBOSSING ON SIDE DOORS	MISCELLANEOUS	TYPE
Black-finished wood retained by fenders. Each fender creates a cup effect.	Well-defined. Continues onto the hood.	Expensive to assemble, but die work to make parts was simpler. Can be multicolored.	1
Wooden. Retaining washers.	Elaborate.	Tabs (see "Hood") can be seen from underside of truck. Purpose of tab not known, but may possibly be related to operating headlight. Battery may have had strip or rubber band around it to hold it in place. Rear fenders on top of chassis.	2
Wooden.	Elaborate.		3
Wooden. Retaining washers.	Minimal.	Clean lines at intersection of hood and window. New rear fenders strap about 3/16" below top of chassis.	4
Wooden. No retaining washers (but body has long tabs to retain the wheels).	Minimal.	Grille has horizontal embossed bars. Bumper has bumper guards. Headlights bent over to follow contours of fender. Clean lines at intersection of hood and window. Headlights are embossed with ribs.	5
Wooden. No retaining washers (but body has tabs to restrict front wheel movement). Red metal hubcaps on rear wheels. Rear wheels mounted on outside of frame.	Minimal.	No rear fenders. Grille has horizontal embossed bars. Bumper has bumper guards. Headlights bent over to follow contours of fender. Different from Type 5 in that headlights are smooth and rounded in front.	6

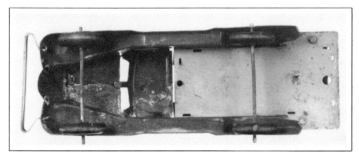

A view of the underside of the Deluxe Delivery Truck. T. Riley Collection.

Compare the fronts of a Type 3 and a Type 4 truck. T. Riley Collection.

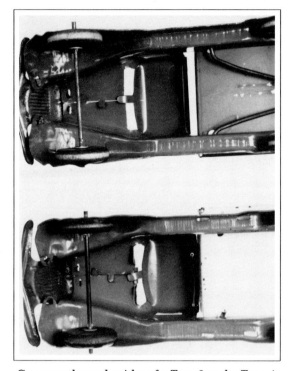

Compare the undersides of a Type 3 and a Type 4 truck. T. Riley Collection.

This Meadow Brook Dairy Truck is an example of a Type 4 truck. Made around 1940, it is 10" long. It has an off-white body and a tin hood strip. (For the Meadow Brook Dairy Trailer, see the photo of the Motor Market Trailer, Type 6, on page 76.) T. Riley Collection.

This 13" Ice Truck is an example of a Type 3 truck made in the 1940s. The rear of the body is bent down to form a step. "Ice" is rubber-stamped in large letters. See listing on page 82. T. Riley Collection.

This Type 5 Sand Truck has "Sand Gravel" rubber-stamped onto the truck. It has an aluminum dumper body, a red shaker screen, and an eccentric lever. T. Riley Collection. See listing on page 84.

ABOVE LEFT: *The base of the Sand Truck. T. Riley Collection.* **ABOVE RIGHT:** *This example of a Type 6 truck is a 1939 Motor Market Truck. The 10" truck has a white chassis, cab, and body. "Made in U. S. A." and "Marx Toys" are rubber-stamped onto the truck, while "Made in U. S. A." is embossed onto the lower right side of the truck. T. Riley Collection. C. Myer photograph. See listing on page 83.* **LEFT:** *The base of the Type 6 Motor Market Truck. T. Riley Collection. C. Myer photograph.*

The Ice Trailer on the right has a rear step, similar to the Ice Truck. It is 6-1/4" long with the step. The trailer does not have a Marx logo on it. Also shown on the left is the Baggage Express Trailer. T. Riley Collection. C. Myer photograph.

On the left, this white Motor Market Trailer has the same body as the Motor Market Truck. The center strip horizontally divides the storage area. On the right is the Meadow Brook Dairy Trailer. Both trailers have Marx logo embossing. T. Riley Collection. C. Myer photograph. See listings on pages 82 and 83.

This Army Truck has rear benches, a canopy, and wooden wheels. There is no visible lettering on the toy. T. Riley Collection.

The 10" Medical Corps Ambulance Truck has an opening rear door. T. Riley Collection. C. Myer photograph.

ARMY TRUCKS

	Good	Exc

ARMY TRUCK: Circa 1950. About 12" long. This olive drab plastic truck, marked "U. S. Army" on the hood, has a plastic Army driver with a head that turns. The truck has a steel frame, an opening tailgate, and rubber tires. The front wheels can go straight or turn the truck in a circle. It closely resembles the Auto Mac Truck (see opposite page).   **30   75**

ARMY TRUCK with REAR BENCHES and CANOPY: 10" long. According to Trip Riley, this Type 2 truck has a hole on each of its side doors. The left side has a tab that forms a hole. The olive drab-painted truck has no operating headlights, benches inside the truck, and a canvas canopy stretched over two wire supports. There is visible lettering on the truck and the canopy. The truck has wooden wheels with retainer washers on the inside of the wheels where the axles are crimped.   **50   125**

MACK ARMY TRUCKS: See Mack Trucks section.

MEDICAL CORPS AMBULANCE TRUCK: 1940s. This Type 4 truck has an olive drab body, cab, and chassis and an extended body with an opening rear door. (The same truck body was used on at least one other truck, but has no windows.) "Medical Corps" is rubber-stamped onto the sides of the truck in black. (For more ambulances, see Mack Trucks section and the Automobiles chapter.)   **75   175**

MILITARY CANNON TRUCK: Circa 1939. 10" long. This Type 4 truck has an olive drab cab and chassis, a medium blue deck, and an olive drab gun base. The red cannon, which is also used on the Marx Military Train, has a 5/8" bore and a black spring-loaded firing mechanism with an olive drab end plate. The rear window of the cab is formed from the base.   **75   175**

The cannon of the 10" Military Cannon Truck, made around 1939, is also used on the Marx Military Train. T. Riley Collection. C. Myer photograph.

Good   Exc   **Good   Exc**

ARTILLERY SET (Three-piece): 1930. This set, listed for 98 cents in the 1930 Sears Fall/Winter catalog, is described as having a "10 inch cannon that actually shoots the four wood pellets included. There is also a 9 inch caisson with two lithographed metal soldiers and a 6 1/2 inch typical Army wagon with a standard Army wagon cover, all parts made of metal in Army colors." The Army wagon cover reads "U. S. Army". Two soldiers in World War I uniforms sit on a caisson pulled by the Army wagon. A cannon is mounted on the caisson.   **90   190**

ASSORTED TRUCKS

AUTO MAC TRUCK: 1950. 12" long. The yellow and red Auto Mac comes with a card that reads, "I drive this truck, I start it, stop it, dump it, my head turns to check the delivery. Signed Auto Mac". [2]   Priced at $2.89, this Studebaker-style truck is described in the 1950 Sears catalog: "Watch him ride along in his truck ... pull to a quick stop ... dump his load ... turn his head to check results ... then speed along to his next stop ... all this automatically! Mac and his big truck molded of bright sturdy plastic. Truck has strong steel frame, tail-gate that opens. Adjustable front wheels. Rubber tires protect floors. Clockspring motor, brake."

Although the Army Truck with Rear Benches is very similar, it is not included in the advertisement.   **40   85**

CARPENTER'S TRUCK: Early 1940s. 14" long. This red and blue stake truck is made of pressed steel. A decal on the side of the truck shows various tools, including a saw. The truck is thought to have come with tools, but it is not known at the present time what they are. The box reads "Carpenter's Truck" and has a realistic drawing of the truck. Excellent price includes original box.   **125   275**

CITY DELIVERY VAN: 11" long. This yellow steel truck with red fenders has a separate tin grille attached to the body. "City Delivery" is black rubber-stamped on the truck's side.
                                              110   225

The Army Cannon Trailer has no visible lettering or embossing. It has the same cannon as the Mack Cannon Army Truck. or the Military Cannon Truck. T. Riley Collection. C. Myer photograph.

---

[2] Rick Rubis (no title), *Marx Toys Collector Newsletter*, Vol. 2, No. 4, p. 17.

This 1950 Curtiss Candy Truck still has its original ten rolls of candy! The 9" plastic truck has rubber wheels. J. Newbraugh Collection.

	Good	**Exc**

COAL TRUCK (First): About 11-1/2" to 12-1/2". This truck has a red cab and chassis, and a lithographed blue and yellow dumper with "Coal" in yellow. It has covered fenders, wheels, a separate tin grille, small cab windows, and embossing on the door. A lever on the side tilts the dumper.

110   225

COAL TRUCK (Second): This light blue truck has a coal dumper with the same shape as the truck above, but different lithography. The red coal dumper has black and white accents and "Coal" in white on the side. This truck also has a separate tin grille and side lever with embossing on the door. Excellent price includes original box.

120   250

This 10" Dump Truck has a lever tilt. The name "Contractors and Builders" is rubber-stamped in black on the dumper. T. Riley Collection. C. Myer photograph.

A colorful magazine advertisement for the Curtiss Candy Truck. Courtesy of Paul Kruska.

	Good	Exc

COAL TRUCK (Third): 1939. 10" long. This Lumar Coal Co. Truck is a Type 4 truck with a shute and a rear door.

A dumper with the same lithography and color comes with "Coke" and "Sand" (see Coke Truck on the next page). The same dumper with "Coke" was used on a Marx tractor as well. Excellent price includes original box. **120 250**

COCA-COLA TRUCK (First): Late 1940s. 20" long. This is a large yellow stamped-steel stake truck, with covered wheels and a separate tin grille attached to the body. On the front side of the bin is a primarily red decal with a figure's head. Wording on the decal says "Coca-Cola, Take Some Home Today". Beside the figure, who is wearing the Coca-Cola bottle top as a hat, is a picture of a Coca-Cola bottle.

This truck and another very similar truck made by Richard Murray in the late 1940s is discussed in an interesting article by William Allen, Jr. in the *Marx Toy Collector Newsletter*. Mr. Allen describes the Murray truck as being the same size as the Marx truck and having a decal on the door which reads, "A Radar Flash Product — Richard Murray Co., Butler, Penna."

He writes, "Both trucks have the same cab, chassis and stake body. The rear 'bullet' fenders have been trimmed away on the Murray truck. The grille work on both trucks is nearly identical. There are differences in the tires, however. The Murray truck has large solid rubber tires, while the Marx truck has tin litho tires with "Louis Marx & Co., N. Y." on them. The Murray truck is dark red and blue, almost dull. The Marx truck is bright red and yellow."

	Good	Exc

(Some Marx Coca-Cola trucks have been seen in all yellow, with a red decal. Trucks with solid black wheels have also been seen.)

Mr. Allen asks why the two trucks are so similar: "Did Mr. Murray work for Marx, then go out on his own? Was he on his own to begin with, and sold a successful design to Marx? Did he acquire the Marx stampings?"[3]

It is possible that Marx either acquired the Murray dies or company, or used the Murray dies or lent dies from the Marx Company, all for a fee, of course. It is known that Marx shared tools and dies with at least one other company, Unique Art, and shared a patent with another, the Hoge Company.

170 350

COCA-COLA TRUCK (Second): Late 1940s or early 1950s. 17" long. This truck is smaller than the First Coca-Cola Truck described above. It has a red cab and chassis, and the same decal as the larger truck. However, the yellow stake body is lithographed instead of having open slots. The front wheels are covered with fenders, but the rear wheels are not. The catalog number for this truck is #1005. The truck comes in a plain box lettered "Metal Coca-Cola Truck". **90 200**

COCA-COLA TRUCK (Plastic): 1950. This Coca-Cola truck, which sold originally for $1.29, is described in the 1950 Sears Christmas catalog as "Gleaming plastic in authentic

---

[3] William Allen, Jr., "How? Why?", *Marx Toy Collector Newsletter*, Vol. 2, No. 1, p. 15.

The 14" "Run Right to Read's" Stake Truck, made around 1940, has fender-covered wheels. T. Riley Collection. C. Myer photograph.

Good   Exc

colors, decorated with Coca-Cola trade marks. Two open shelves hold 6 miniature Coca-Cola cases. Truck about 11" long, has rubber wheels."   **80   175**

Variations: Two yellow variations, #829 and #1087, have green bottles, black wheels, and a red sign board at the top of the truck which reads "Delicious Coca-Cola Refreshing".

Both trucks have slightly different fender arrangements than the one shown in the ad. The ad illustration shows uncovered front wheels and covered rear wheels which suggests the possibility of a third variation.

Variation #829, the shelves of which most resemble the Sears ad, has red front fenders, and rear fenders that cover the wheels. It has an extra protruding ledge which reads "Coca-Cola" (four times) all along the length of the ledge.

Variation #1087 has uncovered rear wheels, no red fenders or protruding ledge, and more shelves.

COKE TRUCK: Circa 1940s. 11-1/2" long. This red steel truck has wooden wheels. The dumper, which is also used on a Marx tractor, is the same as in the Coal Truck but it is now marked "Coke". The Marx logo is at the end of the word. Like the other trucks, this one has a separately attached grille, side lever, door embossing, and covered wheels.   **80   175**

CONTRACTORS and BUILDERS TRUCK: 10" long. This Type 4 truck has a lever tilt, red cab and chassis, and a medium blue dump body, rubber-stamped "Contractors and Builders". The truck is similar in shape to the little unlettered 4-1/2" dump truck which came on a Marx train flatcar.
    60   125

CURTISS CANDY TRUCK: 1950. 9" long. This red plastic truck with black rubber wheels sold for 83 cents in 1950. The truck is marked in white on the door, "Curtiss Candy Company". However, what makes this truck so unique is that it came with ten packages of real Curtiss candy in its dumper.

Good   Exc

Needless to say, it is difficult to find the original candy along with the truck!

The Curtiss Candy Truck comes in a mostly red box lithographed to look like a building.

Marx was not the only manufacturer to combine candy with a truck. In the 1930s Hubley made a Life Saver Truck. There was a hole in the truck's rear to hold a pack of Life Savers candy.   **110   225**

DELUXE DELIVERY TRUCK: 1948. 13-1/4" long. The truck is stamped steel, with a banner-like decal on the side marked "Deluxe Delivery". The 1948 Montgomery Ward Christmas catalog advertises the truck for 89 cents and describes it as having a "Modern design, open rack delivery body, movable tailgate. Metal enamel finish, 13-1/4 in. long."

A photograph of a 10" Deluxe Delivery Truck is on page 71. There are also other Deluxe Delivery Trucks and a Deluxe Delivery Rider Truck from the 1950s.   **75   175**

This Coal Truck (Second) from the 1940s is about 12-1/2" long and has an attached tin grille and covered wheels. The same dumper with different lettering is used on other trucks. E. Owens Collection.

Good   Exc

GRAVEL TRUCK (First): 1930s to early 1940s. 10" long. This gravel truck, as described by Frances and James Nichols, has a gray pressed-steel cab, a red tin lithographed dump bin with "Gravel" on the side, a separate tin grille, and wooden wheels covered by fenders. The dump bin is similar to those on the Coal and Coke Trucks.   **75   175**

GRAVEL TRUCK (Second): 1940s. 8-1/2" long. This metal truck, as described by Frances and James Nichols, has a tin grille, red cab, blue dump bin, running boards, black rubber tires, and decals. "Gravel" is in red on the side of the dumper.

50   110

GRAVEL TRUCK (Third): 1930s. 10" long. Instead of a dump bin, this metal truck has a moving drum marked "Gravel Mixer". The Marx logo and "Made in U. S. A." are underneath.   **75   175**

HI-WAY EXPRESS TRUCK: Late 1940s to mid 1950s. 16" long.

First Version: Late 1940s. This metal truck, as described by Frances and James Nichols, has a blue cab, red and yellow body, tin wheels, and grille. The yellow back door opens. The back door also comes in blue. "Hi-Way Express" is on the side of the enclosed van with a white strip underneath with the

The Sand Truck (Second Version) has the same dump bin as the first version, but differs in other ways. E. Owens Collection.

Good   Exc

names of the cities "New York", "Chicago", and "San Francisco". Underneath the city names is an attractive map and "Cross Country Services".

Although the truck was manufactured in the late 1940s, no ads were found for this toy until 1950, when it sold for 94 cents. Later (after 1950), Marx made a Hi-Way Express Tractor Trailer Truck.   **80   175**

Second Version: Mid-1950s. An English version of the Hi-Way Express Truck is shown in David Pressland's book, *The*

These Sand and Coal Trucks, made around the 1940s, are about 12-1/2" long. Although the dump bins are similar, the trucks themselves have different cabs, fenders, and windows. E. Owens Collection.

This 10" Truck with Searchlight has a battery holder under the deck and a toolbox behind the cab. T. Riley Collection. C. Myer photograph.

	Good	Exc

Art of the Tin Toy. This truck is similar to the first American version. The lithography on the English version has the name and strip, but the city names are replaced with "Nation Wide Delivery". The map is replaced by a wheel-like shape over which the words "Service Over The World" climb in a snake-like fashion. The front fender is more rounded and smaller than in the American truck. [4]   **80   175**

ICE TRUCK: 1940s. 13" long. This "Polar Ice Company" Truck comes with two blown-glass ice blocks and a set of ice tongs. (Extra blocks could be purchased originally.) The truck has a red cab, yellow stake body, and tin grille. (Some trucks are all platic with a metal stake body.) A decal on the stake body shows a polar bear and "Polar Ice Company".

A 1946 *Fortune* magazine article states that the sales of the truck were revitalized when the truck was turned into an ice truck with glass ice blocks and tongs. [5]   **90   200**

JEEPS: See Automobiles chapter.

LUMAR MOTOR TRANSPORT: 1942. 13" long. The 1942 Sears Christmas catalog describes this truck listed at 56 cents as having a modern airflow design and various lithography on the side. "Lumar Motor Transport" is on the truck's side. Fenders cover the wheels and the attached metal grille has a horizontal design. The truck has an open bed.

The Lumar Motor Transport Truck is very similar to the Deluxe Delivery Truck. (See Tractor Trailers for more Lumar trucks.)   **70   160**

MAGNETIC CRANE and TRUCK: 1950. This interesting metal toy, listed for $2.79 in the 1950 Montgomery Ward Christmas catalog, is described as follows: "Swing the revolving cabin around and pick up any metal load to about 2 lbs. A strong electromagnet fastened to the lifting hook operates on a standard flashlight battery that fits in the cabin ... 14 inch 3-position steel boom revolves. Line with die-cast cargo hook, operated by hand crank, raises or lowers loads. Size 25 in. long, 4-3/4 in. wide, 13-1/2 in. high to top of boom."

The all-red truck has black tin wheels, a yellow cabin and crane; a blue/green cabin roof and on the side of the cabin, enclosed in a red badge-like shape, "Magnetic Crane". "Magnetic" is printed horizontally while the word "Crane" is vertical. Both words are cleverly designed to intersect at the letter "E".   **125   300**

MARCREST DAIRY TRUCK: 14" long. This white truck comes with three glass milk bottles. It is the same truck as the Motor Market Truck, except for color and decals. The Marcrest Dairy Truck has its name on the decal.

In the 1960s Marx made a Marcrest Livestock Lines Truck. Excellent price includes original box.   **125   300**

MEADOW BROOK DAIRY TRUCK: Circa 1940. 10" long.
First Version: This Type 4 truck has fenders covering both front and rear wheels and two holes above the running board. (For a photograph, see page 74.)

---

[4] David Pressland, *The Art of the Tin Toy*, (New York: Crown Publishers, Inc., 1976), p. 200.
[5] "Louis Marx: Toy King," *Fortune*, 1946, p. 124.

	Good	Exc

Second Version: This truck is shown in the book, *Past Joys*, by Ken Botto. [6] Unlike the first version, the truck has only front wheels covered by fenders and only one hole above the running board. The truck is loaded with corked milk bottles in what appears to be a carrier and it is possible that variations could have been sold both with and without these bottles. Excellent price includes original box.   **125   300**

MOTOR MARKET TRUCK: 1939. 10" long.
First Version: This Type 6 truck has a white chassis, cab, and body, rubber-stamped with "Made in U. S. A." and "Marx Toys". The truck fenders are a rounded shape covering only the front wheels. (For a photograph, see page 75.)   **75   200**

Second Version: As described by Frances and James Nichols, this 13" truck has a bright red cab, blue stake body, tin lithographed wheels and grille, and primarily yellow decal with a figure carrying a box marked "Delivery". At the top and bottom of the decal is "Motor Market" in red. This version has less rounded larger fenders than the first version that cover both front and rear wheels.   **75   200**

Third Version: This 18" truck has a removable partition. The 1940 Christmas Sears catalog advertises this truck as selling for 79 cents. The truck resembles the first version with the stamped name and logo, but again the fenders differ in that they cover both the front and rear wheels.

The most interesting feature, however, of this advertised truck is the addition of a miniature scale and pan on a metal bracket to weigh orders. The truck comes with a supply of name brand cartons. (The first version, and probably the second, also comes with these cartons.)   **75   200**

---

[6] Ken Botto, *Past Joys*, (San Francisco: Prism Editions, Chronicle Books, 1978), p. 12.

	Good	Exc

PET SHOP TRUCK: 11" long. This delightful truck is very similar to the plastic Coca Cola Truck listed on page 80. The 1950 Sears Christmas catalog describes the truck, priced at $1.45, as: "Plastic truck has movable, transparent sides that reveal 6 compartments, each holds a different breed [removable] dog of vinyl plastic about 1 3/4" long. Truck has rubber wheels." On the top of the truck is a sign that reads "Pet Shop".   **75   200**

RAILWAY EXPRESS AGENCY TRUCK: 1940s to 1950s. Markings on this green closed van truck include "Railway Express Agency" on the side, a large "Air Express" decal with a globe above the name, and on either side "Railway Express Agency" in diamond-shaped decals. The truck has a hydraulic tailgate and comes with a dolly and name brand packages.   **65   150**

R. C. A. TELEVISION SERVICE TRUCK: Circa 1948 to 1950. 8-1/4" long. This dark blue or light green plastic Ford panel truck has a metal red-painted chassis, black-painted wooden wheels, and ladder brackets on the roof which hold a yellow extension ladder that extends to over 13". Authentic R C A logos appear on the sides and rear door along with Nipper, the R C A dog, and "his master's voice." The rear door opens and inside is a tear-off work order pad lettered "... This customer wants:" and lists such things as "Complete Coverage Contract" and "Outdoor Antenna Installation". Inside the truck at the center on the top is the Marx logo.

On the bottom of the box is an assembly diagram that shows how to install the ladder and ladder brackets. Excellent price includes original box.   **120   250**

ROAD BUILDER TRUCK #1033: 1950.
First Version: This interesting truck consists of a yellow cab and chassis, yellow dump bed, red underframe, black rubber wheels, and a red scoop loader attached to the front. Markings

The transport part of this 11-1/2" windup Auto Transport, made in 1932, can be separated from the truck section, but the cars are permanently tabbed to the transporter. (See listing on page 96.) Dr. M. Kates Collection. R. Grubb photograph.

Good Exc

on the truck include "Dump" and an arrow on the door near a lever. "Dump Truck" and other illegible words are repeated on a flap that sticks up behind the cab. **65 150**

Second Version: In the same 1950 Sears catalog that advertised the Pet Shop toy is this similar Road Builder Truck, priced at $1.94, which is likely another Marx version or possibly a Wyandotte toy. The toy is described: "Scoop loader picks up loads, dumps into the body. Release spring lever, body dumps automatically, tailgate opens. Heavy gauge steel, enamel finish, steel wheels, dummy headlights, grille and bumper. 20 1/2 inches overall." The ad illustration shows the scoop loader handle that covers the wheels and a flap that juts out horizontally on the dump bin front. Unlike the ad illustration, however, examples of the actual toy do not have wheels covered by the handle and have a vertical dump flap.[7] **65 150**

"RUN RIGHT TO READ'S" TRUCK: Circa 1940. 14" long. This truck has a red cab and chassis, a blue stake body, a shiny metal one-piece bumper, radiator grille, headlights, another

---

[7] In the 1950s Marx was still loading trucks such as the "Deluxe Delivery Service Truck" with cartons marked with well-known name brands.

Good Exc

shiny metal piece running down the center of the hood, black metal wheels, and a green decal with "Run Right To Read's" in yellow and a yellow border. It is not known whether Read's or Marx put on the decal, although it was probably Marx. (Read's was a Baltimore Drug Store chain now known as Rite Aid.) Marx occasionally used the name of a store on a toy (see Bamberger Truck (Small) in the Mack Truck section). The truck also comes with an assortment of product boxes for cargo.

The four-piece truck frame is spot-welded, which was a new technique in the late 1940s. A crossbar on the base holds the rear wheels in position so bent tabs are not needed. The truck is embossed with the Marx logo both on the crossbar and on the body.

In the 1950s a plastic Dump Truck was made using the same slogan. **75 200**

SAND TRUCK: 1940s. About 12-1/2" long. The sand truck may have come in other sizes (see Third Version).

First Version: It has a red and gray cab and chassis, a red underframe, and a red dump body with "Sand" in large white letters, and a black and white design on the lower side of the dump bin. The same dump bin is used with different wording

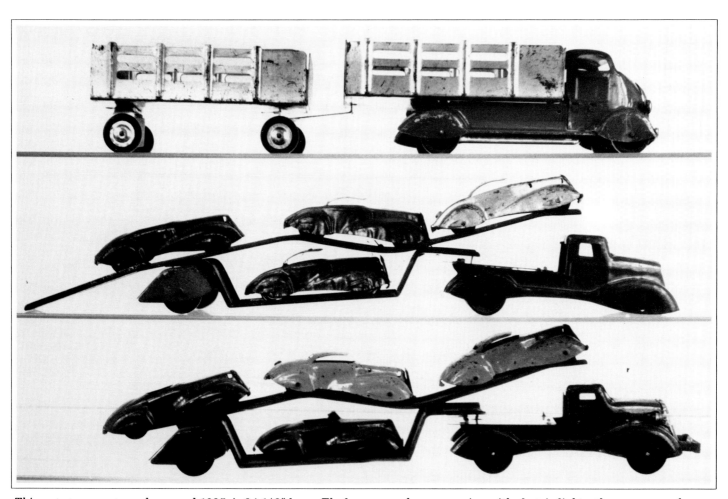

This auto transport, made around 1935, is 24-1/2" long. The lower row shows a version with electric lights; the upper row shows a version without lights. Also shown is the stake truck and trailer. (See listing on page 86.) T. Riley Collection.

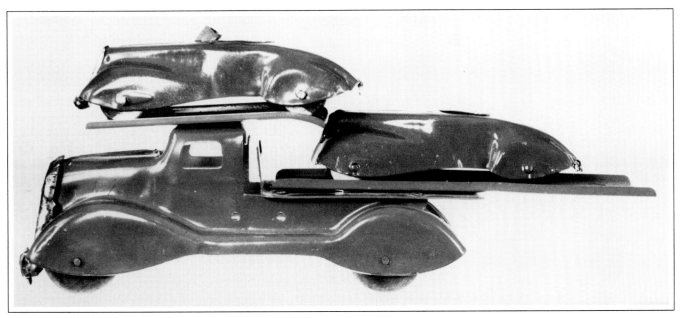

The 10-1/4" Truck circa 1948 has two metal cars. There is also a version of this toy with plastic cars. T. Riley Collection. C. Myer photograph.

Good   Exc

and sometimes different lithography on other trucks. Excellent price includes original box.   **75   200**

Second Version: This sand truck has the identical dump bin to the first version, but the truck is blue and the fenders do not cover the wooden wheels. Excellent price includes original box.   **75   200**

Third Version: 9" long. Selling for 67 cents in 1948, this truck has a different dump bin and, unlike the first two versions, does not come to a point at the back end. The side of the bin has a different design. The body of the truck resembles the Coal Truck pictured with the Sand Truck (on page 81), but it has slightly different back fenders.   **65   150**

Fourth Version: This Type 5 truck has a red cab, chassis, and underframe, an aluminum dumper body, a red shaker screen, and an eccentric lever. It has black wooden wheels with covered fenders. "Sand-Gravel" is rubber-stamped onto the sides of the dumper body. (See chart on pages 72-73 and two photographs on page 75.)   **65   150**

TOYLAND DAIRY TRUCK: 10" long. This Type 2 truck has four holes on each side of the chassis and cab. The truck has a red cab and chassis, a light blue bumper, deck, and body, and very faint (probably gold) stamping.   **75   200**

TRUCK with SEARCHLIGHT: 1930s. 10" long. This interesting unmarked truck has a red cab and chassis, a bumper, and wire handrails. There is a toolbox behind the cab which appears to be the same as those found with certain early toy railroad stations.

Mounted towards the rear of the truck is a searchlight which has a tinned back, a front lens holder with a red handle, and a glass focusing lens, similar to lenses found on early railroad searchlight cars and searchlight towers.

Good   Exc

The truck's blue deck goes up to meet the cab, forming the rear part of the cab. There is a tinned battery holder under the deck. Excellent price includes original box.   **110   250**

AUTO TRANSPORTS

Like other manufacturers, Marx made many auto transports over the years, starting around 1931. *The auto transports below are listed chronologically from 1931 to 1950.* Values include the racers, cars, and trucks that come with them.

1931 and 1932 AUTO TRANSPORTS: 22-3/4" long x 4-1/4" wide x 4" high. This red and black toy has a detachable dray trailer with drop front wheels and a start/stop lever. The transport carries three small removable driverless windup racers with lithographed exhausts and pointed rears as shown in the Butler Brothers catalog in October 1931. Though not shown in ads, each small racer bears the number "61". It is possible that the racer was made in a version without numbers. (See Racers (Miniature) on page 63.) The wheels of the transport have lithographed orange spokes with "28 x 4.75 Balloon Cord". By 1932 the smaller 11-1/2" Mack auto transport carrying three small rounded race cars (see listing on page 96) was being advertised.   **175   400**

1933 AUTO TRANSPORT: 22" long. Marx tried something new with this transport, adding battery-powered headlights which could be switched from bright to dim. (Marx also made other toys with electric lights at this same time.) The transport has three detachable cars, but instead of racers they are coupes measuring 5-7/8" x 2-1/4" x 2-1/2". Both the tractor and trailer have embossing on the sides and balloon-type rubber-tired wheels.

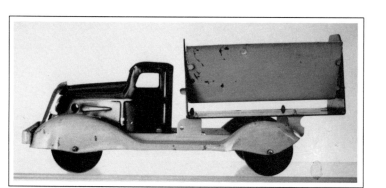

This 1930s 10" Side Dump Truck with wooden wheels is an unlighted version without the electric light terminal bar. T. Riley Collection.

Good   Exc

The set including two batteries is listed for 69 cents in the 1933 Sears Fall/Winter catalog. The same toy comes in what appears to be a non-electric version called the Auto Transwalk #T50447-B. The front of the trailer is used to make a wrecker, according to the June 1977 PB 84 auction catalog. Girard made an auto transport strikingly similar to this one. **175   400**

Good   Exc

1935-1937 AUTO TRANSPORTS: 24-1/2" long. This double-decker transport with electric headlights first appears in the 1935 Sears Fall/Winter catalog selling for 98 cents. The same version also comes without the electric lights.

The loading platform can be dropped to allow the three cars on the top level to roll down. The streamlined cars have sloping radiators and are each about 6" long. On the lower platform, there is a similar dump truck which really dumps. The auto transport truck comes in two variations, either with a red and green base and no electric lights or with a green and blue base, electric lights, and a red bumper. Similar cars and trucks were sold in sets by themselves.

As shown in the photograph (on page 84), the auto transport also comes with all cars (four in various colors) instead of three cars and one dump truck. **225   500**

1938 AUTO TRANSPORT: 30-1/2". The shape of the auto transport changes this year. Sides and a roof on the top are added, making the transport much sturdier and giving it an appearance almost like a bus. This new shape will be the basic shape for many years to come. By 1938 the size of the auto transport has increased to 30-1/2" with the two runways attached to load or unload the top level. There is also an unloading platform on the bottom. The transport carries three

14-1/2" windup Fire Truck, made around the 1940s, has an aluminum ladder that rotates and rises. T. Riley Collection. C. Myer photograph.

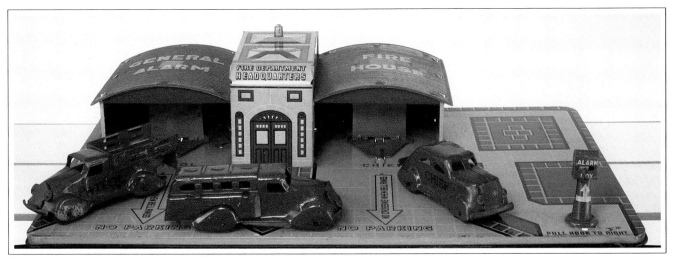

Made in 1938, the General Alarm Fire House ejects the emergency vehicles when the alarm bell rings. T. Riley Collection.

Good   **Exc**

vehicles of the same size as before: a coupe, a roadster, and a dump truck. Two of these are on the top and one is inside the trailer. The toy has eight wheels and a spare, according to the 1938 Sears Fall/Winter catalog. **225**   **500**

1940-1942 AUTO TRANSPORT: 21" long. This three-car transport is similar in shape to the 1938 Auto Transport. Selling for 94 cents, the toy is described in the 1940 Sears Christmas catalog as: "New cab-over engine hauler. 8 wheel trailer . . . Lower the ramp, let car roll out from lower deck, then attach the 12" skid rails and let the streamlined cars roll down." The catalog emphasizes that the toy is made from "Colorful auto fender steel". The trailer can be detached by lifting a hand lever. (There are markings on the bottom of the trailer near the back wheels, but these markings are illegible.)

In 1941 the same auto transport is advertised, but it has only two cars instead of three. (Marx was apparently trying to keep the price down.) By 1942 Marx gave up the price struggle and the price of the toy increased from 98 cents in 1941 to $1.29. **200**   **450**

1947-1948 AUTO TRANSPORT: This auto transport is the same as the 1942 Auto Transport. Ads mention that the detachable trailer has collapsible support. By 1948 a sign at the top of the trailer reads "Deluxe Auto Transport". The trailer can carry cars inside or on top and the tractor can be detached from the trailer and played with separately.

Also in 1948 a completely new auto transport appears. Selling for 97 cents, the toy is described in the 1948 Sears Christmas catalog as having "Two plastic sedans [that] ride on individual platforms [on truck]. Lower platform connects with upper for loading . . . unloading. 10-1/4" long." This transport has no separate trailer for the cars; the cars rest on platforms which are on the truck itself. The yellow cars shown in the ads have a more modern look than previously. Apparently this transport also comes with metal cars as shown by the photograph on page 85. The cars have the same streamlined look as those in earlier ads. It is possible that an all-metal version was sold just before 1948. The two-car auto carrier truck has a tilt back and a red chassis and cab. The two red convertibles have

Good   **Exc**

one-piece bodies with separate grilles and windshields. As in the other cars of these types, they do not have drivers, hood, or side trim. **125**   **300**

1950 AUTO TRANSPORT: 13-3/4" long. This transport is in a new size with wooden wheels. Unlike the version described above, it has a double-deck trailer with metal ramps and two 3-7/8" plastic sedans which are more modern in appearance than previous cars on the big transports. The 1950 Montgomery Ward Christmas catalog appears to show the toy, priced at 94 cents, without the words "Deluxe Auto Transport".

The transport has a gray truck cab and chassis, a red and blue auto carrier, and two yellow plastic cars. (For more information on this transport, see Tractor Trailers: Sets and Groups.) Also in 1950 the 10-1/4" and 22" transports continued to be sold. **75**   **150**

DUMP TRUCKS

Dump trucks are listed by size.

6" DUMP TRUCK: Mid-1930s.
First Version: This stamped-steel rubber-wheeled truck has dummy headlights and a vertical grille, but its fenders do not cover the wheels. It probably came as part of a set as well as being sold separately. **40**   **90**

Second Version: This truck has a red cab and chassis, a green dumper, and a side lever to move the dumper. **40**   **90**

6-1/4" DUMP TRUCK: From 6-1/4 to 6-1/2" long. 4" wheel base. This truck has a one-piece red cab and chassis with a separate tin grille and green body, a white tailgate, and wooden wheels. There are no Marx markings on the truck, but "Made In U. S. A." is embossed on the right-hand door.

Marx also made a very similar tow truck. (For a photograph of both the dump truck and the tow truck, see page 102.) **35**   **80**

Marx made Mack trucks in small, medium, and large sizes. The small 5" truck pictured was made in 1930. Dr. M. Kates Collection. R. Grubb photograph.

	Good	Exc

7" PROTOTYPE DUMP TRUCK: 1949. This non-powered prototype is plastic with red cab and chassis, yellow dumper and black wooden wheels with uncovered fenders. "3383X 2/15/49 Glen Dale" is hand-painted on the base of the truck. **NRS**

9-3/4" TIPPER DUMP TRUCK: 1950. Listed at 89 cents in the 1950 Montgomery Ward Christmas catalog, this windup truck has a side lever to dump loads. A characteristic Marx touch is the addition of a steel wheelbarrow and a shovel. **75 125**

10" SIDE DUMP TRUCK: 1930s. This light blue, red, green, and yellow truck has two intersecting curved slots on the ends of the body, turned wooden wheels, and a separate stamped-steel bumper tabbed onto the front of the fender. The truck has an early-style Type 1 chassis with a battery cavity and a small 7/32" hole on each side of the hood to accommodate an electric light terminal bar. **75 160**

11-1/4" TIPPER DUMP TRUCK PROTOTYPE: Longer than the production toy, this non-powered plastic truck has a green cab and chassis, a yellow dumper, and black rubber wheels. A cab protector, the piece on the front of the dumper, overhangs the cab. The part of the dumper directly behind the cab is hand-painted "#1838 Glendale 7/11/50 12.8.3 GR". "PL 304" is on the base of the toy. (For a photograph of this truck, see page 104.) **NRS**

DUMP TRUCK #1013: Circa 1950. About 18" long. Similar to the 11-1/4" Tipper Dump truck Prototype, this truck has a red cab, yellow bed, and gray dumper with a cab protector over the cab. However, it has a slightly different raised design on the dump bin. On the back of the dump bin is a red opening tailgate which is hinged on top. The wheels have silver centers instead of spokes. **60 150**

	Good	Exc

DUMP TRUCK #1081: Circa 1950. About 18" long. This truck is similar to Dump Truck #1013, but it has a yellow cab, red bed, and blue dumper.

The front part of the dumper juts straight up rather than overhanging the cab. The truck has all-black wheels without spokes.

(Also see Dump Trucks under the specific name of the toy and the Mack Trucks section.) **80 175**

EMERGENCY SERVICE TOW TRUCKS

The two friction-powered tin trucks, #2691 and #2692, have the same basic body as the Fire Trucks, but different lithography and towing units instead of ladders.

EMERGENCY SERVICE TRUCK #2691: This truck has "N. Y. 12" on the hood, the Marx logo above to the right, and a headlight on top of the cab. Pictured on the side of the truck under "Emergency Service" and the "5" are a simulated gas canister and compressed air tanks. It is not known whether this truck has a siren. **110 225**

EMERGENCY SERVICE TRUCK #2692: This truck is similar to #2691, except it has a searchlight behind the cab and a siren. **125 250**

FIRE TRUCKS

FIRE TRUCK: 1940s. This metal fire truck has a ladder that rotates and rises, a snorkel on the ladder tip, and two aluminum ladders. It is a windup with turnable front wheels.

Good   Exc

The side of the hood has embossing and "V. F. D.", simulated controls and hoses towards the rear, and the Marx logo near the front fender. The black wheels have silver centers.

110   225

FIRE TRUCK: 1948. 14-1/2" long. Priced at $3.89 in the 1948 Montgomery Ward Christmas catalog is this fire truck which closely resembles the 1940s Fire Truck. Although it may have been out before 1948, it is described in the catalog as: "Heavy gauge steel, red baked enamel finish. Loud siren, heavy duty clockspring motor equipped with brake. Two eight inch ladders, two dummy fire extinguishers. 12-1/2 [inch] fire tower raised and lowered by gear and crank arrangement mounted on swivel ... can be turned in any direction. 14-1/2 inches long." No headlights are illustrated in the catalog ad, but a fireman, who appears to be made of tin, is shown driving the truck.

110   225

FIRE TRUCK #2637: Circa 1945 to 1950. About 14" long. All metal, this friction-powered truck has a yellow plastic aerial ladder and a lithographed driver, plus three white plastic figures which perch on the end of the truck. A yellow headlight is on the top of the cab, but there is a version without

The 5" friction-powered Army Truck, made in 1930, has a canvas top. Dr. M. Kates Collection. R. Grubb photograph.

The 5" friction-powered American Trucking Co. Mack Truck has similar design perforations to the medium-sized Royal Van Co. Mack Truck. Dr. M. Kates Collection. R. Grubb photograph.

Good   Exc

the headlight and possibly without the plastic figures. On the side of the hood, enclosed in a badge outline, is a "1". "V. F. D." is enclosed in an oval on the door. Various simulated controls, fire hoses, and an axe are pictured on the side of the truck.

65   140

FIRE TRUCK "EMERGENCY SQUAD": This all-metal electrically-powered truck has the same basic body and aerial ladder as Fire Truck #2637, but different lithography. The door is lettered "V. F. D." without the badge outline. "Emergency Squad" and "No. 2", enclosed in a box, are on the side of the vehicle. Below these markings, enclosed in a box, are "Tools" and "Flares" and simulated dials and hoses.

65   140

HOOK and LADDER FIRE TRUCK: This Fire Truck with a similar body to the Emergency Service Truck #2692 is shown in an ad reprinted in the *Marx Toy Collector Newsletter*. The ad shows what appears to be embossing on the door and

Good   Exc

differently-shaped fenders. The Fire Truck also has three lithographed fireman that appear to be tin.

The ad states "Three firemen hop on running board and away they go, bell clanging as you push this truck along the floor to the 'fire'. Modern cab-over-engine Hook and Ladder Truck 13-1/2 inches long. Run up three 8 inch interlocking ladders for the truck to 'rescue' folks. Two realistic fire extinguishers and hose reel. Heavy steel, finished bright red."[8] No date is shown in the ad, but as indicated by the price (49 cents) and tin firemen, this toy is probably of an earlier manufacture than the Fire Truck described previously.

80   175

HOOK and LADDER FIRE TRUCK #3211 (Articulated): Circa 1950. About 24" long. On top of the truck is an operating plastic ladder which can be raised or lowered. On the side are simulated extension ladders and "Nozzles" and

---

[8] Ad reprint, *Marx Toy Collector Newsletter*, Vol. 3, No. 6, p. 4.

The 5" Bamberger Mack Truck (Small), made in the late 1920s to 1930, was sometimes used as a Christmas promotional special. Dr. M. Kates Collection. R. Grubb photograph.

DIRECTIONS *for* OPERATION

This box contain one Fire House **(1)**, one Patrol Car **(2)**, one Chief Car **(3)** and one Weather Vane key winder **(4)**

1 Place cars in the middle of their respective stalls and push them against metal slides "A" until slide reaches rear of stall and locks.

2 Wind toy, using Weather Vane winder as shown. Give it approximately one full turn in a clockwise direction until it touches the stop lock.

3 Now pull the lever or hook in the Alarm Box "B" to the RIGHT and the cars will shoot out to answer the alarm

Made in the United States of America by

LOUIS MARX & CO.

200 Fifth Avenue, NEW YORK

This 9-3/4" Mack Truck marked "Armored Trucking Co." belongs to the medium-sized series of Mack trucks. The toy is a windup. Dr. M. Kates Collection. R. Grubb photograph.

	Good	Exc

"Tools". "9" is on the cab door and a red warning light is on the top of the cab. **80 175**

HOOK and LADDER FIRE TRUCK #3217 (Articulated): About 33" long.

First Version: This truck has a "9" enclosed in a black and yellow emblem on the door and an ornately-styled "V. F. D." on the side of the hood. On the hook and ladder section is "No. 9" over another "V. F. D." Between the letters and the number is a banner that reads "Hook & Ladder".

On the front of the trailer is a white ladder which can be raised. The mount to which the ladder is attached comes in red

This medium 10-1/2" windup Mack Army Truck, although similar to the 5" Army Truck, differs in several other ways from the smaller Army Truck. Dr. M. Kates Collection. R. Grubb photograph.

or white. Another ladder, silver-colored, is underneath, situated further back on the trailer.

A yellow-lithographed decorative design runs from the hood on though the side. Also on the side are yellow plastic simulated tanks, a fire extinguisher, an axe, and lithographed ladders.

The black rubber or vinyl wheels marked "Lumar" and "11.00 x 20" have silver centers. At the point where the trailer attaches to the truck, there are dual wheels for extra strength.

The truck has lithographed lights on the top and bumpers and dummy lights on the grille. On the back of the trailer is a rear driver's seat. A simulated diamond plate is on the running boards.

Some versions may have come with plastic firemen. **130 275**

Second Version: Circa 1950. 33" long. Similar to the first version, this truck has "9" on the cab and the letters, banner sign, and "No. 9" repeated on the side along with the same decorative design. However, it has a fire extinguisher, portable light, and other fire extinguishers on the side. Above these items are simulated extension ladders. (For more information on Fire Chief Cars and Fire Houses, see the Automobiles chapter.) **130 275**

GENERAL ALARM FIRE HOUSE: 1938. First listed in catalogs in 1938 selling for 94 cents, the General Alarm Fire House is predominantly red and yellow, has a windup mechanism that rings an alarm bell, and ejects the Chief Car and then the Patrol Truck from the garages. The ejection mechanisms are metal plates that are spring-loaded. To operate, the plates are manually reset. The Alarm Box on the right front corner has a small lever. The 17" x 11" base has lettering that includes

Made around 1927-1933, the bright blue of the 10" City Hospital Ambulance is an unusual color for an ambulance. The rear of the ambulance opens up. E. and L. Schafle Collection.

"Chief", "No Crossing When Bell Rings", "No Parking", and "Pull Hook to Right". The rear is lettered "Training School".

The toy comes with a red sedan that is rubber-stamped "Chief" in black and with a red stake truck that is rubber-stamped "Patrol" in black. Both vehicles are otherwise unmarked.

Ads of the time showed the Fire House with just two vehicles, but it is possible that the toy came with an ambulance as a third vehicle (see photograph on page 87). The vehicles are made of heavy gauge steel. The car consists of a one-piece body with grille, while the stake truck and ambulance have one-piece bodies each with separate grille and back sections.

The Fire House structure consists of a central building with a lithographed entrance and "Fire Department Headquar-

ters" at the top front and two red-roofed garages. The left garage roof is lettered "General Alarm" and the right garage roof is lettered "Fire House".

The Fire House shares some features in common with other Marx toys. The City Airport and the Greyhound Bus Terminal have the same garage stampings and, in addition, the Greyhound Bus Terminal has the same central building. The large base is also used on the Airport and Bus Terminal.

The patent for the Fire House, #2,135,584, which was applied for in 1937, shows no vehicles in the drawing, but mentions them in the description. Excellent price includes original box.   **175   400**

This colorful mechanically-operated Dump Truck, made around 1926-1928, is 10" long and has a manually-operated dumper body. Dr. M. Kates Collection. R. Grubb photograph.

The colorful 8-1/4" Royal Oil Company Truck, made in 1927, is mechanically-powered. Notice the way the Marx logo is used in the word "GAS O LENE" on the rear of the tank. Dr. M. Kates Collection. R. Grubb photograph.

The 9" mechanically-operated Royal Van Co. Truck, made around 1928, has opening rear doors. The truck comes in other versions. Dr. M. Kates Collection. R. Grubb photograph.

MACK TRUCKS

Marx made a great number of Mack trucks in all types and sizes. The toy manufacturer, Chein, also made Mack trucks that are similar enough to Marx trucks that they are often mistaken for one another.

Mack Trucks are listed alphabetically and are grouped according to size: small (5"-5-1/2"), medium (8"-10-1/2"), or large (12"-19").

AERO OIL COMPANY (Small): 1930. 5" long. This friction-powered truck is advertised in a 1930 Butler Brothers catalog as part of an assortment of other small toys including an airplane, a zeppelin, a moving van, a racer, and an Army truck, and selling for 80 cents a dozen wholesale.

The attractive box for the Royal Van Co. Truck. C. Holley Collection.

Good   Exc

The attractive Aero Oil Company Truck has a blue hood and cab with pale yellow detailing, a brown underframe and fenders, and blue wheels. A star is on the roof and door; "F. 64" is below the star on the door. The Marx logo is lithographed onto the front of the hood. The orange oil tank has stripes, reads "Aero Oil Company", and has a stamped-metal top.

80   175

AMERICAN TRUCKING COMPANY (Small): 5" long. This friction-powered truck has a blue body and hood with pale green lettering. "American Trucking Co." and "Moving Shipping Storing" are on the side. "Padded Van" appears above the lithographed door and "65" appears underneath. "Coast TO Coast" are above the windshield area. The Marx logo is on the front of the hood. The design of perforations is similar to the medium-sized Mack truck, the Royal Van Co. (see page 100). It has a dark blue rear door and wheels, and a dark green underframe and fenders. On the roof are three stars. The truck has an opening rear door.

90   190

ARMY TRUCK (Small): 1930. 5" long. This friction-powered truck has a khaki brown cab and hood with black printing and striping which includes "U. S. Army F. 63" on the cab door. There is a star on the roof, the Marx logo on the front of the hood, and a canvas top on the truck. The truck has a brown underframe, fenders, and wheels (they have also been seen in red).

50   175

Good   Exc

AUTO TRANSPORT (Small): 1932. 11-1/2" long (truck and trailer).

First Version: This red-wheeled windup toy has a dark blue tractor cab with no lithography and a medium blue hood outlined in pale yellow. The Marx logo is on the front of the grille. The brown underframe is similar to the underframes of other trucks in the small Mack Truck series.

The dark green trailer of the transport carries three small red racing-type cars with unpainted metal wheels. The individual cars which have no drivers are permanently tabbed to the trailer. Ads have been seen for this toy stating that the cars are removable, thus suggesting the likelihood of another variation.

The trailer can be separated from the truck by rotating a lever on the side. A small pair of dolly wheels can be extended to support the truck so the piece can stand by itself.

90   250

Second Version: This friction-powered transport has a medium blue cab and hood with the usual pale outlining, a star on top of the cab and on the door, and "F. 64" on the door. (The Aero Oil Company Truck bears the same "F. 64" designation.) It has a dark green underframe and blue wheels.   **90   275**

Third Version: This windup transport has a dark blue cab and underframe with no lithography, a medium blue hood, and red wheels. It appears to have the same cab and underframe as the first version.

90   250

The crane hook of this 8" mechanically-operated Towing Truck, made in 1926, can be manually-operated. Dr. M. Kates Collection. R. Grubb photograph.

This 10-1/4" Toyland's Farm Products Milk Truck is spring-wound and originally came with removable wooden milk cases and twelve wooden milk bottles, 2" high. Notice the illustration which is unusual for a Mack truck. T. Riley Collection. C. Myer photograph.

	Good	Exc

BAMBERGER MACK TRUCK (Small): Late 1920s to 1930. 5" long. This uncommon windup truck has a dark green body and hood with pale yellow lettering. "L. Bamberger & Co." is lithographed in large letters on the side with "One of America's Great Stores, Newark, N. J." in smaller letters beneath the name. "219" appears beneath the windows of the side door. "WOR" is in a circle on the front of the grille. (These were the call letters of the Bamberger radio station.) Five vertical lines indicate the radiator vents on the side of the hood. The dark green rear opens. Like the American Trucking Co. truck, four perforations simulate a window on the side of the cab. The toy has a black underframe and bright red wheels.

The Bamberger Truck along with another Marx toy, the Movie Theatre from the Home Town series, were Christmas promotional specials for the Bamberger Department Store of Newark, New Jersey. According to Eric Matzke, the store gave these toys with larger purchases in a carton marked "Merry Christmas".   **175   375**

U. S. TRUCKING CO. (Small): Circa 1930. 5-1/2" long. This friction truck has a dark maroon cab and roof, a yellow and green-checked body, and cut-out sides marked "U. S. Trucking Co." on the lower part. It has a khaki underframe and black wheels with lithographed orange spokes.
75   150

ARMORED TRUCKING CO. (Medium): 9-3/4" long. Similar to other trucks of the series, this handsome windup truck has a red hood with black lettering, a black Marx logo on the front, and a dark green underframe and bumpers. The driver, however, is of the series found in the Marx Stutz Racers (see Automobiles chapter). The one-piece body and cab are mostly

black with yellow printing and outlining. Indicating the door are hinges and four cut-out windows with "5" in a box underneath. Rivets on the side suggest a steel body. "Armored Trucking Co." is in a shield in the middle side of the truck and also on the lower side of the truck. On either side of the shield, which also appears on the opening rear door, are six small windows. A step is attached to the bottom of the rear truck body.

Like the U. S. Mail Truck (described on page 102), the black wheels are lithographed with red spokes and "28 x 4.75 Balloon Cord", and "Armored Truck" appears on the visor of the roof above the front window of the cab. These two vehicles appear to be of similar age. On the roof are raised yellow stripes. The front wheels can be set in three different positions.
100   350

ARMY TRUCK (Medium): 10-1/2" long. This windup truck has a khaki brown body, truck bed, cab, hood, and wheels, "U. S. A. Army D-105" in black on the side of the cab, the Marx logo on the front of the hood, and "U. S. A. Army Truck" on the canvas top. The driver may have come from such a similar series as the Rex and King Racers.

Unlike the small Army Truck, the medium Army Truck has front fenders, wording on its canvas top, a driver, and no star on top of the cab. Also, there are different markings on the doors and a raised design of spokes on its wheels. (Also see Army Trucks (Large).)   **90   200**

CANNON ARMY TRUCK (Medium): Circa 1930s. About 9" long. This truck has been described as: "Large size, cannon used on other toys, including Army Train and Target Sets.

This windup U. S. Mail Truck is 9-1/2" long. The front wheels can be set in three different positions and the rear door opens. Dr. M. Kates Collection. R. Grubb photograph.

	Good	Exc

Same #D-105 [on door on medium-sized Army Truck] but wheels plain, key wound, firing gun". [9]

The truck also comes in a version with "7" on the door and lithographed spokes on the wheels. The truck may also come in other sizes. **100 220**

CITY HOSPITAL AMBULANCE (Medium): Circa 1927-33. 10" long. This windup truck has a blue body, an unusual color for an ambulance, with red markings and trim. "City Hospital" on the side of the ambulance has a red cross between the two words. Beneath these markings, in larger letters, is "Ambulance". The windows on the door and sides are cut out. Under the door windows is a "4". "Ambulance" is repeated on the top of the cab. The lithographed driver wears a tan cap.

The khaki hood and chassis very likely came from the medium Army Truck described above. The black wheels have

The 13" Big Load Van Co. Truck, made in 1928, is a windup and has opening rear doors. Dr. M. Kates Collection. R. Grubb photograph.

	Good	Exc

lithographed orange spokes and "28 x 4-75 Balloon Cord". The rear of the ambulance opens up and has handrails. **120 350**

DUMP TRUCK (Medium): 1928. 10" long. This colorful windup truck has a dark red cab and hood with black outlining, the Marx logo on the front of the hood, an orange underframe similar to the Royal Oil Co. Truck (described below), a dark green bumper and wheels, and a manually-operated dumper body. The front wheels can be set in three different positions. The bed of the truck is medium blue on the outside and red on the inside.

The black-dressed driver of the truck is made out of the same piece of metal as the steering wheel. This truck also comes in a version with a green underframe.

In 1926 the Sears catalog advertised another Marx Dump Truck of the same size which was sold with a working Sand Crane. Both items sold for 48 cents, a bargain price even in those days. [10] **100 250**

MERCHANTS TRANSFER TRUCK (Medium): 10" long. This red open-stake truck has "Merchants Transfer" on a solid panel at the front near the cab, a "7" on the door, and a bed that is orange outside and blue inside. The orange and black wheels have lithographed spokes. A slightly different larger version was made also (see page 106.) **175 400**

POLICE PATROL (Medium): 10" long. This windup truck has a perforated window on the cab door and lithographed spokes similar to those on the U. S. Mail Truck described on page 102. It has two small perforated windows on the side of the truck.

Other markings on the truck side are "Police Patrol" in large letters, "3rd Precinct" in smaller letters, and "Dept. of Police" on the cab door. At the rear of the truck is a platform and handrail. The color of the vehicle is not known (reader information requested). **150 350**

ROYAL OIL COMPANY TRUCK (Medium): 1927. 8-1/4" long. This windup truck, like the Royal Van Co. Truck (see next entry), has a dark red cab and hood, black outlining, the Marx logo on the front of the hood, and an orange underframe and wheels. The wheels have the same raised spoke design as the medium Army Truck. Although there are perforations for a bumper, there does not appear to have been one (catalog illustrations do not show one).

The medium green tank has pale orange/yellow outlining and "Royal Oil Company" on the side of the truck.

The rear of the tank is yellow with red printing. A particularly appealing touch is the way the word "Gasolene" is formed. (The spelling "gasolene" was current at the time and

---

[9] Gerritt Beverwyk, "Mack Trucks," *Marx Toy Collector Newsletter*, Vol. 1, No. 2, p. 10.
[10] If the nearby Bucyrus-Erie Company, which manufactures construction and mining equipment, was in business at this time, it is quite possible the Marx toy crane may have been a copy of one of this company's cranes.

This #550 Dump Truck, made in 1936, is a 12-3/4" windup with a manually-operated dump body. There are two other Marx trucks with the same wording and similar dump bodies. Dr. M. Kates Collection. R. Grubb photograph.

This 14" windup truck was made in 1934 and has battery-powered front headlights. The driver is missing from the example pictured. Dr. M. Kates Collection. R. Grubb photograph.

The 13" windup green and blue #11 Dump Truck was manufactured circa 1934. The cab and coloring are different from the #550 Dump Truck shown in the top photograph on page 99, but the dump beds are the same. Dr. M. Kates Collection. R. Grubb photograph.

	Good	Exc

used by the Sinclair Oil Company, but is not generally in use today.) The first letters "GAS" are followed by the letter "O", which is formed from the Marx logo, and then the letters "LENE". Three lithographed spigots appear beneath "GAS O LENE". There are two unpainted, stamped metal oil spouts on top of the tank.   **150   350**

ROYAL VAN CO. TRUCK (Medium): 1928. 9" long.
First Version: This windup truck has a medium red cab and hood with black outlining, four raised orange/yellow stripes on the red roof, red accents on the orange/yellow body of the truck, "Royal Van Co." on the lower part of the body below rectangular perforations which are similar to those in the American Trucking Co. truck in the small Mack series. The driver can also be found in the racer series.

This second Stake Truck, made around 1940, has a silver-painted bumper and wooden wheels. T. Riley Collection.

This third Stake Truck, made around 1947, is shown here with replacement wheels. T. Riley Collection. C. Myer photograph.

Good   Exc

The orange/yellow rear opening door has two cut-out oval windows, the Marx logo in red beneath each window, and a bright blue door knob on the right-hand door. The underframe, bumpers, and wheels are dark green. The underframe also comes in blue.   **140   300**

Second Version: 1928. Instead of the rectangular perforations, this red and yellow truck has closed sides with "We Haul Anything Anywhere" inside an oval. The wheels have lithographed spokes like the Armored Trucking Co. Truck, but no raised design. "7" is on the door.   **140   300**

Third Version: This version is a larger 12" Hauler and Trailer. (See large Mack Trucks starting on the next page for more information.)   **140   300**

TOWING TRUCK (Medium): 1926. 8" long. This windup truck is one of the earliest of the Marx Mack trucks. It is

Good   Exc

advertised, along with a car, in the 1926 Sears catalog for 48 cents and described as: "...the Wrecker, which has a crank that unwinds and winds up the cord holding the wrecking hook, is 9-1/4 inches". Actually, the truck is closer to 8". (Minor discrepancies in size do sometimes exist between an ad description and the actual toy.) By 1928 the truck was being sold without the car and was listed as 8" long.

The truck has a dark red hood with black outlining, similar to the hoods of the Royal Oil Company and Royal Van Co. Trucks, and the Marx logo; dark green cab, underframe, bumper, and wheels; double sets of rear wheels; a dark blue and yellow crane and crane mechanism on the truck bed; a mechanically-operated crane hook; and a towing mechanism that can be set in two positions: extended for towing, or collapsed into the truck chassis when not in operation. The driver is similar to the drivers of the Marx Racers.   **140   300**

10" Tow Truck has a crank to raise and lower the hook. T. Riley Collection.

Auto Carrier and Lumar Lines Tractor Trailers, made around 1948-50, are about 14" long. T. Riley Collection.

Good   Exc

TOYLAND'S FARM PRODUCTS MILK TRUCK (Medium): 1931. 10-1/4" long. This interesting truck, produced somewhat later than the other medium Mack trucks, is listed in the 1931 Sears Fall/Winter catalog for 47 cents. The catalog states: "[It has a wooden] milk case containing 12 wooden milk bottles each about 2 in. tall. Made of metal, handsomely colored. Assorted design decorations. Has Marx spring". The milk boxes can be removed from the truck. Although the advertising copy does not mention a bumper, the illustration shows one. A bumper is mentioned in other ads as well, so it is possible that the toy was made both ways.

The ad also mentions "assorted decorations" and shows a number "5" on the door. However, the toy has been seen with a "7".

The truck has cream, white, red, and blue lithography and a driver in the cab, "Butter Eggs" on one side and "Milk Cheese" on the other. Two-thirds of the truck body has rectangular perforations, while the front third has an illustration reminiscent of the one on the horse-pulled milk wagon also named "Toyland's Farm Products".

The tires are marked "28 x 4.75 Balloon Cord" and have lithographed spokes similar to the Armored Trucking Co. Truck. There are two white and blue dividers for the body, a cream cab and hood with red trim, "7" on the door, and the Marx logo is on the hood. The front axle can be set to go either straight or around a curve. Price does not include milk bottles.

170   350

U. S. MAIL TRUCK (Medium): 9-1/2" long. This rarely seen windup truck has a black body with pale yellow outlining and a blue bumper, "3" in a box beneath the windows of the cab door which is lithographed in pale yellow and outlines the four square windows, and a number of small perforations along the side of the truck. "U. S. Mail" appears along the lower side of the truck, on the cab roof, and on the pale yellow opening rear door. The khaki underframe has black outlining and the Marx logo is on the front of the hood.

The black wheels have orange/yellow-lithographed spokes and are lettered "28 x 4.75 Balloon Cord". The front wheels can be set in three different positions: to go straight, or circle to the left, or circle to the right. The driver has a cap and appears to be from an early series of toys. **200   450**

ARMY TRUCK (Large): 1929. This Marx Army Truck is advertised for 59 cents in 1929 in various catalogs. A 1930 Butler Brothers catalog describes the truck as: "13-1/2 inches long. 2-tone khaki color enameled, black trim, disc wheels, mud guards, running board, bumper, chauffeur, removable khaki canvas top." In the ad illustration, "U.S.A. Army Truck" is on the side of the canvas top and a star is on top of the cab. The cab door has "U. S. A. Army", "No. 10", and other markings that are impossible to distinguish. **175   400**

These similar dump and tow trucks have a one-piece cab and chassis and separate tin grille and body. T. Riley Collection. C. Myer photograph.

The Stake Truck and Sunshine Fruit Growers Truck are about 14" long and are identical except for the upper half of the trailers. T. Riley Collection. C. Myer photograph.

	Good	Exc

BIG LOAD VAN COMPANY (Large): 1928. 13" long. *First Version:* Advertised for 48 cents in 1928, this windup truck has a cab and body which are similar in construction to the #11 Mack Dump Truck, but they are pale orange with black outlining. There is black outlining on the roof ribs, the Marx logo on the front of the hood, "We Haul Anything" on the side above the Marx logo, and "Anywhere Anytime" underneath. Three cut-out windows are on either side of these markings with "Big Load Van Company" beneath the windows. The truck has a medium green underframe, running boards, front bumper, and fenders; black wheels with raised spokes; and two pale yellow opening doors at the rear with oval windows like those of the medium Mack Royal Van Co. Truck. The truck has also been seen with "11" on the door.   **175   400**

Second Version: 1927. 12-3/4" long. The Big Load Van is also advertised as a Hauler and Trailer selling for $4.25 a dozen wholesale. The trailer as shown comes loaded with "little cartons of nationally known products." "Big Load Van Co." is on the trailer, but in place of the slogan, "We Haul Anything Anywhere Anytime", are perforated rectangles.[11]

150   350

CITY COAL CO. DUMP TRUCK (Large): 1934. 14" long. This may be a Mack truck, but the cab and hood are different from the other Mack trucks described. This dump truck has an enclosed cab and a grille with straight sides and a round top. The other trucks are narrow at the top with grilles that slant outward towards the bumpers. Priced at $3.80 a dozen wholesale in a 1934 Butler Brothers catalog, the truck is described as having a "red body, green, black and yellow chassis, dummy lights, driver, strong spring motor, automatic lever action dump body." The ad illustration substantially resembles the actual toy except that it does not show the holes in the hubcaps.

This Tractor Trailer with Dumpster has a lithographed driver, grille, and headlights. E. Owens Collection.

---

[11] Edw. K. Tryon Toy catalog, Philadelphia, 1927.

The 11-1/4" Tipper Dump Truck and 9-3/4" Van Truck prototypes, made in 1950, are plastic with rubber wheels. (For more information on the Tipper Dump Truck, see page 88.) W. Maeder Collection. R. Grubb photograph.

Each vehicle in the Miniature Pull Toy Assortment, made in 1937, measures about 6". **TOP SHELF:** *The Tank Truck, the Van or Stake Truck, and the Roadster.* **MIDDLE SHELF:** *The Limousine (which may not be part of the original assortment) and the Greyhound Bus.* **BOTTOM SHELF:** *The Coal Truck and the Coast to Coast Greyhound Van. C. and C. Weber Collection.*

Good   Exc

The medium red cab and hood have black and white outlining, "Marx" on the side of the radiator, a black cab roof, and the Marx logo on the top of the off-white grille with red and black outlining. The truck has a black underframe, running boards, and fenders; a black front bumper held by two metal bars extending from the grille that juts out further than the other bumpers in the Mack series; black rubber wheels with pale yellow hubcaps; and a provision for a battery underneath to power the front headlights. The green color mentioned in the advertisement has not yet been reported. The bed of the truck is identical to the other large Mack Dump Trucks, but it is dark red with black outlining with "City Coal Co.", "Coal", and "Coke".   **150   450**

#11 DUMP TRUCK (Large): Circa 1934. 13" long. This windup truck sold for 50 cents in 1934, but was probably produced earlier. The medium blue cab is higher than the cab of the #550 Dump Truck and has pale yellow outlining, "11" on the cab door, a green star on top of the cab roof, and the Marx logo on the hood front, and a shape similar to the Big Load Van cab. The driver is orange and black. The medium blue truck has a medium green underframe, running boards, front fenders, and bumper; pale yellow outlining; and black wheels with orange or green centers, similar to those of the #550 Dump Truck. The front wheels can be set in three different positions. The dump bed is identical to that of the #550 Dump Truck and is manually-operated.

In the 1928 Butler Brothers catalog, a Marx Dump Truck is advertised with a similar shape and size, but a different color

The Armored Bank Truck is part of the Miniature Pull Toy Assortment and may have been sold separately. It has a coin slot in its roof and a removable base. T. Riley Collection.

Good   Exc

and none of the markings. Priced at $4.25 a dozen wholesale in the catalog, it is described as having a "Yellow body, red trimmed, black wheels ..." This version is thought to have been made, but little else is known about it. (Also see Mack Lincoln Transfer Truck.)   **160   350**

#550 DUMP TRUCK (Large): 1936. 12-3/4" long. This windup truck has a medium blue hood with pale yellow outlining, the Marx logo on the front of the grille, a silver cab with blue outlining, a "550" on the side of the cab door, and a dark blue star on the cab roof. The driver wears a red cap. The truck has a black front bumper, green and black wheels, and a silver underframe, running boards, and front fenders.

This Group of Four 6" Trucks, made in the 1930s, includes a cement mixer truck and a stake truck (above), and a tow truck and an Army truck (below). T. Riley Collection.

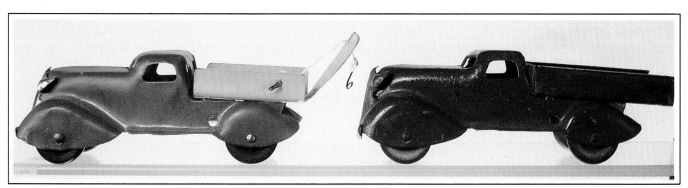

Good   Exc

The medium blue dump bed has pale yellow outlining. The lettering is in three partitions and reads from front to back: "City Coal Co." in the first partition, "Coal" in the second, and "Coke" in the third. The dump body is manually-operated.

200   425

#1520 DUMP TRUCK (Large): 1930. 19" long. The 1930 Montgomery Ward catalog shows an unusually large 19" Marx Mack Truck selling for $1.39, higher than the cost of the average Marx toy. Unlike the other large Mack Trucks, the truck does not have a driver. (This possibly was a cost-cutting measure.)

Although the truck resembles the other Mack trucks, it lacks bumpers. The dump bed has an interesting paneled design with vertical lithographed ribs and six dots between each pair of ribs. "3" is at the base of the door. The wheels have solid hubs and balloon-style tires. The colors of the truck are not known, but the ad names the toy "Big Silver".

175   550

LINCOLN TRANSFER and STORAGE CO. (Large): This unusual windup Mack truck is shown in the outstanding book, *American Toy Cars & Trucks*, by Lillian Gottschalk. The front of the truck is almost the same as the #11 Dump Truck. However, there is a fire extinguisher lithographed on the door instead of a geometric shape. Instead of the solid wheels of the #11 Dump Truck, the wheels have cut-out spokes.

Good   Exc

The biggest difference between the two trucks is the Lincoln Transfer's two large billboards that cover the sides. They read from the top down: "Across the Street — Or Across the Continent / Lincoln Transfer and Storage Co. Movers & Shippers of Pianos & Household Goods / Gramercy 2773 / Padded Van". [12]

175   650

LONE EAGLE OIL COMPANY (Large): Circa 1930. 12" long. This handsome windup truck has a bright blue cab and hood, yellow outlining, a yellow star on the top of the cab, a yellow "11" on the door, and a lithographed fire extinguisher to the rear of the door. The truck has a khaki underframe and black wheels.

The green gas storage tank has three dark orange bands. "Lone Eagle Oil Company" in orange is on the side of the tank. Below these words to the left is "Oils" and to the right "Gasolene" (sic). There are three unpainted metal oil intake domes on top of the tank.

175   400

MERCHANTS TRANSFER TRUCK (Large): 1928. 13-1/3" long. This truck has a covered top (unlike the medium

---

[12] Lillian Gottschalk, *American Toy Cars & Trucks* (New York: Abbeville Press, 1986), p. 251. This engagingly comprehensive book covers a wide range of vehicles including Marx toys.

This Group of Four Vehicles, made in 1940, are each 4" long. The bus also comes as part of a Marx bus station set. T. Riley Collection.

Good   Exc

Merchants Transfer Truck) and three side rectangular slots on either side of an oval which is lettered "Merchants Transfer" with the Marx logo between the two words. On the lower side of the truck is "Merchants Van Co." Priced at $4.50 a dozen wholesale, the toy is described in a 1928 Butler Brothers catalog as: "13-1/3 in. 3-color enameled, hinged doors, chauffeur". The smaller version is described on page 98.

           200   **450**

ROYAL VAN CO. TRUCK (Large): 1927. As well as coming in the medium version described on page 100, the truck also appears as a Hauler and Trailer. It is advertised in a 1927 Butler Brothers catalog, priced at $4.20 a dozen wholesale, and described as: "12 3/4 x 5 1/4 inches, red, green and yellow enameled. Extra strong spring, chauffeur. Trailer loaded with small cartons of advertised products." The trailer resembles the body of the medium-sized Royal Van Co. Truck.

           200   **450**

STAKE TRUCKS

STAKE TRUCK (First): (For photograph, see page 71.) This Stake Truck has a Type 1 light yellow chassis, light blue cab and frame, and a light green stake body with a rubber-stamped chick on one side and a bunny on the other. Marx likely made this truck for the Easter season with spring pastel colors, possibly at the same time as the Bunny Express Train (1936).

    The manufacturer Wyandotte also made a truck in Easter colors consisting of a pink cab and chassis and a green dump body. It comes with candy and Easter eggs covered with tinted cellophane and bedded in green Easter grass. **65**   **150**

STAKE TRUCK (Second): Circa 1940. 10" long. This Type 2 truck has three holes on each side. It does not have a second hole (which is the tab hole) on the side of the hood.

    The truck has a medium blue chassis and cab, aluminum-painted bumper, red stake body, and wooden fender-covered wheels. Although there might have been lettering originally, none exists now.   **65**   **150**

STAKE TRUCK (Third): 1947. 20" long. The unmarked truck consists of a red cab front and two side chassis pieces, a one-piece green stake body, and a copper-colored grille. The 2-1/2" diameter wheels are lithographed scrap. The wheel spacing on the axles is maintained by tabs. The cab represented contemporary truck design at the time. **65**   **150**

STAKE TRUCK and TRAILER: This is a flat-nosed red truck, with a tin grille and bumper assembly and fender-covered wheels. The truck has a silver-painted stake body with no apparent lettering and comes with a matching aluminum-painted trailer. A photograph of the trailer is shown on page 84. (Also see First, Second and Third Stake Trucks above.)

           75   **200**

TOW TRUCKS

Good   Exc

TOW TRUCK: 6-1/4 to 6-1/2" long cab with a 4" wheel base. This aluminum-finished truck has a one-piece cab and chassis with a separate tin grille body, wooden wheels, a windup motor, and vertical barred grille with dummy headlights. There are no Marx markings but "Made In U. S. A." is embossed on the right-hand door. (Also see the 6-1/4" Dump Truck on page 87.)

           45   **100**

TOW TRUCK: 10" long. This green and medium blue Tow Truck has no apparent lettering and a narrower body than the Ice or Stake Trucks. The red window is formed from the body. The tow boom, the same as used on the railroad car, has a crank to raise and lower the hook. **65**   **170**

TOW TRUCK #T-16: Circa 1935. About 10" long. This is a rather strange looking truck, since it appears to have some part of it missing. The reason for the odd appearance is that the cab and chassis of this truck is used on another tractor trailer. The part where the trailer rests now has towing equipment. There is side embossing on the hood and exposed wheels, as shown in the June 1977 PB 84 auction catalog. **75**   **200**

TRACTOR TRAILERS: SETS and GROUPS

AUTO CARRIER: 1950. 14" long. The red and blue Auto Carrier has two yellow plastic cars marked "Made In U. S. A." and two ramp tracks. The cab and chassis are gray, an unusual color for a Marx truck. The Marx logo is stamped on the inside of the trailer. **75**   **200**

LUMAR LINES TRUCK: 14" long. This toy has the same dimensions as the Auto Carrier above. It has a red cab and chassis and an aluminum-finished trailer with a yellow decal lettered "Lumar Lines" in red. The same large "L" from the word "Lumar" is used in "Lines" and underlines the word. A black Marx logo is also on the decal. The toy comes in a box marked "Open Van Trailer Truck". The toy also comes in a closed van version.

    The truck section of both the Auto Carrier and the Lumar Lines Truck is the same as the lower half of the trailers. **75**   **200**

LUMAR LINES and GASOLINE SET: 1948. The Lumar Lines Tractor Trailer was sold along with another tractor trailer marked "Gasoline". The Auto Carrier described above was probably sold around the same time and may also have come as part of a set. Both toys, priced at $1.95 a pair in the 1948 Montgomery Ward Christmas catalog, are described as: "Gas trailer has red and yellow enamel finish, is 8-1/2 in. long, has lever to prop trailer up when hauler is disconnected. Back drops for unloading cargo. Red hauler is 8 in. long, has strong windup motor. Tool box in back of cab." There is a similar description for the Lumar Lines Truck except that it does not

Good **Exc**

have the toolbox and the van trailer is red and blue. Both trucks have wooden wheels.

In the 1950s Lumar Lines Trucks of various designs continued to be sold both as part of a set and separately. (Also see Lumar Motor Transport on page 82.) **175** **400**

STAKE TRUCK and SUNSHINE FRUIT GROWERS TRUCK: 14" long. The Stake Truck has a red cab and chassis, and a trailer in which the top slotted half is yellow, while the lower half is red. The unmarked toy comes in a box lettered "Open Body Trailer Truck".

The Sunshine Fruit Growers Truck has the same red cab and chassis, and yellow rear deck as the Stake Truck. The upper half of the trailer is yellow and white with a blue roof, while the lower half is red.

Markings on the side of the truck include "Sunshine Fruit Growers", a pineapple underneath, "Trucking Service", and a telephone number which is indistinct, but appears to be "Call 1364-0 or 1". **100** **175**

STREAMLINE MECHANICAL HAULER, VAN, and TANK TRUCK COMBINATION: 1936. Advertised in the 1936 Blackwell Wielandy catalog as selling for $4.32 a dozen

Good **Exc**

wholesale, these toys are described as: "10 3/8 inches long, made of heavy gauge steel, finished in bright baked enamel colors, equipped with strong clockwork motor. Van is equipped with a back door". The van trailer appears to be closed, while the other truck has ridges across the roof, interspersed with oval shapes. Both trucks have fender-covered wheels, vertical grilles, and dummy headlights. **140** **300**

TRACTOR TRAILERS: SINGLE

NORTH AMERICAN VAN LINES TRACTOR TRAILER: 13" long. This windup Tractor Trailer has a hauler which is similar to the Lumar Lines Truck. It is thought to be colored red and cream.

The trailer has "North American Van Lines, Inc." on the side over a strip which reads "Long Distance Moving". **75** **200**

SIDE DUMP TRUCK and TRAILER #T-4045: Circa 1935. 15" long. This toy has an embossed hood and exposed

This colorful Group of Five Vehicles consists of a tow truck, a bus, a panel truck, a dump truck, and a stake truck. Although each measures 4" long, two types of bodies are used. T. Riley Collection.

Good   Exc

wheels. The hauler part of the toy was also made into a Tow Truck #T-16, according to the June 1977 PB 84 auction catalog.   **75   200**

TRACTOR TRAILER with DUMPSTER: The hauler is blue and yellow with a lithographed grille, headlights, rear view mirror, a lithographed driver, a black underframe and wheels, and a tan dumpster that rests on an aluminum hitch.   **75   200**

TRUCK with ELECTRIC LIGHTS #T-571E: Circa 1935. 10" long. This truck has battery-powered electric headlights.

An electrically-lighted Truck and Trailer Set #T-5733B was also made around the same time, according to the June 1977 PB 84 auction catalog. There is also another electrically-lighted Truck and Trailer Set #T-5715 made in the 1930s which is 15" long. [13]   **75   200**

TRUCK TRAIN: 41" long.

First Version: This impressive toy consists of a stake hauler and five trailers with metal wheels and rubber tires. Priced at 98 cents in the 1933 Sears Fall/Winter catalog, it is described as: "Hauler is equipped with two strong headlights which you can turn on and off and change from dim to bright by moving switch. Train comes complete with two 1 inch diameter dry cell batteries to light these headlights. All made from heavy gauge steel, beautifully colored. Includes hauler, gravel car, stake trailer, dump truck, oil car and van. Trailers average 5 1/2 x 3

Good   Exc

1/2 x 4 inches. Hauler 7 x 4 x 4 1/8 inches." The advertised truck shows holes in the tire centers which the actual truck does not have.   **150   450**

Second Version: In the 1938 Sears Christmas catalog, a more elaborate version of this truck is advertised, still with the same length and price. The truck now has different detachable trailers and is described as having "About 20 pieces. Modern truck; detachable ice trailer with dummy ice, ice tongs; baggage trailer with hand truck and trunk; market trailer with dummy food boxes; milk trailer with dummy milk bottles." This time the wheels illustrated in the ad do not have the holes. Also, a truck with a hook rather than a hauler appears to pull the trailers, which now number four rather than five.   **200   650**

In later years the Truck Train came with a lithographed box which could be made into a 17" platform station. The Truck Train may also have come with trailers (see the two photographs of trailers on pages 75 and 76).

VAN TRUCK PROTOTYPE: 9-1/2" long x 4-1/4" high. This plastic prototype has a green cab and chassis, a detachable closed red van with a hinged door on each side, rubber wheels, and "1643 Louis Marx Glendale 7/31/50" hand-painted on the bottom of the van. The date is repeated on the left side, while on the right are unclear markings which appear to be "TOP 116.2 BOT. 73 0002 8.9." On the base of the toy is an embossed Marx logo.   **NRS**

Vehicle Sets and Groups

Marx sold vehicles in sets and individually. In addition, small toys were sometimes used as parts of larger toys. For example, small buses and trucks were used in the Military Train, the Auto Transport, several garages, and numerous terminals.

MINIATURE PULL TOY ASSORTMENT: 1937. This group consists of twelve vehicles that were sold as a set and individually (for 10 cents each). They are described as "Miniature pull heavy gauge vehicle toys, about 6-1/2" long [actually 6"] which are streamlined in every detail and finished in bright baked enamel colors — shiny radiator and dummy headlights." All of these vehicles have wooden wheels, tab construction, and separate tin grilles with bumpers and non-operating headlights. Many have embossing on doors and hood vents.

The set contains: a coal truck, a tank truck, a van baggage truck (a stake truck), a van, a bus, an armored bank truck, a

roadster, a dump truck, a wrecker, a racer, a fire truck, and an ambulance. [14] Information about seven of the twelve vehicles is available:

1. The coal truck has a light blue chassis and a yellow dumper with an operating coal chute made of tin.   **35   75**

2. The tank truck has a buff-colored chassis with a red tank.   **35   75**

3. The van baggage truck or the stake truck has a red chassis and a light green stake bed.   **30   70**

4. The Greyhound Van has "Coast" on each side of the Marx logo instead of windows. Silver with a red radiator, this bus may also have come in tan. The Greyhound Van does not have cut-out windows like the Greyhound Bus, but it is similar it in that it has a rear bumper which is actually the end of the toy bent into a bumper-like shape, a one-piece tin grille, a 3-11/16" wheel base, and non-operating headlights. **30   65**

5. The Greyhound Bus has a red body, cut-out windows surrounded by an embossed area, a Greyhound embossed onto the left side of the bus, and a rear bumper which is actually the

---

[13] Richard O'Brien, *Collecting Toys* (Alabama: Books Americana, 1982), p. 60.
[14] David Pressland, *The Art of the Tin Toy* (New York: Crown Publishers, Inc., 1976), p. 175.

"Durable and Mechanically Perfect"   5

Size of individual toys approximately 5½ in. long, 2¼ in. wide, 3½ in. high

New Novel Pull Toys

Packed 1 dozen solid of a number to a box; 1 gross to a case.   Sold under individual numbers

LITTLE LINDY
No. 160

No. 162

TANKER
No. 164

YANKEE BOY
No. 161

U. S. ARMY TRUCK
No. 163

RAPID EXPRESS
No. 165

No. 170

ARMY TANK
No. 171

No. 169   Toy Assortment

Consisting of
- 2 doz. No. 160 Aeroplane
- 2 " No. 170 Zeppelin
- 2 " No. 165 Vans
- 2 " No. 161 Racers

- 1 doz. No. 163 Army Truck
- 1 " No. 164 Tanker
- 1 " No. 171 Army Tank

These numbers packed 1 doz. of a number solid to a box, 1 gross assorted as described to a shipping case.

A page from the rare 1930 Marx catalog. Although the toys shown are described as pull toys, they have only been seen in friction versions, except for the tank which comes as a windup.

Good   Exc

end of the toy bent into a bumper-like shape. The bus top has simulated ventilators. This same bus also comes in pale green without the embossed greyhound. According to Trip Riley, this bus is similar to the Greyhound Van in that it has a 3-11/16" wheel base and a separate, one-piece tin grille, bumper, and non-operating headlights.   **30   70**

6. The armored bank truck has a red or green body with a coin slot in its roof, a removable base, and "Armored Bank" in black, rubber-stamped letters on its side.   **50   110**

7. The silver-colored roadster has a red radiator and a red simulated-wood gas cap. The toy does not have side roof support posts. Unlike the other toys in the set, the roadster does not have embossed doors or side vents. However, it does have embossed fenders. The rear bumper is molded out of the end of the car.   **30   70**

A limousine is shown as part of the Miniature Pull Toy Assortment in the photograph on page 104 although it may not be part of the Assortment (but may have been made by Marx). The limousine has a buff-colored chassis and light blue fenders and running board. It differs from the other Assortment toys in its headlights, grille design, and wheel and axle mounts. Instead of a one-piece body with fenders molded from the toy, the limousine has attached fenders.   **30   70**

MINIATURE MECHANICAL TOY ASSORTMENT: 1936. 5" long. This set consists of six windup toys with vertical grilles and non-operating headlights. The toys include a stake truck, a dump truck, a tow truck, a panel truck, a tank truck, and a coupe. The set sold for $1.68 per dozen toys wholesale in the 1936 Blackwell Wielandy catalog.   **200   300**

SIX-STYLE ASSORTMENT: 1934. 10" long. Although called "autos" in a 1934 ad, this set actually contains six trucks. The ad describes it as "Heavy gauge steel, asst. enamel finishes, asst. dump and stake trucks, wrecker, milk truck, etc. Strong spring motor, bumpers, rubber tired disc wheels." Priced at $4.50 a dozen wholesale, the 1934 Butler Brothers catalog shows three of the trucks: a dump truck, a tow truck marked "Service Truck", and a milk truck which resembles a tank truck and which reads "Toyland Dairy".   **250   550**

TRUCKS and GARAGE: In 1936 two 16" trucks, a moving van and a dump truck, and an 18" cardboard garage were sold by Sears for $1.00. The ad makes a point of stating "Sold by Mail Only by Sears." The trucks are described as, "Real dump truck with drop gate, van has opening back door.... Trucks heavy gauge auto steel. New hoods, shiny radiators, dummy headlights, strong bumpers, balloon type wheels." As shown in the ad, both trucks have the same cab and chassis, and what appears to be embossing on the doors. The back of the dump truck slants outward in a diagonal fashion.

The cardboard garage has a lithographed tile roof with "4 MI" in a circle. Going through the circle is a directional arrow. Doors are on the side of the garage. On one door is the word "Office".

A year later in 1937, the same set was repeated but the packing box garage is lithographed differently and reads

The 4-1/2" Army Truck on Marx Military Train has a cardboard insert bent over to resemble a canvas top with "U. S. Army" in silver. D. Allen Collection. R. Grubb photograph.

Good   Exc

"County Highway Dept." . The moving van is now called a tank truck and has "Fuel Oil" on the door.   **200   600**

TRUCKS (Group of Four): 1930s. 6" long, 3-5/8" wheel bases. These conventional trucks have a one-piece cab and chassis, a separate body and grille, and wooden wheels. Although the trucks carry different loads, such as a towing unit, stake bed, etc., the basic body shape is the same. There is no indication on the trucks to suggest that they were made by Marx. The group consists of:

1. A cement mixer truck with a red cab and chassis, a blue cradle frame for the mixer, and a red cradle. The mixing barrel has a tin finish and is turned by a metal crank.   **60   125**

2. A tow truck with a red cab and chassis. Its yellow towing unit contains a rod that holds string for a hook.   **60   130**

3. A 4-1/2" plain olive drab army truck which probably can carry a canopy or a load. A similar but larger army truck is found on the Marx Military Train. But unlike the larger army truck, it has an embossed door and a cab back perpendicular to the truck bed. The stationary dumper has straight sides. A piece of cardboard curves over the bed to resemble a canvas top and reads "U. S. Army" in silver. It was unusual for Marx to make trucks in two similiar sizes, such as 4-1/2" and 6".   **55   125**

4. A stake truck with a red cab and chassis, and a blue stake body, similar to those on a dump truck on a Marx civilian train. In addition, both the stake truck and the dump truck have holes between their doors and fenders. However, the stake truck is larger, has a movable dumper, an embossed door area, and a different shape from the truck on the Military Train.   **60   130**

VEHICLES (Group of Four): 1940. 4" long, 1-13/16" wheel base. The vehicles have one-piece bodies with stamping and a bent-and-tabbed rear door. The grille, the two axles, and the

Good   Exc   Good   Exc

four wheels are separate pieces. Sold as a group, the four vehicles include:

1. A green gas truck with "Gas" in black, rubber-stamped letters.   **25   60**

2. A blue delivery truck with "Delivery" rubber-stamped in black. The underside of the truck is embossed with "Made in U. S. A." A similar red Delivery Truck is shown in a Lionel train catalog the same year.   **35   75**

3. An unmarked red bus which is also part of a Marx bus station set.   **25   60**

4. A white milk truck with "Milk" rubber-stamped in black. The underside of the truck is embossed with "Made in U. S. A."   **20   55**

VEHICLES (Group of Five): 4" long, 2-1/4" wheel bases. Each vehicle has a one-piece cab and chassis with a separate piece with a tin-finished grille, headlight, and bumper. Marx

made a number of different bodies for its trucks. There are two types of cabs: Type 1 with a square windshield and Type 2 with a windshield with rounded corners. (For further information on truck types, see the beginning of the Truck section below.) The five vehicles include:

1. A bus with a Type 1 cab and chassis. The original color of this toy is not known, but appears to be dark blue in the photograph on page 108.

2. A tow truck with a dark green, Type 1 cab and chassis. The body and the towing unit are red. A steel rod winds a piece of string for a hook.

3. A red panel truck with a Type 1 cab and chassis.

4. A stake truck with a light green, Type 2 cab and chassis. The stake unit is pink.

5. A dump truck with a red, Type 2 cab and chassis, and a dark blue dumper body.   **Group: 110   250**

ECCENTRIC CARS

Eccentric cars typify the humor, charm, and variety of Marx toys. These delightful toys are an excellent example of how one idea was continually developed to produce a large number of variations. All of the cars feature a driver trying to control an uncontrollable car. Eccentric cars are known as Funny Cars, Tricky Autos, and Back and Forth Cars, although they are perhaps best known as Crazy Cars. Most of the cars are lithographed tin spring windups with two large rear wheels and two small front wheels. The mechanism that drives the car is under the rear wheels. The front wheels pivot in a complete circle, allowing the car to move erratically or "eccentrically" in any direction. Most of the cars have tin drivers, a few have celluloid figures, such as the Dippy Dumper and the Funny Fire Fighters, and later cars have hollow plastic figures. Almost all the early eccentric cars had celluloid windshields which were discontinued after 1930. The celluloid windshields, along with the suitcases, also not seen after 1930, are the most frequently missing items in the early cars.

The eccentric cars are listed in chronological order.

One of the earliest eccentric cars, the 1926 Funny Flivver does not have a trunk. J. Iannuzzi Collection.

The Snoopy Gus Wild Fireman car is 7" long x 8-1/2" high. As the car moves, the ladder revolves. W. Maeder Collection.

Good   Exc

FUNNY FLIVVER: 1926. 7" long x 5-1/2" high. The Funny Flivver is one of the earliest, if not the first, eccentric car. The driver of the black car is dressed in a yellow jacket with orange-red trim, a white shirt, and yellow hat with red trim. The black and white wheels have lithographed spokes. A suitcase sits on the running board and displays the names of various cities. White lettering all over the car includes "Don't Bring Lulu", "My Lizzie of the Valley", "So's Your Old Man", and "Leap Year Girls Leapin". The radiator reads "Funny Flivver". As shown in the 1926 Sears Fall/Winter catalog, "4 Wheels, No Breaks" (sic), "Louis Marx & Co., N. Y., U. S. A.", the Marx logo, "Pat's Pend'g.", and the license number "X07-11" are on the back of the car.

Although the Funny Flivver resembles the later eccentric cars, it differs in several ways. For example, the large rear wheels are smaller than those on the later cars. The steering wheel post is longer, requiring the driver to sit further back. However, the most noticeable thing about the Funny Flivver, as shown in the 1926 Sears Fall/Winter catalog, is that it has no trunk. Priced at 43 cents, the toy is advertised in the catalog under the heading, "Brand New Funny Flivver — New Sensation," and is described as:

"It travels in every direction, running right or left and then suddenly backs up, only to shoot forward again in some freakish way. The head of its comical looking driver keeps turning in different directions with a puzzled look on his face. A dog (colored brown, black, and white) sits on the running board."

The next year, a 1927 Sears catalog shows the same car with a trunk. The price was raised to 48 cents. The toy is believed to be the Funny Flivver because "Private Property"

appears on the left side of the seat and a dog is on the running board. Neither of these features were on the toy that followed the Funny Flivver, the Joy Rider.

The box illustration for the toy differs somewhat from the actual toy. In the drawing, the driver wears a checked coat and the license plate on the radiator reads "1949". Near the windshield is the word "Honk". Meanwhile, a young boy and chickens scatter out of the car's way as other children watch.

Although the 1927 Sears catalog pictures the car with a trunk, neither the few examples of the Funny Flivver that have been seen nor the patent from which the toy was taken (#72,694, dated May 24, 1927 by Samuel Berger) show a trunk. However, it would have been logical to add one in order to improve the existing toy. Perhaps the Funny Flivver with a trunk was a plan that was canceled before production, although the advertisement had already been placed.   **350   500**

SNOOPY GUS WILD FIREMAN: 1926. 7" long x 8-1/2" high. Although both the Snoopy Gus and the Funny Flivver were on the market at the same time, they were not advertised together in either the Sears or Montgomery Ward catalogs for 1926. The Snoopy Gus is shown alone in the 1926 Montgomery Ward catalog, priced at 47 cents, and is described as follows: "While the truck dashes madly over the floor, the heroic fireman clings to the top of the ladder, which revolves in circles, trying to locate a fire." The ad mentions a Marx spring, one of the first times that a toy is identified with the Marx company.

Because the red car has no trunk, it accommodates a revolving ladder with a fireman clinging to it. A metal base supports the 6" long ladder so that the ladder can pivot when the car moves.

Good   **Exc**

Although the ladder is very impressive, it was not used again until the early 1940s on the Funny Fire Fighters. Since it has only thin yellow pin stripes, yellow lettering, and no slogans, the car has a neat appearance. "Snoopy Gus" is on the radiator and on the back of the seat. Also on the back of the seat are "Louis Marx & Co., New York, N. Y., U. S. A." and the Marx logo. "Hook & Ladder" is on both sides of the hood.

In some of the eccentric cars, large drivers completely fill their seats. In the Snoopy Gus, however, both a small fireman and a dog sit on a 1/2" high seat. The dog is also used on other eccentric cars. The firemen are realistically lithographed with mustaches, red coats and helmets, navy pants, and black boots.

In addition to the rotating ladder, the Snoopy Gus car differs in other ways from the rest of the eccentric cars. To allow space for the ladder, the steering wheel's post is higher than that on most eccentric cars. While it has the eccentric cars' design and small front wheels, its lithographed rear wheels, like those on the Funny Flivver, are smaller. It also has embossed dots at the ends of the spokes and unusual hub caps on its rear wheels. The hub caps, mounted onto the inside of the wheels by four tabs, and the axle can be seen from the outside of the car. The two firemen, one on the ladder and one driving, are also smaller than other eccentric car figures.

The box in which the car was sold is amusingly illustrated with busy firemen and reads "Snoopy Gus Wild Fireman". The Snoopy Gus car is difficult to find and is priced accordingly.

450   **1000**

JOY RIDER: 1928. 8" long x 5-1/2" high. As advertised in the 1928 Montgomery Ward catalog, the Joy Rider sold for 48 cents. In the ad, several words appear on the car's hood.

Although most are difficult to distinguish, "your" and "baby" are legible. Because the actual car is different from the car shown in the ad, it is possible that a variation exists.

The Joy Rider is a black car with lithographed wheel spokes, similar to the Funny Flivver. The driver of the Joy Rider is also the same as the driver of the Funny Flivver; however, he is dressed differently in a red jacket, a white shirt, and a red and green hat. Among the most detailed of all of the eccentric car drivers, the Joy Rider's face has a creased brow and a toothy smile.

The red trunk and suitcase have lithographed labels marked with the names of cities from all over the world. The license plate reads "7-11 N. Y." "The Ride'm Rough Tire Co. 31 x 1" is on the wheels; "Use No Hooks", "Thanks For The Buggy Ride", "Don't Bump Me I'll Go", and "I Do Not Choose To Run" are in white on the car; "Joy Rider" is on the car's radiator; "Louis Marx & Co., N. Y., U. S. A. Patent Pending" is on the back of the driver's seat.

The box illustration shows a huge, rearing car with a driver. It is knocking over the top of a building while tiny people, including a policeman, run around in panic.

The words "4 Owners All Broke" beneath the trunk are difficult to read without disassembling the car. This suggests that the Joy Rider was originally made without a trunk. However, the trunk is necessary to balance the car when it tips back on its rear wheels. The car performs this "eccentric" feature when a gear engages the axle of the rear wheels, causing the wheels to turn alternately forward and backward. Most of the car's weight is concentrated in the rear because of the trunk, the motor, and the driver. As a result of the forward and

The 1928 Joy Rider, 8" long x 5-1/2" high, has the same driver as the Funny Flivver. J. Iannuzzi Collection.

The boldly lithographed 1931 Coo Coo Car is 8" long. The driver has movable legs that enable him to stand up and sit down. J. Iannuzzi Collection.

Good   Exc

backward motion and the heavier weight in the rear, the car tilts up on its rear wheels. It comes to rest on a 1/2" strip of metal that protrudes from the trunk bottom. This strip has been made into the license plate. Excellent price includes original box. (The price of the toy in Excellent condition without the original box is $450.)   **350   650**

The 1930 Komical Kop car is 7" long x 6-1/2" high. It is possible that the driver was meant to resemble one of the actual Keystone Kops of the silent films. W. Maeder Collection.

WHOOPEE CAR: 1930. 8" long x 5-1/2" high. This car, which is shown on the front cover, is often thought to be one of the most attractive of the eccentric cars. Priced at 49 cents, the toy is described in the 1930 Sears catalog as "No telling which direction the car will go." For some reason, the driver is described as "grotesque." His girlfriends are "holding on for dear life," but they actually appear to be sitting calmly. This toy has the same car body and driver type as the Joy Rider but different lithography. The driver's turning head is lithographed in detail. He wears the popular 1920s raccoon coat, a natty white shirt with orange stripes, an orange bow tie, and the same red and green hat as the Joy Rider. The driver, who is balding, appears to be older than a college-age student, although there are college pennants lithographed onto the suitcase, the large back wheels, and the trunk. One possible explanation for this incongruity is that the company had the figures on hand and decided to use them. Although somewhat hard to see, the Marx name is on the back of the seat.

A major structural difference between the Joy Rider and the Whoopee car is the addition of two identical female figures to the trunk. These flat, two-dimensional figures are dressed in red, wearing hats, long scarves, and short skirts.

Marx was not the only manufacturer to place a figure on the trunk of a vehicle, to use large and small wheels, and to make use of an "eccentric" action. Although not identical, a 1924 imported toy called Dizzy Dan uses all of these features and may well have been an inspiration for the eccentric cars. [1]

---

[1] Earnest A. Long, *Dictionary of Toys Sold in America*, Vol. 1, 1971, p. 79.

The 1938 Charlie McCarthy in His Benzine Buggy car features the dummy of the famous ventriloquist, Edgar Bergen. W. Maeder Collection. R. Grubb photograph.

Good   Exc

The box for the Whoopee car accurately depicts the two female figures on the trunk. However, the box panel illustrations incorrectly show the front and back wheels as the same size.

A 1929 Montgomery Ward catalog suggests that there may be a variation to the Whoopee Car with an advertisement charmingly entitled "Joy Riders Elope". It mentions only one girl. Excellent price includes original box.   **250   750**

KOMICAL KOP: 1930. 7" long x 6-1/2" high. The Komical Kop car is very reminiscent of the Keystone Kops in the great silent comedies by Mack Sennett. The driver is probably the popular Ford Sterling, chief of the Kops, but no copyright credit is given, and the representation is not exact — Sterling wore a goatee at that time, not a mustache. (Another example of Marx's informal use of film characters is the Marx toy Funny Face, popularly thought to depict the film comedian Harold Lloyd. For this toy, as well as for the Komical Kop, no copyright credit is given.) As further evidence, "Beat It" and "The Komical Kop" with a "K", appear on the back of the trunk.

Although lithographed differently, the 1932 Whoopee Cowboy Car has the same car body and driver as the Coo Coo Car. The car also comes in another version with minor variations. W. Maeder Collection.

Good   Exc

The Komical Kop is similar to the Joy Rider. The same bodies are used for the driver and the car, and a dog sits on the running board (although it was later discontinued). However the lithography of the two toys differs, and the Kop's head is stamped in a longer shape.

The black car has red wheels, edged in black. The Kop wears a blue uniform with "P. D." on his cap. He has boldly drawn features on a ruddy complexion, eye glasses, a white mustache, and a red nose. The car has "P. D." on the radiator, "Traffic-B" on the hood, the Marx logo on the side of the trunk, and the Marx name and address on the back. The license plate reads "P. D. 7000". The number "7" on the sides of the seat appears for the first time on this car, and was subsequently used on several other eccentric cars.

The ad in the 1930 Montgomery Ward catalog, which priced the toy at 49 cents, emphasizes its "Marx unbreakable spring motor." Excellent price includes original box.

350   800

COO COO CAR: 1931. 8" long x 6-1/4" high. Listed for 59 cents in the 1931 Sears catalog, the toy is described as "unique," "new," and "clever." The ad continues: "forwards, backwards, in circles and all kinds of 'curly cues' goes the car, then the man stands up with an excited expression then falls back into his seat with front wheels high off the ground, acts like a 'bucking bronco'." Soon after, Marx introduced the Whoopee Cowboy car where "bucking bronco" was an even more apt description.

The mobility of the Coo Coo Car driver is the biggest difference from the earlier eccentric cars. He has movable legs that enable him to stand up and sit down, an action which is facilitated by a movable steering wheel post, in an upward position. The Snoopy Gus car has a similarly positioned but stationary post. In earlier cars, the seats were built so that only the upper half of the driver could be seen (with the exception of the Snoopy Gus car).

The red and black Coo Coo Car has a red steering wheel and red wheels with white dots and a white rim. The driver is nattily dressed in striped pants and a black coat with red trim.

Good   Exc

A newspaper is in his left jacket pocket. He is dressed humorously with a crooked tie, an open collar that sticks up on one side, and no hat. The driver's stationary head has a surprised expression.

The Coo Coo Car has several new features. While previous eccentric cars have square windshields with the outside corners extending upwards, this car has a smaller windshield with three horizontal bars and no protruding corners. In addition, a diagonal support is under the windshield. Some later eccentric cars also have this type of windshield. Earlier cars had lithographed radiators (except for the Komical Kop), but the Coo Coo Car has a grille design and the Marx logo embossed into the metal. The grille, pointed hood, and small wheels can also be found on the Amos 'n Andy Fresh Air Taxicab (see page 95 in Volume I). Instead of the square trunk of earlier cars, the Coo Coo Car has a smaller round trunk or, more likely, a gas tank. On the back of the gas tank, fancy lettering reads "Coo Coo Car". The Marx logo appears on the sides of the tank. As on the Komical Kop, a stripe and a "7" appear on the sides of the seat. In place of a license plate is a hook. There is a variation of this toy that does not have the stripe, the number on the seat, or the logo on the gas tank.

The "Coo Coo" box is quite striking. The Coo Coo Car is shown driving up a road which turns into a bird which resembles a cuckoo bird. "Coo Coo" probably comes from the bird on the box. By the late 1930s, "coo coo" was slang for crazy. Excellent price includes original box.   **350   800**

WHOOPEE COWBOY: 1932. 8" long x 6-1/2" high. This car appeared the year after the 'bucking bronco' Coo Coo Car and was priced at 59 cents in the 1932 Sears catalog. Other mail

The 1935 Uncle Wiggily Car was inspired by the stories of Howard R Garis that feature Uncle Wiggily, a rabbit. The driver is the first in a series to have lithographed arms instead of three-dimensional ones The trunk is missing from the example shown. W. Maeder Collection

Manufactured in 1939, the 7-1/2" long Mortimer Snerd's Tricky Auto is identical to the Charlie McCarthy car, but the driver depicts another dummy of the famous ventriloquist Edgar Bergen. W. Maeder Collection. R. Grubb photograph.

Good   Exc

order houses ran ads for this toy through 1934. The toy uses the same red and black car and figure as the Coo Coo Car, but different lithography. The driver has a tan-colored band around his head that is shaped into a hat brim. The top of the cowboy's head is lithographed to match so that it appears as if he is wearing a cowboy hat. He wears a red shirt, tan chaps, and a gun on his belt.

The front of the car has a raised grille design stamped into the metal. Laughing cows are lithographed onto the wheels and steering wheel. The back of the gas tank reads "Whoopee Car" and "Louis Marx & Co., N. Y." in the same fancy lettering as the Coo Coo Car. A variation of the Whoopee Cowboy Car has dots on the steering wheel, "7" on the seat, and the Marx logo on both sides of the gas tank. This car's lithography, except on the driver, is identical to the variation Coo Coo Car. Excellent price includes original box.   **200   500**

UNCLE WIGGILY, HE GOES A RIDIN' CAR: 1935. 7-1/2" long x 7" high. This delightful car comes from the Uncle Wiggily rabbit stories of Howard R. Garis. Under the car's windshield is "Uncle Wiggily Trademark 1935 Howard R. Garis".

The lithography of this car is softer and has more illustrations than many eccentric cars. Rather than the usual graffiti, Uncle Wiggily appears to be holding several multicolored eggs in a basket on his lap. The egg motif is repeated on the hood and on the trunk. Various animals are also pictured: one knits, another paints, a third runs. The heads of different animals are lithographed onto the wheels. The box is similarly illustrated, showing Uncle Wiggily driving the car near the

Good   Exc

words "Uncle Wiggily he goes a ridin' ". To the right, on a sign post, is the Marx name and address, while beneath the address an arrow points to "town". A fox lurks in the distance. In a different illustration captioned "Uncle Wiggily and his car", Uncle Wiggily raises his hat to a hen and a duck.

For the first time in eccentric cars, the driver's arms are lithographed onto the car, rather than being separate metal ones. Most of the cars that follow Uncle Wiggily have lithographed arms. Like earlier drivers, Uncle Wiggily's head revolves. His hat reads "Uncle Wiggily".

A German manufacturer marketed another Uncle Wiggily car in 1925. This toy is a larger, more expensive car, that is also driven by a rabbit. The imported car, which is referred to in ads as a "crazy car," has an erratic action like the Marx cars, which were developed later. Excellent price includes original box.   **350   850**

COLLEGE BOY CAR: Mid-1930s. 8" long. The College Boy Car looks different from the earlier eccentric cars and the Uncle Wiggily car, although manufactured about the same time.

The blue car with yellow trim and wheels is described as follows: "A college boy wears the 'beanie' cap and a silly look probably due to his wringing neck which can turn in a complete circle. He steers in an erratic manner." [2]

---

[2] Lillian Gottschalk, *American Toy Cars & Trucks* (New York: Abbeville Press, 1986), pp. 178 and 181. Additional information from Lillian Gottschalk.

A celluloid Popeye drives the Dippy Dumper. Manufactured in 1940, the car is 8-3/4" long. W. Maeder Collection.

Good   Exc

The College Boy wears a black cap with red dots and a red bowtie with black dots. His body is red and yellow with yellow arms. His face and neck are white. The neck is longer than that of most eccentric car drivers. Mortimer Snerd in the Private car has a similar neck with an Adam's Apple (see page 97 in Volume I). The car is unusual in several respects: it is low to the ground, and it has four similarly-sized wheels instead of two small front wheels and two large rear wheels. Like the later eccentric cars, the one-piece car body is rounded at the ends. Moreover, the steering wheel post stands up straight. Excellent price includes original box.   **250   750**

CHARLIE MCCARTHY in HIS BENZINE BUGGY: 1938. 7-1/2" long x 6-1/2" high. The Charlie McCarthy car is based on the well-known dummy of the famous ventriloquist, Edgar Bergen. The friendship between Louis Marx and Edgar Bergen is evident in the special care that was taken in the design of the car. Listing the toy at 49 cents, the 1938 Sears Christmas catalog describes Charlie's head turning as he goes forward, in reverse, or around in circles. The box shows the encircled head of Charlie McCarthy telling the likewise enclosed head of Edgar Bergen, "I'll Mow You Down!" A full view is shown of Charlie driving his car. Charlie McCarthy In His Benzine Buggy is more common than the Charlie McCarthy Walker in which Charlie's mouth moves (see Volume I).

In contrast to the other eccentric cars, the Charlie McCarthy buggy is almost entirely black and white. This elegant appearance is brightened by Charlie's face and by a red and

Good   Exc

white steering wheel. (A variation has also been seen with a black and white steering wheel.) This is the first car to have wooden hub caps instead of the standard metal, but a version with metal hub caps has also been seen. Charlie, dressed in tails and a top hat, wears a monocle. His lithographed face is carefully detailed. "Charlie McCarthy" is on the front and sides of the car and on the back of the trunk, "Charlie McCarthy" and "Edgar Bergen" on the back of the trunk, and "Pat's Pend'g, Made in U. S. A." on the sides of the trunk. The Marx logo is on the radiator and the trunk.

Rick Rubis owns a fascinating eccentric car prototype that was never produced. The *Marx Toy Collector Newsletter* describes the prototype as a New York World's Fair 1939-40 toy. Mr. Rubis notes that the prototype looks like the Charlie McCarthy car repainted, except for the head, which is a globe with a smiling face. "9/18/38 17/10 Erie" appear on the underside of the car. [3]   Excellent price includes original box.

	Good	Exc
With white wheels:	400	1000
With red wheels:	500	1200

MORTIMER SNERD'S TRICKY AUTO: 1939. 7-1/2" long x 6-1/2" high. Like Charlie McCarthy, Mortimer Snerd was a dummy of the ventriloquist Edgar Bergen. The Mortimer Snerd car is almost identical to the Charlie McCarthy car.

---

[3] Rick Rubis, "Prototypes," *Marx Toy Collector Newsletter*, Vol. 1, No. 4, p. 14.

Good Exc

Only the lithography and the driver's head differ. Like the Charlie McCarthy car, the lithography of the head is finely detailed. However, Mortimer has yellow-orange hair, lithographed eyelashes, and a big smile. Mortimer wears no hat, although he does in the Mortimer Walker (see page 97 in Volume I). He is colorfully dressed in a yellow jacket with red and black checks, a yellow-spotted shirt, and a red tie with yellow and black stripes.

The Mortimer Snerd toy is outstanding for its fine use of the colors mauve, blue, blue-green, red, yellow, yellow-orange, cream, and black. The purple car has cream trim, red wheels with cream rims, and blue running boards, fenders, and floor. Some cars appear to be faded; if possible, it is best to avoid buying the toy in this condition. The fading on this toy is more noticeable than on other toys because the original colors are so bright.

The Marx logo and "1939 Edgar Bergen" are on the sides of the blue-green trunk and "Mortimer Snerd" and "Louis Marx & Co., New York, N. Y., Made in U. S. A. Pat's Pend'g" are on the back of the trunk. Three labels, "M. Snerd, U. S. A.", "Vermont", and another illegible label are on the top of the trunk. "Vermont" on the wooden dummy's car is a touch of humor, since Marx had once worked for a wood products company in Vermont. The car also has wooden hub caps.

350   800

At 8", the Dagwood the Driver toy is one of the longest of the eccentric cars. It was manufactured around 1941. Dagwood's hat is made of wood. W. Maeder Collection.

Good Exc

DIPPY DUMPER: 1940. 8-3/4" long x 5-3/4" high. This car differs from all the previous eccentric cars in that the drivers are made of celluloid and the rear of the vehicle is a movable dump cart.

The red Dippy Dumper has blue and white trim and red wheels with white edging. The toy has a raised radiator design, a stamped Marx logo, and a barred windshield, all of which remain from the earlier cars. White-lettered "Dippy Dumper", "Pat's Pend'g", and "Made in U. S. A." are on the sides and the back of the dumper along with the Marx logo.

One version has Popeye driving, another, his arch-rival, Brutus. These celluloid characters are molded in one piece, except for the arms. In other Popeye and Brutus toys, the arms are fastened through the body by a pin, which lets the arms move. But in the Dippy Dumper, the arms do not move because they are fastened to the steering wheel with wire. Thus, when the dumper moves, the figures can be raised without falling from the toy.

Popeye wears a sailor costume with a white cap. Brutus wears a navy cap, a flesh-colored sweater over a red shirt, and brown pants. "7/82" is on their backs with an unidentifiable logo. The boxing gloves on the figures' hands indicate that they were used in Marx's earlier toy, Popeye The Champ. Despite the fragility and the flammability of celluloid, Marx managed to make considerable use of these two figures' bodies. They were used in the Funny Fire Fighters (see next page) and the Popeye Horse and Cart (see page 73 in Volume I).

The patent for the Dippy Dumper, #2,175,845, is dated October 10, 1939. Despite the popularity of the Popeye character, Brutus is shown in the patent drawing.

300   650

The 1941 Funny Fire Fighters is 7" long and uses the same celluloid Popeye and Brutus figures as the Dippy Dumper. W. Maeder Collection. R. Grubb photograph.

A celluloid Brutus drives this variation of the Dippy Dumper. W. Maeder Collection. R. Grubb photograph.

Good Exc

FUNNY FIRE FIGHTERS: 1941. 7" long x 10-1/2" high.

First Version: In the 1943 Montgomery Ward Christmas catalog, the car, priced at 52 cents, is described as a fire truck that "bucks, rears and twists but Popeye atop his ladder hangs right on through all sorts of reckless driving."

The red Funny Fire Fighter is similar to the Dippy Dumper. Both toys have the same celluloid figures, red wheels edged with white, a radiator with a raised design, and the same hoods. There are several differences, however. The Funny Fire Fighters car has a steering wheel without a post instead of a windshield. A trunk and a revolving ladder replace the dumper body, steering wheel, and post. The ladder is narrower, more like the Snoopy Gus car. Brutus is at the wheel of the truck, and Popeye is on the ladder. Fire fighting equipment is lithographed in yellow on several parts of the car. "Funny Fire Fighters" is in yellow on the sides of the hood, and on the top, back, and sides of the trunk. In addition, "Louis Marx & Co., Inc., New York, N. Y., U. S. A. Made in U. S. A." is written on the back of the trunk. The toy comes in a plain, unillustrated box.

The Funny Fire Fighters is one of the rarest and consequently most expensive eccentric cars. Its scarcity may be due to the fact that the manufacture of toys was interrupted during World War II to produce weapons parts. Excellent price includes original box. (The price of the toy in Excellent condition without the original box is $1200.) **750 2000**

Second Version: The only known variation of the Funny Fire Fighters car, this version is also rare. Instead of the Popeye and Brutus figures there are two celluloid black children who are boxing. Like the Popeye and Brutus figures, the child boxers have jointed arms and wear boxing gloves. These figures are repeated from the Marx Knockout Champs, a toy similar to the Popeye the Champ toy. It is possible that the Funny Fire Fighters toy was produced with white boxers because the Knockout Champs came in a white version. The Black Funny Fire Fighters toy was made around 1941, about

This Funny Fire Fighters version has the celluloid, child boxers from the Marx Knockout Champs toy. It is similar to the Popeye the Champ toy. One figure may have been attached to the ladder. W. Maeder Collection.

With the exception of the lithography, the 1950 Old Jalopy is identical to the Jumpin Jeep. The names on the car refer to key people who worked at the Marx Company. W. Maeder Collection. R. Grubb photograph.

	Good	Exc

the same time as the Popeye and Brutus Funny Fire Fighters. Excellent price includes original box. (The price of the toy in Excellent condition without the original box is $1200.)

	750	**2000**

DAGWOOD THE DRIVER: 1941. 8" long x 6" high. This amusing and colorful car was taken from the comic strip *Blondie,* created by Chic Young. The car used for family outings is typical of cars that appeared in the comics in the 1940s. It has exposed tires, minimal fenders, and a simple body.

The Dagwood car, probably the longest eccentric car Marx produced, was styled from an oblong block. Earlier cars have a more defined car shape. This multicolored car is predominantly red. The front wheels are orange, white, and black, while the back wheels are red, silver, and black. The larger back wheels have a stamped tread design, and the front wheels have a lithographed tire tread. The hubcaps on the back wheels have silver discs to match the fenders above them, but the front wheels have thin white circles. These types of fenders were discontinued after this car.

Baby Dumpling and Blondie appear on the hood, Cookie and Mr. Dithers are on the side of the hood, and Daisy the Dog and her puppies are on the trunk. Except for Mr. Dithers, all of the characters' names are on the car. The Marx logo and "Made in United States of America" are used together for the first time on this car. Although this trademark is on the box of the earlier Mortimer Snerd Tricky Auto, it is not on the toy itself. A "learner's permit" is lithographed around the left side of the windshield frame to look as if it has been hung there, and "123" is lithographed onto the front and back of the car. As in

Plastic was introduced in the 1949 Sheriff Sam and His Whoopee Car, which measures about 5-3/4" long. J. Iannuzzi Collection.

This version of the Old Jalopy, driven by a student wearing glasses, is profusely lettered with names and slogans. W. Maeder Collection.

the earlier Uncle Wiggily car, Dagwood's arms and his big red bow tie are lithographed. Dagwood is the only eccentric car driver to wear a wooden hat, which is red. Dagwood's revolving head is also used in the airplane toy "Dagwood's Solo Flight" and in the rare "Blondie's Jalopy". The box for this toy is illustrated in a lively fashion with *Blondie* characters. Large red letters on the attractive box read "Dagwood the Driver".

Gerritt Beverwyk, former editor of the *Marx Toy Collector Newsletter*, pointed out that the Cookie character illustrated on this car was not created until 1941. [4] Thus, this car was probably produced in 1941. The copyright dates "1930, 1934, 1935 by King Features Syndicate, Inc." on the side of the car are for the rights to use the characters and thus tend to be misleading. As a late eccentric car, the Dagwood car shows the shape of cars to come. Its "modern" windshield is a simple rectangular shape. No longer used are a barred windshield,

[4] Gerritt Beverwyk, "Blondie Dagwood," *Marx Toy Collector Newsletter,* Vol. 2, No. 3, p. 4.

gas tank, running board, and raised radiator design. Excellent price includes original box. (The price of the toy in Excellent condition without the original box is $250.)   **150   450**

JUMPIN JEEP: 1947. 5-3/4" long x 4-1/2" high. The Jumpin Jeep was probably developed by Marx in response to the country's patriotic feelings of post-World War II. Advertised for 79 cents in the 1947 Sears Christmas catalog, the toy is described as "[running] in all directions, backwards, forwards, tips back on rear wheels." The Jumpin Jeep ad also appears in the 1948 Montgomery Ward catalog and is priced at two cents less than the 1947 Sears Jeep. The June 1977 PB 84 auction catalog lists 741, 741-2, and 742 as catalog numbers for this toy which suggests the existence of different versions.

This khaki car has large black and khaki or black and rust metal rear wheels with stamped tire treads. The tire treads of the smaller wheels are lithographed in black and khaki, black and red, or black and rust, similar to the lithography on the Dagwood car. The Jumpin Jeep is shorter and narrower than the Dagwood car by about a 1/4". A noticeable spring is on the

The 1947 Jumpin Jeep is about 5-3/4" long. It was the first in a series of cars made with four figures. W. Maeder Collection.

The Smoky Sam the Wild Fireman Car is similar to Sheriff Sam, minus the driver's legs. J. Iannuzzi Collection.

Good   Exc

underside. Even more than the Dagwood car, the Jeep is closer in size and shape to the later eccentric cars.

A new feature for the eccentric cars, the car has a driver with three passengers, all soldiers. Only their heads can be seen. (The same heads were also used in Marx racers.) In most of the later eccentric cars, the bodies are lithographed. One soldier drives while the other three hold guns. Lettering on the hood reads "Jumpin Jeep" and "22 C". The Marx logo is on the sides of the jeep.

The toy's colorful box shows soldiers watching the jeep rear in a cloud of smoke. Behind the vehicle is a large circle which contains the word "Jeep". "Jumpin" is to the left of the circle, "Action" to the right. Excellent price includes original box.

100   250

SHERIFF SAM and HIS WHOOPEE CAR: 1949. 5-3/4" long x 6-1/2" high. Priced at 94 cents in the Sears 1949 and 1950 catalogs, the car "streaks around in circle and back and forth. Head turns from side to side, big hat flops up and down." The June 1977 PB 84 auction catalog lists 744 as the number for this car.

The Sheriff Sam car is the first eccentric car to use plastic. In an amusing touch, the driver's feet are sticking out of the car. The red plastic car has cattle horns on the hood. The driver has a plastic body, a red plastic cowboy hat, and a tin head. Like the Old Jalopy car, the large tin back wheels have white spokes edged with red discs and black and white stripes. The front wheels are red with yellow- or white-lithographed treads.

Good   Exc

Sheriff Sam and his Whoopee Car is similar to the Smoky Sam the Wild Fireman car. Both toys came in red, yellow, white, and black boxes with similar illustrations. The front of the box shows the smiling sheriff driving with the car's front wheels off the ground. On one side of the box the sheriff holds a rope, a design which is cleverly continued around the entire box. The other side shows an unsmiling sheriff near a man on horseback and a cactus. The box also comes in a slightly different design that does not have the rope pattern. Excellent price includes original box.

150   325

OLD JALOPY: 1950.

First Version: The Old Jalopy is the same car as the Jumpin Jeep, but with different lithography. The dominant colors of the car are red and yellow, with some black, white, and brown. Four college students ride in the car. As in other eccentric cars, each set of wheels is different. The large rear wheels have white spokes edged with red discs and black and white stripes. The front wheels are red, with yellow- or white-lithographed tire treads. Excellent price includes original box.

250   750

Second Version: In this version, each student holds something in his lithographed hand: the steering wheel, a piece of paper, a book, a sandwich (?). The car is lettered "Queen of the Campus" and "Engine Room" on the hood; "Air Brakes" on the side; and "Town and Country" and "Army Surplus" on the trunk. Also on the trunk is the license plate, "FO 4", and, in small and hard-to-read letters, the Marx logo. A lithographed patch mends the radiator. The 1950 Montgomery Ward catalog lists the Old Jalopy for 79 cents.

Good   Exc

Of great interest are the names printed on the car. They include "Louie" [Marx] and "Archie", which probably refers to Archie Marcus, vice-president of the firm, financial expert, and frequent visitor to the plant. Other names are "Ray" for Ray Lohr, head of research and development in Erie; "Monty" for Monty Feist, general manager, treasurer, and assistant secretary of the firm in Pennsylvania; "B. K." for either Bill Keller, general manager of the Erie factory, or Bill Kalsch, head of the lithography department and later plant superintendent; and "Dick C." for Dick Carver, design foreman, toy designer, and model maker. Other letters and names cannot be attributed to Marx personnel as easily. (For more information on the names listed above, see Volume 1.) Excellent price includes original box.   **250   750**

Third Version: In this version, the four heads of the college students are in reversed positions, having probably been switched by Marx assembly line workers. The student with glasses, who sat to the right in the back seat, now drives. The June 1977 PB 84 auction catalog lists 747 as its number.
100   250

Good   Exc

Fourth Version: This major variation has one student holding a piece of paper that reads "History" and another a school pennant. The radiator has "deteriorated" to such a degree that it has several holes instead of just one; none are patched. The wire on the trunk shows chickens and an advertisement for fresh eggs. "Queen of the Campus" and "Louie" are still on the car, but much of the lettering is different. For example, "Leapin' Lena" has replaced "Louie", which is now on the lower left side of the car. The license plate reads "P U 109". Hanging on a corner of the windshield, as on a few previous cars, is a lithographed diploma, "G. I. Diploma Upside Down College". A minor variation of this car does not have a student with glasses and all of the students wear beanies.

The toy's name "Old Jalopy" is on the box, but not on the toy. The Old Jalopy eccentric car should not be confused with another 1950 Marx sedan of the same name which has a completely different appearance (see page 33). The Old Jalopy also comes in a version with the four students seated in a small black convertible covered with jalopy markings. Excellent price includes original box.   **250   750**

The Peter Rabbit Eccentric Car, 5-1/2" long, was manufactured in the 1950s. The rabbit figure, with movable ears, is made entirely of plastic. B. Allan Collection.

The Jolly Joe Jeep is 5-3/4" long and was made in the 1950s. The driver's plastic helmet is missing in the example shown. W. Maeder Collection.

Good   Exc

SMOKY SAM the WILD FIREMAN CAR: 1950. 6-1/2" long x 6-1/2" high.

First Version: The Smoky Sam car is made of red plastic and has white plastic ladders on the sides. There is a non-operational white plastic bell on the hood, which is decorated with a design of embossed flowers. The driver has a plastic body and wears a red plastic fire helmet on his tin head. A gold decal on his hat reads "Chief". The tin wheels are black and olive drab. The tread of the larger rear wheels is stamped into the metal; the smaller front wheels are lithographed. A small, pivoting wheel is located on the rear of the car.

Smoky Sam is listed for 94 cents in the 1950 Montgomery Ward catalog. The Smoky Sam and the Sheriff Sam toys come in red, yellow, black, and white boxes with similar illustrations. The Smoky Sam box shows the driver in a red helmet. One side of the box shows a farmer who is angry because Smoky Sam is frightening one of his chickens. The other side shows Smoky Sam driving with his hands off the steering wheel.

The June 1977 PB 84 auction catalog lists 746 as its catalog number. Excellent price includes original box. **75   200**

Second Version: Smoky Sam wears a yellow plastic helmet in this version. The large tin rear wheels have lithographed spokes edged in red and black and white stripes. The front wheels are red, with yellow- or white-lithographed tire treads. Excellent price includes original box. **75   200**

Third Version: A metal version of the Smoky Sam has been seen. When a plastic Marx toy was reproduced in metal, it was

Good   Exc

usually manufactured by Linemar, Marx's Japanese subsidiary. Therefore it is likely that the metal version of the Smoky Sam was made by Linemar. Excellent price includes original box. **75   200**

PETER RABBIT ECCENTRIC CAR: 1950s. 5-1/2" long. Because the Peter Rabbit car is entirely made of plastic, it is thought to have been made later than the Sheriff Sam and Smoky Sam toys. Though of more recent manufacture, the Peter Rabbit car is not found as easily as the earlier cars. The June 1977 PB 84 auction catalog lists 779 and 799 as catalog numbers for this car. The box is similar to but more colorful than the boxes for the Smoky Sam and Sheriff Sam toys. Wording on the box emphasizes that the toy is "molded of plastic with long running motor". "Eccentric Car" and the Marx slogan, "One of the many Marx toys — have you all of them?" are also on the box. Some sides show just a rabbit's head; others a driver frightening a running chicken. This popular theme was used on boxes as early as the 1920s. The

With the exception of the lithography and Milton's plastic hat, the Milton Berle Car is identical to the Jolly Joe Jeep. It was manufactured in the 1950s. P. Rolin Collection.

This Dora Dipsy Car is lithographed with familiar Disney characters. W. Maeder Collection. R. Grubb photograph.

The Dan Dipsy Car is similar to the Dora Dipsy Car but with a young boy, dressed in red, driving. P. Rolin Collection.

Good   Exc

Peter Rabbit car body is identical to the Sheriff Sam and Smoky Sam cars, except for the large plastic carrot in place of the radiator cap. Peter Rabbit is brightly colored with his pink head, movable yellow ears, white body, large blue eyes, and buck teeth. A pair of two-dimensional, yellow plastic ducks is on one side of the hood; a similar pair of chickens is on the other. The large tin back wheels have black- and white-striped treads, yellow hubcaps, and white-lithographed spokes edged with red discs. The red and white front wheels are lithographed with white tire treads. A small wood wheel castor hangs down at the rear of the car so that the back will not drag on the ground. The front of the car lifts up when the drive mechanism abruptly changes from reverse to forward. Excellent price includes original box. **150   500**

JOLLY JOE JEEP: 1950s. 5-3/4" long x 5-1/2" high. The style of the Jolly Joe Jeep indicates that it was made in the 1950s. With the same car body as the Jumpin Jeep, it is lithographed in olive drab and black with rust-colored wheel centers. Headlights are lithographed onto the radiator. Mounted on the hood of the car is a plastic machine gun; two others are lithographed onto the hood and trunk. The driver's stripes indicate that he is a corporal. He has a smiling face

Good   Exc

with caricature features, a plastic helmet, lithographed arms, and a turning head, which is larger than those used on the Jumpin Jeep.

The hood reads "Jolly Joe" and "13079A". On one side of the trunk is "5"; on the other side, a star; "U. S. 25, 7-A" is on the top; and "U. S." on the back. The Marx logo is on the right side of the hood. Variations are thought to exist with and without a metal gun. **100   250**

MILTON BERLE CAR: 1950s. The Milton Berle car, named for the well-known comedian, is the same car as the Jolly Joe Jeep. The car's dominant colors are yellow, red, and white. Headlights are lithographed onto the radiator, and the large back wheels have white spokes edged with red discs and black and white stripes. The small front wheels are red, or olive drab and black, with a lithographed tread. The car has been seen with wooden wheels.

Except for his toothy grin, the face of the driver does not resemble Milton Berle. However, a caricature on the back of the trunk and a drawing on the top of the trunk do bear a resemblance. The Milton figure has blue-lithographed arms and a large plastic cowboy hat in yellow, red, or pale beige. The hat (which is easily cracked) is also used on the Marx Porky Pig the Cowboy (see Volume I). The turning head is the

The 5-3/4" Dora Dipsy Car has a spring in the figure's neck which causes her head to nod and shake. W. Maeder Collection.

The Mickey Mouse Disney Dipsy car was manufactured in 1953 and is 5-3/4" long. The car is the same as a variation of the Dora Dipsy Car with lithographed Disney figures. W. Maeder Collection.

	Good	Exc

same as that used for Jolly Joe. Black lettering on the car reads "What The Hey", "I'll Give You a Shot In Th' Head!", and "I'm Milton, Who Are You?" Some of these are repeated on the red, yellow, black, and white box.

The June 1977 PB 84 auction catalog lists 782 as the catalog number for this car. The Milton Berle car is one of the easiest cars for collectors to obtain. Excellent price includes original box. **150   350**

DAN and DORA DIPSY CARS: 1950s. 5-3/4" long x 6" high.

First Version: The Dan Dipsy Car is the masculine version of the Dora Dipsy Car. Both the Dan and Dora figures have springs in their necks which make their heads nod and shake. The spring is partially hidden by a piece of plastic that covers the neck, but can be seen under the headpiece.

The dominant colors of the tin cars are red and yellow.

Both cars have lithography similar to that on one of the versions of the Old Jalopy. The only difference between these cars is in the space on top of the trunk. In the Old Jalopy, this space is occupied by two other figures. In the Dan and Dora cars, this space is covered with "Hot Dawg!" and "Cap. 25 Gals". Hood lettering on both of the Dipsy cars reads "Queen of the Campus" and "Engine Room". The initials "J. C." (which probably stand for Jay Campbell, the head artist at the Erie plant) appear on the radiator.

	Good	Exc

Both the Dan and the Dora figures also come in small yellow and red convertibles with lithography different from that of the other eccentric cars. The undercarriage details of the cars are lithographed on the bottoms of these convertibles. The figures' heads and upper bodies are made of plastic.

Shown to her waist, the Dora figure is a little girl with two brown pigtails and a blue and white dress with a white collar. She holds a plastic steering wheel. Dan has brown hair and is dressed in a red sweater and cap.

The large tin back wheels have lithographed spokes edged with red discs, and black and white stripes. The front wheels are red and white with white-lithographed tire treads.

The June 1977 PB 84 auction catalog lists 796 as the catalog number for the Dan Dipsy car. While the Dora Car is quite common, the Dan Dipsy Car is unaccountably scarce.

	Good	Exc
Dora:	100	250
Dan:	200	450

Second Version: This mostly red Dora car is covered with Disney characters. Goofy and Pluto are on top of the hood, Mickey Mouse is on the left side of the car, and Thumper is on the right. On the left side of the trunk is Donald; on the right side, Minnie. Curiously, only one of the two chipmunks, probably Chip, is shown on the top of the trunk. Pluto is pictured on the back. Lettering reads "Mickey Mouse" on the radiator. "Walt Disney Prod." appear in very small letters on the trunk. Dora has reddish-colored pigtails, but her hair may have come in other colors. A "Disney" version of the Dan car has not been seen, although it is likely the car was made.

	Good	Exc
Dora:	100	250

This variation of the Disney Dipsy Car has Donald Duck driving. W. Maeder Collection.

MICKEY MOUSE DISNEY DIPSY CAR and DONALD DUCK DISNEY DIPSY CAR: 1953. 5-3/4" long x 6" high. Both toys sold in 1953 for about one dollar. The illustrated box for the Donald Duck car, labeled "Disney Dipsy Car", shows both Donald and Mickey, so it may have been used for either toy.

These cars are identical to the Disney version of the Dora Dipsy Car. The predominantly red and yellow multicolored car has Goofy and Pluto on top of the hood, Mickey Mouse on the left side of the car, and Thumper on the right. On the left side of the trunk is Donald, on the right side, Minnie. Only one of the two chipmunks, Chip, is shown on the top of the trunk, while Pluto is pictured on the back. The large rear wheels have white spokes edged with red discs and black and white stripes. The small front wheels are red and white. "Mickey Mouse" is on the radiator.

The car comes with either a plastic Mickey Mouse or a plastic Donald Duck. Unlike the Dora figure, the Mickey and Donald figures have arms that appear to be waving. Because the arms stick out of the car, they are frequently found to be broken or missing. The neck springs that make the characters' necks nod are visible since there is no neckpiece covering them.

The Mickey figure is also used in a small convertible called Mickey The Driver (see page 80 in Volume I). Similar to other convertibles of this kind, the automobile works are lithographed onto the bottom of the car. Disney characters are found on the convertible, too, but the lithography is different from the Dipsy Car. It is very likely Donald Duck was also used as the driver of this car.

Linemar, Marx's Japanese subsidiary, made tin versions of the Mickey Mouse and Donald Duck Dipsy cars. Linemar also produced a tin Donald The Driver Car.

The June 1977 PB 84 auction catalog lists 794 and 794-2 as the numbers for both the Mickey and Donald Disney Dipsy cars. [5] Excellent price includes original box.   **350   800**

---

[5] The Sotheby Parke Bernet Eight-Four Auction Catalog from June 1977 refers to a No. 188 Dottie the Driver Tricky Action Driving Car. Female figures in Marx toys are scarce; Dottie and Dora, from the Dora Dipsy Car, are the same figures. The number 188 is not close to the numbers used for the eccentric cars; it may refer to the convertible this figure drove.

⑤

MOTORCYCLES AND RELATED TOYS

Marx motorcycles are fun to play with. Some motorcycles, if tipped over, right themselves. Others will not run off the edge of a table. Still others have sirens and/or sidecars, but, oddly, most of the sidecars have no passengers. (Perhaps adding a passenger would have made the toy too expensive to produce.) In addition, open sidecars can carry small loads. Beginning with the Police Tipover Motorcycle, almost all of the motorcycles are made from one 8" long die. Currently, many Marx motorcycles are easy to find and reasonably priced.

All of the following toys are lithographed, tin windups, except for the plastic Speeding Car and Motorcycle Policeman.

Although ads for Marx toys began to appear in 1924, it was not until 1933 that motorcycles were advertised.

The following toys are arranged chronologically.

POLICE TIPOVER MOTORCYCLE: 1933. Approximately 8" long x 5-3/4" high. Priced at 59 cents in 1933 ads, this motorcycle is first referred to as a Tipover Motorcycle in the 1934 Sears Fall/Winter catalog. It contains a new type of "very fine clock spring motor," probably the one referred to in patent #1,972,713, filed by Wilbur W. Kelch on October 6, 1931.[1] This motorcycle was to be the basic design for a number of future variations.

Marx made many Police Motorcycles, but this one does a unique trick: It travels a short distance, falls over, and returns to an upright position, assisted by the 2-1/4" long handles of its

---

[1] Some of the later eccentric cars, such as the Old Jalopy, have differently lithographed front and rear wheels.

The small Mystic Motorcycle, measuring only 4-1/4" long x 3-1/4" high, was made in the mid-1930s It is one of the most easily found Marx motorcycles. P. Rolin Collection.

winding key, which goes through the toy. The motorcycle needs about six feet to perform this action.

The boldly-lithographed motorcycle is driven by a policeman dressed in a navy blue uniform with patches and three stripes on each of his arms, a tan-striped hat, and a lithographed gun belt. The red motorcycle has lithographed gears and a start/stop lever. On each side of the motorcycle is "Marx" in large black letters, its only reference to the name. "PAT'S PENDG (sic)" is near the back wheels, and "Made In U. S. A." is on the back fenders. The motorcycle has two types of wheels. The front three-dimensional wheel is fixed at an angle to enable the motorcycle to travel in circles. The rear wheels are in two

Good   Exc

separate flat sections that are attached to the motorcycle. The Police Tipover Motorcycle is believed be the only motorcycle to have this type of back wheel. All of the wheels are lithographed similarly. (Some of the later Eccentric Cars, such as the Old Jalopy, have differently lithographed front and rear wheels.) They are navy and white with lithographed spokes and are marked "Marx-Balloon-U. S. A.-34x5". Excellent price includes original box.   **100   375**

MYSTIC MOTORCYCLE: 1936. 4-1/4" long x 3-1/4" high. *First Version:* Selling for 25 cents in 1936, this motorcycle is entirely different from the Tipover Motorcycle. Popularly known as the Tricky Motorcycle, the name on the box is the Mystic Motorcycle. This toy may have been available prior to 1936.

The motorcycle has lithographed front and rear wheels, and two small, white metal working wheels on each side, close to the back wheels. Under the base are two more wheels; one is on the left side of the base, and the other is placed horizontally at the front.

Produced in 1933, the Police Tipover Motorcycle's winding key handles return the motorcycle to an upright position when tipped. W. Maeder Collection.

The dark-haired policeman wears a dark blue uniform. On his arms are yellow stripes and a patch which reads "P. D." He rides a blue, orange, yellow, and white motorcycle, with "Louis Marx & Co. N. Y., U. S. A." on the back. The Mystic Motorcycle is one of the most easily found of the Marx motorcycles.

Like the Marx Tricky Taxi, the Mystic Motorcycle rarely runs off the edge of a table. It also runs in circles. Both toys have patent #2,001,625, submitted by Heinrich Muller of Nuremburg, Germany on September 17, 1934. This is unusual in that Heinrich Muller did not work for the Marx Company. The box for the Mystic Motorcycle describes the toy: "Will scoot around in a mysterious manner in all directions on a smooth table or base without falling off. It will also do many tricks on small surfaces." Excellent price includes original box.

70   175

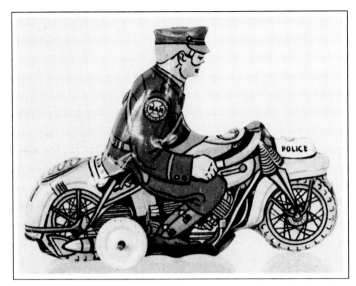

Another version of the Mystic Motorcycle. E. Owens Collection. G. Stern photograph.

Good   Exc

Second Version: Not as common as the first version, this motorcycle is driven by a blue-uniformed policeman with blond hair and goggles. On his arm is a patch with the Marx logo. The front of the motorcycle reads "Police". Excellent price includes original box.   **100   375**

Good   Exc

POLICE SIREN MOTORCYCLE: 1938. 8" long x 5-3/4" high. In 1938 this Police Siren Motorcycle was advertised as selling for 57 cents. The illustrated box for the toy shows a policeman driving in the country while the siren screams "whee-e-e". The front of the box says "Police Mechanical Motorcycle" and the side says "Police Siren Motorcycle".

Similar to the Tipover Motorcycle, the vividly lithographed Police Siren Motorcycle features a policeman in a navy blue uniform with "P. D." under the patches on each of his arms. He wears white gloves, brown boots, and a hat with a tan stripe. "7" appears on the back fender. The motorcycle has two different types of wheels. The front wheel is three-dimensional and fixed at an angle to enable the motorcycle to travel in circles. The back wheel is lithographed. The motorcycle differs from the Tipover Motorcycle in several ways: It has gray wheels with lithographed tire treads; a siren on its left side; a start/stop lever on its right side; and a small wheel on its left side.

Its most unusual features are the various meters and dials lithographed on the fender with the Marx logo. Since they are directly in front of the headlight, the policeman cannot see them! Although the Marx Company rarely made this type of mistake, it was repeated with several motorcycles.

125   275

POLICE MOTORCYCLE with SIDECAR: Late 1930s. 8" long x 5-3/4" high. This toy is very similar to the Police Siren Motorcycle. The most noticeable difference is the addition of a

The attractive Police Motorcycle with Sidecar, made in the late 1930s, has various meters and dials lithographed on the front of the fender which are "hidden" from the driver by the large headlight. The toy also comes in a version without the sidecar. Dr. M. Kates Collection. R. Grubb photograph.

Police Squad Motorcycle with Sidecar, made by Marx's Mexican branch, Plastimarx, is almost identical to the American version of the toy. W. Maeder Collection. R. Grubb photograph.

Good   Exc

sidecar. According to Dr. Malcom Kates, the driver of the red motorcycle is wearing a navy blue uniform, a striped hat, brown boots, and white gloves. On his arms are tan "P. D." arm patches and three tan stripes. Like the Police Siren Motorcycle, the wheels are gray with lithographed treads. A three-dimensional front wheel is fixed in a turning position and the rear wheel is lithographed.

The sidecar has a movable steering wheel, and although the passenger in the sidecar does not drive, the wheel helps to balance and move the toy. The sidecar has a yellow interior and a red exterior, with "Police Siren Squad" in a shield on the side of the car. On the front is a police shield inscribed with "Police" and crowned with an eagle. "P. D." is on the rear of the sidecar behind the seat.

Like the Police Siren Motorcycle, the design mistake in which the driver cannot see the controls of his motorcycle because of the headlight is repeated. The various dials and meters are now blocked by an even larger headlight with a sparkler beneath it. Excellent price includes original box.

125   375

POLICE MOTORCYCLE WITH SIDECAR (Miniature): Late 1930s. 3-1/2" long x 2-3/4" high x 1-1/4" wide. This appealing toy is one of the smallest of the Marx motorcycles. Although the motorcycle was originally inexpensive, it is not found as frequently as some of the other motorcycles, such as the Mystic Motorcycle.

The motorcycle policeman is dressed in a blue uniform with a "P. D." badge on his chest. Despite his small size, details of

The Police Motorcycle and Sidecar, made in the late 1930s, is one of the smallest Marx motorcycles, measuring only 3-1/2" long x 2-3/4" high. W. Maeder Collection. R. Grubb photograph.

	Good	Exc

the policeman's uniform are shown, including buttons and a belt. His leg on the motorcycle side is lithographed; on the other side is the sidecar. The mostly red motorcycle has three-dimensional wooden wheels and no headlight. The dials and the Marx logo on the front can easily be "viewed" by the driver.

The sidecar has a lithographed interior with "Police" on the side in white letters. In small black letters at the bottom is "Made In United States Of America". The rear of the sidecar reads "P. D." in white and has an on/off switch. **80   175**

SPARKLING SOLDIER MOTORCYCLE: Circa 1940. 8" long x 5-3/4" high. This colorful motorcycle was made around 1940 and is similar to the larger motorcycles. One noticeable difference is a camouflage shield with a protruding spark-shooting gun in front of the soldier. The motorcycle also has fenders with a camouflage design. As indicated by the chevrons on the soldier's red uniform, he is a corporal. He also has three stripes on his coat, several stripes on his pants, and one stripe on his hat. All of the stripes are predominantly yellow. Like the Police Siren Motorcycle, the wheels are gray with litho-graphed treads; a three-dimensional front wheel is fixed in a turning position and the back wheel is lithographed. This toy comes in a plain, unillustrated box. **150   350**

	Good	Exc

ROOKIE COP (No. 216): 1950. 8" long x 5-3/4" high. Made in 1950, this toy is a new version of the Tipover Motorcycle. Both tip over and right themselves. The box advertises the toy with the line "See Him Flop". Both run in a circle, but the lithography differs and the Rookie Cop has a siren.

The Rookie Cop is dressed in a gray shirt with a keystone on his left arm (indicating that he is a Pennsylvania State Trooper) and the Marx logo on his right arm. He also wears goggles, red pants, a red cap with yellow stripes, gray gloves, and brown boots. The detailed motorcycle is yellow, red, silver, and black. The policeman's view of the controls is not blocked, as in previous motorcycles, because the controls are properly placed behind the headlight instead of on the fender. The motorcycle has a large "3" on the fender and the license number, "102D", on the back of the motorcycle. The front wheel is three-dimensional and fixed at an angle to enable the motorcy-cle to turn in a circle. The back wheel is lithographed and has a small rubber wheel on each of its sides. Excellent price includes original box. **130   325**

POLICE SQUAD MOTORCYCLE SIDECAR: 1950. This set comes with a sidecar in yellow, orange, red, and black and has the same motorcycle as the Rookie Cop with a larger headlight. A keystone and "Police" are on the side of the car.

The Police Motorcycle with Sidecar is similar to the Police Squad Motorcycle with Sidecar except for the driver's uniform and the headlight. Dr. M. Kates Collection. R. Grubb photograph.

Made in the early 1930s, this 9-1/2" Motorcycle Delivery toy has battery-operated headlights and taillights. Dr. M. Kates Collection. R. Grubb photograph.

	Good	Exc

In smaller letters, "Police" is repeated on the front with the Marx logo. A large "3" is behind the sidecar seat. The controls are below the large headlight, which blocks the view of the controls. A sparkler is adjacent to the controls. The policeman wears the same uniform as the Rookie Cop: a gray shirt with a keystone on his left arm. The Marx logo is on his right arm. He also wears goggles, red pants, a red cap with yellow stripes, gray gloves, and brown boots. The Police Squad Motorcycle with Sidecar comes in an illustrated red, white, and blue box that mentions the toy's sparkling siren. Excellent price includes original box. **120 350**

POLICE SQUAD MOTORCYCLE with SIDECAR (Mexican Version): 1950. 8" long x 5-3/4" high. Almost identical to the Police Squad Motorcycle with Sidecar, this toy was manufactured by Marx's Mexican branch, Plastimarx. In the Mexican version, "Policia" replaces "Police" and the Marx logos on the officer's right arm and sidecar are "Plastimarx", enclosed in triangles. **80 200**

POLICE MOTORCYCLE with SIDECAR: Circa 1950. 8" long x 5-3/4" high. This motorcycle was probably manufactured around the same time as the Police Squad Motorcycle with Sidecar because the lithography is very similar. However,

according to Dr. Malcolm Kates, this policeman has a blue cap and blue pants with yellow stripes. The small headlight is made of lithographed, stamped metal rather than the larger sparkling headlight of the other toy. The motorcycle comes with a sidecar in yellow, orange, red, and black. A keystone and "Police" are on the side of the car. The latter is repeated on the front with the Marx logo in small letters. A large "3" is located behind the sidecar seat. This motorcycle probably came in a version without the sidecar. Excellent price includes original box. **120 350**

MOTORCYCLE DELIVERY TOY: 1932-?. 9-1/2" long x 4-1/2" wide x 5-1/2" high. This toy consists of a driver and the front three-quarters of a motorcycle attached to a two-wheeled delivery cart. There are five versions of this toy and two known prototypes.

First Version: This toy was first advertised in the 1932 Sears Fall/Winter catalog, although it is possible that it was available before then. Sold with three other toys, the set cost $1.00. Some of the other toys shown in the Sears ad were not manufactured by Marx. In the 1934 Sears Fall/Winter catalog, the Motorcycle Delivery toy is described as having electric headlights and taillights which can be turned on and off. The toy and two 10-cent, 1" batteries sold for 59 cents.

This later version of the Motorcycle Speed Boy Delivery, manufactured in the late 1930s to 1940s, features a driver wearing a cap and goggles instead of a helmet. Dr. M. Kates Collection. R. Grubb photograph.

Good   Exc

One of the earliest models is orange with black and gray trim. "Speed Boy 4" is on its side and "Speed Boy Delivery" is on the rear with the Marx logo. The orange wheels have black tires. It comes with a perforated orange cart trimmed in black. Underneath the car is a battery box for the headlights and taillights. The driver wears a blue helmet, a blue jacket, black gloves, and brown pants which, like his helmet, have an orange stripe.   **125   300**

Second Version: Though similar to the first version, this toy's sides and ends are not perforated and the colors differ. The cart is red with black trim, and the wheels are green or yellow with black tires. The headlight is stamped metal and does not operate. In the 1935 Sears Fall/Winter catalog, Speed Boy Delivery toys with non-operating headlights are priced at 25 cents.

The driver wears a blue helmet, a blue jacket, black gloves, and brown pants which, like his hat, have an orange stripe. Although this outfit is the same as the first version, the clothing is much more vivid. The difference in colors may be due to a change in manufacturing or perhaps the colors in the first version have faded.   **125   300**

Third Version: This motorcycle is similar to the first two versions, but it has a perforated yellow cart, an orange motorcycle, and orange wheels with black tires.   **125   300**

Fourth Version: By 1936 this 11" version, called the Lightning Express Speed Boy Delivery, was made. It sold for $8.00 a dozen wholesale in the Blackwell Wielandy Company catalog. The size is slightly larger than the others, but a new die was not used for this toy. The addition of a rod in the rear is perhaps another reason this version is slightly larger.

Good   Exc

The catalog describes the toy as: "Rod in rear of toy is pressed down and when released, the truck proceeds to run a considerable distance at a fast rate of speed . . . Toy contains miniature cartons of nationally known products . . ."

The rod for the toy has a ball at the top. The press-and-run action is similar to the method used for the Marx Mystery Pluto, where the dog's tail is pushed down and the toy speeds along. The colors of the Lightning Express are not known.

125   300

Fifth Version: This version of the Speed Boy Delivery toy was probably manufactured in the late 1930s or 1940s. In later years, a plastic version of this toy was made.

The driver wears a striped red and gray cap, and goggles instead of a helmet. He is dressed in a red jacket, blue pants, gray gloves, and brown boots. Unlike the other versions, this motorcycle is yellow with orange, white, and black trim and has red and black wheels. "Speed Boy 4" is no longer on the motorcycle, but "Speed Boy Delivery" is on the sides of the cart. The sides and ends of the cart are not perforated, but they are lithographed in a yellow wood design with brown wood inserts. The license plate "2-68" is on the rear of the vehicle. The toy has a stamped metal headlight that does not operate, and the Marx logo appears on the cart sides. Unlike earlier versions with black fenders, this toy has no fenders.   **150   350**

First Prototype: Never put into production, this prototype has a similar driver and the same unperforated sides as the second version. However, the brand name "Purity Bakery" is

---

[2] Gerritt Beverwyk (no title), *Marx Toy Collector Newsletter*, Vol. 3, No. 3, p. 12. Marx could have used as many names as companies would allow for promotion.

Good   Exc

on the side of the bed. [2] (Marx also used brand names on the fourth version.) **NRS**

Second Prototype: This intriguing prototype with lever action is similar to the first prototype. The figure of the dog Pluto is used as the lever/rod, while an incompletely painted Mickey Mouse is the driver. Had this prototype been produced, it would have made a delightful toy.[3] **NRS**

SPEEDING CAR and MOTORCYCLE POLICEMAN: 1939 (patent), 1953. Priced at $2.79 in a 1953 Sears Christmas catalog, the Speeding Car and Motorcycle Policeman has a car with a motorcycle attached to the rear like an interesting toy

---

[3] Information from Philip Stillmacher (no title) in *Marx Toy Collector Newsletter*, Vol. 2, No. 3, p. 10.
[4] On May 30, 1939, the *Patent Gazette* published patent #2,159,974 by Louis Marx & Company.

Good   Exc

patent, dated 1939. [4] (The car in the patent drawing, however, has a different shape.) The Sears catalog describes the toy: "Pull motorcycle away from the car and car speeds away..... motorcycle follows with siren wailing. As the motorcycle policeman reaches the car, speeder comes to a halt. Both motorcycle and car made of durable plastic." The ad does not credit this car to Marx, but the toy appears on a page with many other Marx toys so there is a strong chance that it is a Marx toy. Since there is so much time between the date of the patent, 1939, and the date of the advertised toy, 1953, it is possible that an earlier version of the toy was made. Like a number of Marx toys, it may not have been advertised in the catalogs of the large mail order houses. The Japanese manufacturer Yonezawa made a similar toy, but it is not known if this toy was copied or if there is a connection between the toy and the Marx patent.

45   100

TRICKY MOTORCYCLE: See Mystic Motorcycle on page 134.

This vividly colored Motorcycle Delivery toy does not have a perforated cart, sides, or an operating headlight. Dr. M. Kates Collection. R. Grubb photograph.

⑥
TANKS

Made in various sizes, Marx tanks really perform! They climb, turn over, and shoot from sparkling guns. Marx used "sparkling" as a synonym for "sparking." The sparkling "gun-fire" adds plenty of drama to the play appeal of the toy. By rubbing a piece of grit bonded to the edge of a wooden disk against an abrasive metal flint, these clever guns create sparks.

Several techniques were used to produce a wide variety of tanks economically. "New" tanks were often created by taking parts originally designed for an existing tank and lithographing them in a different color or pattern. Other tanks were created by using a part from one tank as a different part on another tank. For instance, the hubcap of one tank, when lithographed differently, could become the turret of another. A tank body could be used for both a sparkling tank and a turnover tank once different mechanisms and attachments were added. Surviving prototypes are examples of variations or completely different designs that were considered for production but were never produced.

In January 1930 a two-page spread (see page 26 in Volume I) appeared in *Playthings* magazine in which Louis Marx & Company gave notice that they had received a license for their Climbing Toys with traction belts from the Wolverine Supply & Manufacturing Company (a large, Pittsburgh-based competitor founded in the early 1900s and lasting almost 60 years), under Huth patent #1,334,539. [1] The patent covered the toy versions of the tanks which were used by the British Army in France during World War I. Marx used this patent for many tanks and tractors. In fact, tractors were shown on the notice which was signed by David Marx, Louis Marx's brother. The second page of the spread contains an enthusiastic ad for the company's new Climbing Tank, which was not shown, and other mechanical toys, which were not identified. [2]

By the end of 1930 the Marx Company had come out with three types of tanks: the climbing tank, the doughboy tank, and the turnover tank. The turnover tank resembles the tank shown in the Huth patent. It also resembles a Wolverine tank made around the same time called the "Sunny Andy Tank."

A toy cardboard castle and bridge, made to be used with tanks and tractors, was sold in 1930. (See 9" Turnover Tank on page 148 for more information.)

In all, there are eleven sizes, ranging from 4" to 9", sometimes with only a 1/4" difference in length, when measured from end to end. *Tanks are arranged chronologically within each size grouping.*

Also note that when prototype information is available, it is after the toy it most nearly resembles. *All tanks are lithographed tin windups unless otherwise specified.*

4" TURNOVER TANK: 1942. This colorful little tank, lithographed in khaki, red, and yellow, was advertised in 1942. From the side, it is shaped like a flattened oval with a turret on top. It shoots sparks through a slot between two non-operating guns in the turret.

A large "5" is on the front, a pair of lithographed bogies (wheels) is on the sides, and the Marx logo is on the turret at the rear. The lithographed treads are embossed to give a three-dimensional, realistic look. Underneath the tank is a metal bar which helps to balance and turn the tank over while it performs. Excellent price includes original box. **50**   **150**

---

[1] Instead of the familiar "Co.", the ad reads "Company". This ad is also an example of one of the few times that the Marx Company had any kind of an arrangement with another company.
[2] *Playthings* magazine, January 1930, pages 116-117.

TOP SHELF: 5-1/4" Midget Climbing Fighting Tank was made circa 1930s to 1940s. The treads are missing from the example shown. BOTTOM SHELF: Two 4" tank variations made in the 1940s and 1950s. The khaki-colored tank sparks, while the blue and orange tank turns over. T. Riley Collection.

	Good	Exc

4" SPARKLING TANK: 1948.

First Version: Priced at 95 cents, this tank is described in the 1948 Montgomery Ward catalog as a "Clever toy tank that does a series of backward rolls as it charges forward when wound." This ad, as well as earlier ones, states that the tank comes in a camouflage design, but actually it is khaki-colored. The tank has the same lithography as the 1942 4" Tank. As shown in a 1953 Sears ad, it comes in at least one other color combination, "Lithographed in realistic design." It may have been available prior to 1953.

The Superman Turnover Tank (see page 75 in Volume I) has the same shape, but with different lithography: a Superman figure and "1940". However, this date may refer to the copyright date rather than to the date of manufacture. The flat Superman figure, under the tank, helps to balance and turn the tank over. Excellent price includes original box. **50 150**

Second Version: This lithographed khaki, white, red, yellow, and black tank has a sparkling mechanism, an on/off lever, and a windup motor with the key on its right side. The key has a round cross-section. This version does not turn over, although some of the khaki tanks did, according to ads. The flat tin front wheels have edges that are toothed like gears. Two indents on the front and the back of the hull are designed so that the tank can be attached to a flatcar in later versions of the Marx Army Train. Excellent price includes original box. **50 150**

Third Version: This version of the sparkling tank comes lithographed in blue, orange, yellow, red, and black. The tank's box is illustrated in red, yellow, and black, with a tank moving

	Good	Exc

forward, firing its guns in a battle scene. It has two small wooden wheels in back. Excellent price includes original box. **50 150**

4" TURNOVER TANK: 1948. This tank is the turnover model of the third version of the 4" Sparkling Tank. It has the same blue, orange, yellow, red, and black lithography. It does not have an on/off lever. It has a windup motor with the key on the left side; the key has a square cross-section. It is possible that the difference in the keys' locations between the sparkling tanks and turnover tanks has to do with the space available inside for their respective mechanisms. The turnover tank's predominantly blue turret is the same as that on the Superman Tank (see 4" Sparkling Tank, first version). Its front wheels are smooth wood in contrast to the sparkling tank's toothed front wheels of flat tin; its two small rear wheels are wooden.

The Marx Japanese subsidiary, Linemar, made several other turnover tanks with characters such as Popeye, Casper the Ghost, the Flintstones, and the Jetsons. Excellent price includes original box. **50 150**

4" PROTOTYPE TURNOVER TANK: Never put into production, this tank has an extra panel covering its side panel, both panels with the same lithography. The extra panel may have been used as a target so that when shot at, the panel moves against a metal tab on the inside that trips a lever to make the tank turn over. **NRS**

4-1/2" PROTOTYPE TANK: 4-1/2" long x 1-3/4" high x 1-1/2" wide. The trapezoidal tank is hand-painted in a green, red, and cream camouflage design and has a round turret. The tank

The 4-1/2" prototype hand-painted tank with open hatch cover. J. Ritter Collection. R. Grubb photograph.

	Good	Exc

has three wooden wheels, two in the front and one in the back, all of which have treads painted on the tank's hull. There are no markings on the tank. A metal panel which appears to be the hatch cover sticks up behind the one-gun turret.

John Ritter notes that this tank has a clicker to make a clicking sound. **NRS**

5-1/4" MIDGET CLIMBING FIGHTING TANK: Circa 1930s to 1950s. Despite the small number of ads for the Midget Climbing Fighting Tank, it is possible that they were being produced in many versions throughout the 1930s, 1940s, and later. All of the camouflage design production tanks have lithographed headlights, a driver with goggles, and rubber treads. The earlier tanks come with metal wheels and narrow treads. Postwar tanks have wide treads.

First Version: 1931. This camouflage tank has a gun mounted on its turret. The toy curiously disappeared from catalog pages until 1940, when it appeared lithographed differently in khaki with a red turret. However, it retains its gun and black metal wheels. The front of the hull reads "4 T. C.", while one side reads "U. S. Tank Co. No. 4." and the other side reads "U. S. Army". An ad in the 1940 N. Shure Co. catalog describes the tank as "Equipped with sure-grip endless rubber belts, strong spiral spring motor, with key attached. Has brake for starting and stopping [right side]. Will climb steep grades and run over obstacles." The wholesale cost per dozen was $1.96. Excellent price includes original box. **65 170**

	Good	Exc

Second Version: 1947. This has the same camouflage tank and wheels as the 1931 version. Excellent price includes original box. **65 170**

Third Version: 1951. The Montgomery Ward catalog ads, which priced the toy at 75 cents, describe its "New wide sure-grip treads and wide plastic wheels. With gun turret on top." Excellent price includes original box. **70 200**

Fourth Version: Lithographed in silver, the tank has red metal wheels and a red gun turret. Markings on the tank include the Marx logo and "Licensed / Under / Patent / No. 1,334,539 / Made in U. S. A. / Louis Marx & Co. / New York, N. Y." The key is on the left end and the on/off switch is in the rear. This version may also have come without a gun. The patent number is from the Huth patent referred to in the beginning of the chapter. Excellent price includes original box. **70 200**

In addition, John Ritter notes that around 1933 the British firm Triang made the "Whippet Climbing Tank," which resembles the Marx Midget Climbing Fighting Tank. The shape of the hull and the size of the Triang tank are similar to those of the Marx tank, except that the former does not have the raised circular area on the top rear of the hull. The shape and location of the key and the on/off lever are the same on both tanks. The Triang tank also has a small loop bent out of the rear of the hull to accommodate a towing hook, like the Marx climbing tanks.

5-1/4" Midget Climbing Fighting Tank Versions
Compiled by John Ritter

BODY	TURRET/GUN	WHEELS
Camouflage with matte finish	Black with black gun	Metal with narrow treads, green and white camouflage
	Camouflage with black gun	Metal with narrow treads, black
Khaki with yellow details	Red with black gun	Metal with narrow treads, black
	Black with black gun	
Silver with black details	Black with black gun	Metal with narrow treads, black
	Red with black gun	Metal with narrow treads, red
Red with black details	Black with black gun	Metal with narrow treads, red
Camouflage with matte finish	Black with black gun	Plastic with wide treads, red
	Unpainted	Plastic with wide treads, maroon
	Brown with black gun	Plastic with wide treads, red

Good   Exc

The Triang model has a silver body, a red turret, and red wheels, as does the sixth version of the Marx Midget Climbing Fighting Tank. However, the turret and the wheels differ: The Triang turret swivels and is more conical than that on the Marx tank; the two halves of the Triang wheels are joined where four holes are punched through the hub and then crimped together. Marx wheels normally are fastened in three places. There does not appear to be any welding involved.

First Prototype: 1951. This tank has a camouflage hull and red plastic wheels. A lithographed, spring-loaded armored gun takes the place of the turret. The gun is made from the upper part of the anti-aircraft gun on the military train. Although a shortened version, the gun is still long, and thus is mounted towards the rear of the tank instead of the front, where the turret would be located. The date on this prototype is "6/18/51." The tank also reads "X-2400 Erie." **NRS**

Second Prototype: This tank is painted in Army colors, rather than lithographed in camouflage colors. On the side of the tank is a white star and a "2". The top front of the tank is yellow. The long gun barrel is a full-length version of the anti-aircraft gun on the military train. The underside of the prototype reads "X2400A Erie 9/24/51." With the gun, the tank is 6-3/4" long. **NRS**

From left to right: *The 1951 6-3/4" Prototype Tank and two versions of the 5-1/4" Midget Climbing Fighting Tanks made in the 1940s. P. Rolin Collection.*

Two versions of the 5-1/2" Midget Tank, pictured with the smaller 4" Tank. The larger sparkling tanks were manufactured around 1937. B. Allan Collection.

	Good	Exc

5-1/2" MIDGET TANK (Also known as the Midget Climbing Fighting Tank): 1937. When viewed from the side, the shape of this sparkling tank resembles an elongated diamond. The sides are most frequently red, yellow, and black. The middle panel has a predominantly red, yellow, and green camouflage pattern, similar to that used for the Marx Kneeling Soldier with Gun. The tank was also used on the Marx Military Train and in the Marx Army Train Set in khaki. Lithographed treads and bogies (wheels), cogs, and small Marx logos appear on the sides of the tank. The dome-shaped turret, most often seen in silver or khaki, is lithographed with the heads of two soldiers in viewports, like the 9-1/2" No. E 12 Tank, and may come with a towing hook behind the turret. The twin sparkling guns are red or olive, either a solid color or with black- and white-lithographed details of cooling fins and a round ammunition carrier, similar to those used on the Marx airplanes. The tank has a brake lever on the left side. This tank also has been seen either with all-red or all-yellow center sections and no towing hook or with the same olive drab paint used on the Army Train.[3]

The earliest ads for this toy appeared in 1937, and it was still being sold in 1941. The box is illustrated in colors that match the toy. The name on this box is the "Midget Climbing Fighting Tank". The tank has also been seen in a plain box marked "Midget Tank" in red and black. Excellent price includes original box.   **75   200**

Prototype: This red, yellow, and black tank has a 1-1/2" long x 3/4" wide "cannon," instead of a gun. On either side "Flamethrower" is hand-lettered, and "Erie b - 5 - 40" is printed on the back.   **NRS**

5-1/2" JAPANESE MINIATURE DOUGHBOY TANK: See 10" Doughboy Tank on page 150.

6-3/4" PROTOTYPE TANK: This tin tank reads "Tank Corps." on its left side, "Army" on its right side, and "20" on its front. The tank has rubber treads and one gun mount on top. Unusual markings on the base read "Die cost $2,400. Prod. cost $33.50. Erie, Pa. #1487 10-25-3? (partially obscured) 7".

The front of the prototype has a more pronounced flat area above the wheels than does the 5-1/2" Midget Tank. The wheels appear to be the same size as those used on the larger climbing tanks. The turret uses the same wedge-shaped stamping as the side gun housings on the 9-1/2" Doughboy Tank.   **NRS**

7" PROTOTYPE SPARKLING TANK: 7" long x 2-3/4" high. It is not certain if this sparkling tank, which was never produced, was made by Marx. The front end of the tank is higher than the back end. Made of tin, the tank is spray-painted in mustard and brown. The toy resembles the smaller flattened 10" Doughboy Tank in profile, except that the turret is at the rear of the tank instead of at the front. A two-gun turret is at the rear of the tank.

The wheels of the tank are made of metal and the bottom is hand-cut tin. Lines are inscribed on one side of the tank and were probably used to determine the sizes and proportions of the tank during manufacture.

6-3/4" Prototype Tank says "Tank Corp." on the left side and "Army" on the right. Notes on the base state that the die cost $2,400 and the production cost was $33.50. P. Rolin Collection.

---

[3] The 4" and 5-1/2" tanks use exactly the same windup sparkling mechanism. This is possible because both are the same width. Further, parts inventory savings are realized by using the same die-cast pinion gear in five places, four with the same sheet tin-gear attached. The sheet tin-gear is also used five times, but the one which is different is attached to the spring drum rather than a pinion gear.

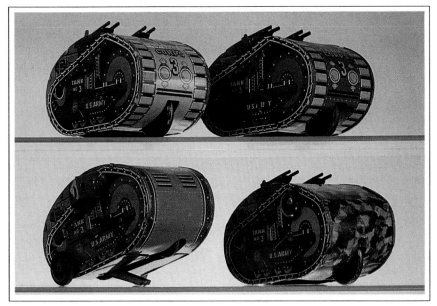

Four versions of the No. 3 Army Tank are about 8" long and were manufactured between 1938 and 1942. The tank on the lower left turns over. The side guns are missing from this tank. T. Riley Collection.

	Good	Exc

The turret gun and the rectangular structure between the turret and the hull are the same shape as those in a 1931 German toy, a small armored car. Like the prototype tank, this armored car has a fork-shaped gun on top of a sparker wheel.

NRS

8" NO. 3 ARMY TANK: 1938. This series of tanks was produced in at least six major versions. Trip Riley states that all of the tanks are marked "Tank / No. 3 / U. S. Army," and have oval-shaped bodies. The tanks are about 8" long x 3-5/8" wide. Powered with a windup motor, some of the tanks go forward and spark, while others roll over. All of the tanks have the same lithography on their sides, consisting of bogies (wheels), cogs, and springs and treads in red, tan, black, and white. "U.S. Army" and "Tank No. 3" appear in yellow.

First Version (Sparkling): This tank has a tan or khaki hull and two red machine guns on its top, similar to those used on many Marx airplanes. These are also the only guns on the tank that spark. It also comes with khaki gun turrets on the top and small circular red turrets with black guns on the sides. These turrets are similar to those on the 5-1/4" Midget Climbing Tank. On the hull are lithographed headlights, yellow treads, and "Tank Corps. 3". The wheels with yellow treads are arranged so that there is one large metal wheel at the tank front and two small wooden wheels near the middle of the tank. Excellent price includes original box. **60 175**

Second Version (Sparkling): This yellow-hulled tank is lithographed with headlights, "Tank Corps. 3", below which are a lithographed gun and turret. The two red-enameled machine guns are detailed in black and white. Yellow treads are on the hull. A large front wheel is made of metal and two small rear wheels near the middle of the tank are made of wood.

By 1942 a sparkling version that did not turn over, priced at 69 cents and advertised in the 1942 Montgomery Ward catalog next to the No. E 12 Tank and one of the Doughboy Tanks, is described as being smaller and lighter. As shown in the ad, it has two sets of twin machine guns, like those found

	Good	Exc

on the Marx airplanes, but, unlike some guns on earlier tank versions, they are not in a housing by themselves. Excellent price includes original box. **75 200**

Third Version (Sparkling): The tank's hull uses the same camouflage design as a version of the 5-1/2" Midget Tank. The tank has two olive machine guns with black and white details on top. Excellent price includes original box. **70 195**

Fourth Version (Sparkling): This tank has a camouflage hull, two khaki guns on top in wedge-shaped khaki gun housings, with the same shape as those on the 9-1/2" Doughboy Tank and the silver 9" Turnover Tank, according to John Ritter. He also points out that the small black round gun turrets have also been seen in red or khaki. The guns are decorative and do not spark. The turrets are also the same as those on the top of the 5-1/4" Midget Climbing Fighting Tanks. The tank has one large metal wheel in the front and two small wooden wheels near the middle. Excellent price includes original box. **75 200**

Fourth Version (Turnover): A 1938 Sears Christmas catalog ad which describes the tank as "new" priced the toy at 49 cents. Two large wooden wheels are near the rear of the tank. When the bar in the base drops down, the tank turns over.

In 1938 a turnover tank with a camouflaged hull was also illustrated in catalogs. However, by the early 1940s it was illustrated without its camouflaged hull. Excellent price includes original box. **70 190**

Fifth Version (Turnover): With a tan hull lithographed with headlights, "Tank Corps. 3", and a turret, this tank has wedge-shaped khaki gun housings on each side that hold black non-sparking guns. "Turnover Tank" is on the top. It also has two large, wooden wheels near the rear and a bar in the base to turn the tank over. Excellent price includes original box. **75 200**

Good   Exc

Sixth Version (Turnover): This tank has a khaki hull printed with "Turnover Tank No. 3", louvers, a round lithographed hatch pattern in red on top, and a wedge-shaped khaki gun housing on each side. It is the only version with a different lithographed hull. Excellent price includes original box.

75   200

6" Prototype: With the same oval shape as the larger 8" Tank, this hand-painted tank in red, white, brown, and dark blue has "U. S. 5" in white on the brown and red hull, instead of "Tank No. 3". White simulated rivets are on the red part of the hull and continue over most of the tank. There are white treads on the hull and twin khaki guns on each side of the tank.   **NRS**

8-1/2" PROTOTYPE CLIMBING TANK: This hand-painted prototype has a rectangular shape, large brown wooden wheels, open portholes, and a start/stop lever. It is possible that the tank was intended to be amphibious. The brown and green camouflage design is similar to that on some of the versions of the 5-1/4" Midget Climbing Fighting Tank. "E 15" is on the side with a lithographed axe and "Erie 7-264 7/30/41" is on the tank's base.   **NRS**

9" TURNOVER TANK: 1930. This early tank, advertised as "new" in 1930, is described in the Sears Fall/Winter catalog: "Tank climbs on its top or bottom. No other tank does this. Tackles obstacles — if too high, turns over on back and goes right back again. . . . If it falls sideways, will lumber along until it strikes other objects, again getting into its upright position." The tank sold for $1.79 in the Sears catalog, which was a high price at that time. Excellent price includes original box.   **100   250**

9" TURNOVER TANK: 1931. This improved model of the turnover tank has the following features: A powerful motor which could not be overwound, a hook for pulling loads many times its weight, a governor on the motor to control speed, the ability to work a long time on one winding, and sturdy metal construction. The price was reduced to $1.59 in the 1931 Sears Fall/Winter catalog.

The diamond-shaped tank has one top gun, two side guns, and a bottom gun. Somewhat wedge-shaped, the side turrets are the same as those on the 9-1/2" Doughboy Tank and a version of the 8" Tank. When the tank turns over, the bottom of the tank becomes the top of the tank.

Made in gold or silver finishes with lithographed or embossed markings, the tank has narrow white treads or wide black treads. The patent used for this tank is #1,830,799, filed January 23, 1930. Although the side of the tank in the patent drawing appears to be different than the actual tank, the shape and the description are clearly that of the 9" Turnover Tank.

The Marx Company also produced a corrugated cardboard Toy Castle and Bridge for play with tanks and tractors. Available from Sears for 49 cents, this toy is 40" long x 10" high x 10-1/4" wide. The box for the toy (which appears to be red in the faded example that has been seen) reads "Toy Castle and Bridge". The turnover tank is shown on the box; oddly enough, it is the only type of tank illustrated, although several types of tractors are shown. It is possible that no other tanks had been

Good   Exc

made by the company when the Toy Castle and Bridge was made. The back of the box shows an assembly diagram. As described by John Ritter, the toy comes in four pieces: the center "box," two ramps, and an undecorated top panel. The lithography on both sides of the toy consists of a red and tan stone pattern, trees, and several barred windows. The opening doors on each side of the castle are below a window imprinted with the Marx logo. Excellent price includes original box.

100   250

9-1/2" CLIMBING TANK: 1930. The December 1930 Butler Brothers catalog ad for this toy describes it as "Heavy gauge metal, gray with black trim, wide tread, non-slipping rubber traction tires, top turret and three mounted cannons, powerful motor." The tank sold for $12.50 a dozen wholesale in the catalog. The tank side mounts are similar to those on the 8" Tank. Excellent price includes original box.   **100   250**

By 1937 the tank was being advertised with some changes. For instance, the gun on the turret was replaced by a decal showing two doughboys. This tank, with a nickel finish and a brake, sold for 98 cents in the 1937 Sears Fall/Winter catalog. At the same time some ads describe the tank as silver-colored and sparkling. This version may have had sparkling side guns and an unarmed top turret. Excellent price includes original box.   **100   250**

9-1/2" ARMY TANK #12: Early 1940s. This sparkling, climbing tank climbs obstacles, turns, or goes straight ahead. It has rubber treads, black or khaki wheels, and is predominantly khaki, black, and yellow. Yellow lettering reads "Tank Corp. 12" on the hull and "Army 12" on the side. Lithographed soldiers look out from the view port in the round, flat-topped turret. The turret is the same shape as the hubcaps found on some larger climbing tanks as well as the turret on the sparkling 5-1/2" Midget Tank. There is a brake and a hook at the rear of the tank. The trapezoidal shape and the size of this tank resemble the earlier 9-1/2" Climbing Tank. The tank bears Huth patent #1,334,539.

A Sparkling Tank No. 12 which shot wooden shells also came as part of an Anti-Aircraft Tank Set. The patent number for this tank is 2,279,386. It was submitted by Richard Carver, a Marx employee, in September 1941 (see page 7 in Volume I). The patent shows the internal works of the tank and closely resembles the toy. Excellent price includes original box.   **80   250**

ARMY NO. 12 PROTOTYPE TANK:
First Version: This tank is similar to the production Army No. 12 tank. However, the prototype has red wheels with tan hubcaps, while the production toys have either black or khaki wheels with or without hubcaps. The prototype has skids mounted to the bottom of the hull which make the tank zigzag. The skids alternately rotate down to take pressure off of the tread on each side. The tank also has a towing hook.

The prototype's most interesting feature is that a helium balloon may have been attached to the hatch cover since the tank has a winding spool for a balloon cord. (Marx may have seen the balloon used on another toy, a clockwork truck, made by the English firm Triang as part of their Minic line. The truck

The Marx 10" Doughboy Tank with the Japanese Miniature Doughboy Tank. The Marx tank was manufactured around 1937 and is 10" long, while the Japanese Miniature tank is 5-1/2" long. The lithography design of the two tanks is identical. Dr. M. Kates Collection. R. Grubb photograph.

	Good	Exc

came with a gas cylinder trailer and a construction kit for a balloon. In fact, some of the early 1930s Triang Minic tanks resemble the Marx Climbing Tanks.) **NRS**

Second Version: This prototype retains the shape of the first version, but it is hand-painted red with apple green, and has foam-rubber wheels. **NRS**

9-1/2" NO. E 12 TANK: 1942.
First Version: The tank sold for $1.89 in 1942. From then on through 1949, it was widely advertised as making a rat-a-tat-tat noise or a rumbling sound, depending on the ad.

The tank has a World War II trapezoidal shape similar to that of the 1930 9-1/2" Climbing Tank, the 9-1/2" Army Tank No. 12, and the 5-1/4" Midget Climbing Fighting Tank. The tank comes in a camouflage design, including the turret and the wheels. "E 12" appears on the front of the hull in small white letters and on the sides in larger letters. A lithographed axe appears on the left side, and a lithographed shovel appears on the right side. The hull has a lithographed driver, gun, and headlights. As noted by Trip Riley, the No. E 12 Tank has

	Good	Exc

rubber treads, dual sparklers in housings beneath the side guns, a turret gun that can be turned, and a heavy clockwork motor. The sparkling side guns are housed in brown- or camouflage-colored mounts, and are the first mounts to have a basically triangular shape when viewed from the side. (On the previous tanks, the mounts were triangular when viewed from the top or bottom.) The tanks can also climb up substantial inclines. Excellent price includes original box. **60 190**

Second Version: This tank has a front-mounted gun that pulls back and snaps forward as the tank moves and the same lithography as the more common first version. Excellent price includes original box. **60 190**

Third Version: This newer version is green with yellow, red, and white details. It has a stripe and a star on its top turret, exhaust manifolds on the rear of the sides, and two red wheels on each side. On the left side is an axe; on the right, a shovel. The side turrets or gun mounts also have multicolored lithography. Excellent price includes original box. **75 250**

Two 9-1/2" tanks manufactured in the early 1940s with similar shapes and different lithography. The tank on the left reads "E 12", and the tank on the right reads "Army 12". P. Rolin Collection.

	Good	Exc

9-1/2" PROTOTYPE TANK: This hand-painted tank reads "E 173 TC". It has an apple green hull with red, white, and black details, similar in color to the 1937 10" Doughboy Tank. The trapezoidal shape of the hull resembles the 9-1/2" Army Tank #12. The side panels, wheels, and turret are a tan color. The turret has a decal with two figures, and its shape and paint scheme copy the pattern of the turret on a German toy armored car made around 1931. The tank has regular construction grooved metal wheels for treads and red side housings which conceal sparklers. The rear end of the hull bears the Louis Marx name and address. **NRS**

9-1/2" DOUGHBOY TANK: Circa 1930-32.

First Version: Advertised as selling for 95 cents, this tank is one of the earliest of the Marx tanks. It features a doughboy with a gun who pops in and out of the hatch as the tank zigzags along. It is equipped with a start/stop lever. The top two-gun turret turns, and guns on the sides have wedge-shaped mounts similar to those on the turnover 8" Tank. The tank moves in an interesting way since the small rear wheel makes the tank turn as it moves along.

The Doughboy Tank is striking. It has a blue hull, orange sides, and an orange turret with black guns. Its shape, when viewed from the side, resembles an elongated diamond with rounded points. The doughboy wears a red jacket with three chevrons on one sleeve and a brown World War I-style helmet. A 1931 ad describes the tank as an exact reproduction of the tanks used by the doughboys in the World War. The price dropped to 89 cents in the 1931 Montgomery Ward catalog. The Doughboy Tank sold so well that by 1931 Butler Brothers, a wholesale house, said in its sales pitch in "Our Drummer" that the Doughboy Tank had a "Great sales record in 1930 — almost impossible to supply the demand."

Although slightly smaller, a toy manufactured in Germany is remarkably similar to the Doughboy Tank. Experts differ, however, on the date of the German toy. Excellent price includes original box. **100 250**

Second Version: By 1932 Marx had a new idea for the Doughboy Tank by adding a flag behind the turret. When the doughboy pops out, the flag disappears. This tank has a blue-green hull, a red turret, and red sides with yellow detailing. (It is not known if the first version also comes with a flag.) The second version may also have a silver hull, sides, and turret. Excellent price includes original box. **100 250**

9-1/2" PROTOTYPE DOUGHBOY TANK: This unique prototype is similar to the production Doughboy Tanks, but differs in the striking painted design on its sides. This design consists of three soldiers looking out of individual gun ports. The two soldiers at each end hold guns, but the soldier in the middle does not. The tank sides are khaki-colored and are divided into square panels. These panels are bordered by black dots that simulate rivets and red seams. The hull is gray, painted on bare metal. Unlike the Doughboy Tank's round turrets, this prototype has a large, basically triangular turret with a sparkling gun. **NRS**

10" DOUGHBOY TANK: 1937. This sparkling tank has an oval rather than diamond shape like its predecessor, the 9-1/2" Doughboy Tank. The sides of the tank are yellow-tan with black and white details. The tank has an apple green hull with red, black, and white markings. Small white circles with black rims cover most of the tank and are meant to resemble rivets. There is a red hatch cover, a lithographed hatch superstructure, a round turret with one black sparkling gun, and a start/stop lever on the right side. Like the soldiers used on earlier tanks, this soldier wears a red jacket with three chevrons on his sleeve and a brown World War I-style helmet.

The side panels of the Doughboy Tank have the same general pattern as those on a small German climbing tank. On the key side of the German tank, a black-lithographed shape mirrors the cut-out for the key shaft. The Marx Doughboy Tank has black details on the side panel that include a lithographed enlargement of this feature, but with no cut-outs and a different location for the key. Therefore, the details on the sides of the Marx tank are probably copied from the smaller German toy.

As with the earlier tanks, a foreign miniature tank, called the Japanese Miniature Doughboy Tank, was made that closely resembles the 1937 10" Doughboy Tank. This tank was found in one of the Marx plants, but Dr. Malcolm Kates has said that it is not known whether Marx copied this toy from an original Japanese design or if it was made for Marx by a separate Japanese organization. Markings on the tank read "Made in Japan" and show the encircled letter "T" in the upper half of a

The beautiful Rex Marx Planet Patrol Tank is 10" long and was manufactured in the early 1950s. The tank has a pop-out figure and the turret gun sparks. P. Rolin Collection.

triangle. The lithography on the tank is identical to that on the Marx tank. However, the Japanese tank does not have a start/stop switch. But, as its name implies, the biggest difference between the Miniature Doughboy Tank and the Marx tank is size, with the Japanese tank measuring only 5-1/2" long x 2-1/2" high, while the Marx tank is 10" long x 5-1/4" high. Another difference is the color of the hulls; the miniature tank is a lighter green than the Marx tank. Despite these differ-

This 10" Doughboy Tank, manufactured in 1951, sparks, reverses, and makes a rat-a-tat-tat noise. T. Riley Collection. C. Myer photograph.

	Good	Exc

ences, the similarities between the two tanks are striking. Excellent price includes original box. **100 250**

Prototype: This prototype tank has a similar apple green hull with red, black, and white markings, but with a trapezoidal shape more like the 9-1/2" Army Tank #12. **NRS**

10" DOUGHBOY TANK: 1942. This oval tank, advertised for $1.27 in the 1942 Montgomery Ward Christmas catalog, is described as follows: "This tank reverses when you least expect it. Turret flies open, soldier pops out, aims, ducks back. Guns shoot harmless sparks to loud rat-a-tat-tat." It is predominantly tan with lithographed blue sprockets, bogies (wheels), and black and white treads. White-lithographed rivets cover the body of the tank. The top of the hull is camouflaged with yellow and purple random shapes. The front of the hull is lithographed with lifting pins and vents. Excellent price includes original box. **100 250**

10" DOUGHBOY TANK: 1951. Originally priced at $2.37, this tank is commonly marked with a "5", "A", and a large white star on the turret. It has a dark olive matte finish with yellow and red fenders and a lithographed olive hatch cover. The olive hull has a lithographed central viewing port, gray tracks, a lifting pin, and machine guns. The tank has a single pivoting front wheel, two wooden or pressed-steel back wheels, and a lever protruding from alongside one wheel. Unusually realistic lithographed details on the tank body show wheels and springs or bogies (wheels). The underside of the tank is lithographed with the Marx logo and underneath the gun on the turret is a sparkler. The doughboy has also changed from earlier ver-

Good   Exc

sions: His face is lithographed in a different style; he wears a new, tan, small-brimmed, World War II-style helmet; and, as the two chevrons on his sleeve indicate, he has unfortunately been demoted to corporal. Excellent price includes original box. **100   250**

SPARKLING SPACE TANK: Early 1950s. This handsome doughboy tank is light blue with dark blue, red, and bronze accents. It has a matte finish. "Rex Mars Planet Patrol" appears on top of the tank and "X-1" and a lightning bolt appear on the sides. Lithographed rockets, ray guns, exhaust pipes, and bogies (wheels) also appear on the sides. The hull shows two lithographed drivers, while the rear shows lithographed exhaust pipes. The lithographed turret has a sparkling gun, and the tank makes a noise as it moves.

The pop-out doughboy looks more like an astronaut than a soldier and has a different face than those of all previous tank soldiers. The blue and red box shows the tank and driver with an astronaut-like figure standing nearby. A June 1977 PB 84 auction catalog lists number 4003 for this toy. Excellent price includes original box. **200   450**

Prototype: 1950s. 10" long. Similar to the production tank, this tank is a Marx experiment in making a battery-operated model: An unpainted metal hatch cover on the front of the tank can be moved aside so that batteries can be placed underneath. The side of the toy has a switch for the battery-operated electric motor. Like the production tank, the toy has a spring-wound motor, but the spring has been disconnected. Instead of word-

Good   Exc

ing on the base is a piece of blue tape, which may have had a code or writing attached at one time. **NRS**

REX MARS PLANET PATROL TANK (Plastimarx Version): 1950s. 10" long. This Mexican-made tank is similar to its American version, the Sparkling Space Tank, but it has Spanish wording and a glossy finish. The figures have pinker complexions and larger, V-shaped collars. The silver hatch cover compliments the blue metal toy. The blue is brighter than that on the American-made version. **150   300**

ANTI-AIRCRAFT TANK OUTFIT: This set includes a tank which is similar to the 9-1/2" Army Tank #12. However, it sparks and shoots wooden shells from its turret cannon. The tank also has a hook on its back for pulling other toys. The tank was probably sold separately as well as part of the set. The other items in the group include an anti-aircraft gun which shoots wooden shells, four flat metal soldiers, a searchlight trailer, extra ammunition, and a folding lithographed cardboard trench. In the 1941 Sears Christmas catalog, the toys sold for $1.98. For 39 cents more, 15 additional soldiers could be purchased, and for only 5 cents, 15 extra shells could be purchased. Excellent price includes original box. **80   250**

Another tank set contains three tanks made of a heavy cardboard. A spring mechanism inside the tanks makes them "explode"; that is, the spring makes the tanks jump into the air and separate around a center hinge. The Marx Company also made metal boats that explode. Excellent price includes original box. **85   275**

TRACTORS

Marx tractors were sold with a variety of implements as well as in elaborate sets. These sets frequently came in lithographed cardboard boxes that could be made into "barns" or "sheds." The fun for the collector is in tracing the history of Marx tractors to see what features the company would think of next.

One reason for the many designs was that two of Marx's biggest accounts, Sears Roebuck and Montgomery Ward, had many customers in the farming area of the Midwest.

From 1930 on, most Marx tractors would have rubber treads. And all through the years, while bringing out new tractors, Marx repeated designs from earlier years.

Tractors are tin lithographed windups with rubber treads, unless otherwise specified. They are listed in chronological order.

1926 TRACTOR

AMERICAN TRACTOR: 1926. 8" long x 4-1/2" wide x 5-1/2" high.

First Version: This tractor, the earliest one identified as Marx, is illustrated in a 1926 Montgomery Ward catalog. Along with a wagon, rake, and harrow, it is listed for 98 cents. (A very similar tractor, with the same attachments, appeared in 1925, but the motor details are different.) The side design of the tractor, as illustrated in the Montgomery Ward catalog, varies slightly from the actual toy.

This colorful treadless tractor is green with red and yellow stripes. "American Tractor" appears on the radiator although this name is not shown in various advertisements. The two large back wheels and two small front wheels are embossed with red-lithographed spokes. Several ads show the red, yellow, and green wheels with open spokes, but these spokes have not been seen in the actual toy. Around the hubcaps are simulated rivets. The dotted rivet design, reminiscent of the wheels found on circus wagons, continues around the edges of the spokes. The front wheels can be set to travel in a circle or straight. As in many Marx ads that refer to a strong Marx spring, this toy has a large, sturdy spring.

"Motor" is lithographed on the side, "Louis Marx & Co., New York, U. S. A." is in red on the back, along with the Marx logo and "Pat's Pend'g Trade Mark".

The driver, dressed in a red shirt and pinkish-tan overalls, wears a hat with a striped brim. He is similar to the driver in the Marx Balky Mule toy. (See Volume I.)

The driver, seated behind a steering wheel post, is attached by thin metal pieces in small flaps on either side to a red and yellow seat with red stripes on the side.

Its various trailers are detachable. The 6-1/4" wagon is the largest trailer, with a green-, red-, and yellow-striped design on the outside and a blue interior. The wheels have the same pattern as those in some of the Marx Eccentric Cars, such as the Funny Flivver. The wheel pattern is repeated in the harrow and rake. The 4-1/2" long seven-disc harrow (also known simply as a disc) is green with red and yellow stripes. The yellow two-wheeled rake has red accents.   **125   275**

Second Version: This green tractor with yellow stripes lacks the dotted rivet design around the hubcaps that the first version has. The driver wears blue overalls, a yellow shirt, and a yellow hat.

Unlike the first version, the driver has a separate location for the steering wheel post, two metal prongs, sits on an

The multicolored American Tractor set, manufactured in 1926, includes the wagon, rake, and harrow shown. W. Maeder Collection. R. Grubb photograph.

all-yellow seat with red side stripes, and is detachable from a small, square-shaped hole.

In addition to the wagon and disc harrow, Eric Matzke has seen other implements for the second version set, including an all-red hay rake. These extra implements may have come with the first version, although they have not been seen in any ads. The attachments, all with red and yellow wheels, include:

Planter: 4" long x 3" wide. The planter has a wire guide marker, seed reservoirs, and a red frame.

Mower: 8-1/4" wide. The mower has lithographed balloon tires, a lithographed red and white frame, and a long movable sickle bar.

Dump Trailer: 6" long. The dump trailer also has lithographed balloon tires and an enameled blue body.

Gang Plow: 6-1/4" x 3/8". The gang plow has lithographed balloon tires, a red-enameled frame, and dummy elevator levers.

Scraper Blade: 3-1/2" long. The scraper blade is nickel-plated and attaches to the front of the tractor.

	Good	Exc

Shovel: 3-3/8" long, plated steel.

Pitchfork: 4-1/2" long, plated steel.

	Good	Exc
Set:	100	225

1929 TRACTOR

CLIMBING TRACTOR with CHAIN PULL: 1929. In 1929 this tractor, entirely different from the American Tractor and advertised in the 1929 Montgomery Ward catalog as being able to climb over obstacles, is listed for $1.49 and is described as "constructed on the same mechanical principles as the steel tanks used during the war. Tractor will climb almost anything that is not at complete right angles with the floor . . . all metal parts are aluminum except driver at the wheel. Stop and start lever . . . about 7-1/2" long, 3-3/4" wide and 6" high over driver's head. Chains that run over wheels are of heavy black rubber with suction cups that hold tractor to its course in steep ascents." The driver wears a wide-brimmed hat.

1930s Marx Climbing Tractor measures 8-1/2" long. Similar tractors also came in aluminum. The driver is missing from the example shown. C. Holley Collection.

Good   Exc

Differences between the Montgomery Ward ad and other ads of the time suggest the possibility of further variations. For instance, some ads show the same tractor with a different radiator, no key, and ridges on the hood.   **100   175**

1930 TRACTORS

By 1930 Marx decided to expand its tractor toy line. In January 1930 the company took a two-page ad in *Playthings* magazine which stated,

> "We hereby announce to the trade that we have received a license from the Wolverine Supply & Manufacturing Company [Pittsburgh, Pennsylvania] under its Huth patent #1,334,539 for which we are paying substantial royalties.

> "We are manufacturing and selling all of our Climbing Toys having traction belts under this license. Our customers of these toys are therefore protected under this patent.

> "We also announce that we have additional patents pending in the U. S. Patent Office on other features of these Climbing Traction Toys."

The announcement was signed by David Marx, the brother of Louis Marx. Illustrated on the bottom of the announcement were tractors climbing over books. The other page of the announcement concerned the new Marx Climbing Tank. [1]

75   150

CLIMBING TRACTOR: 1930. 8-1/4" long x 3-1/2" wide x 5-1/2" high. This tractor, similar to the one illustrated in the

1930 *Playthings* announcement with three exhausts on the side, was shown in catalogs. It comes in three different versions: first, as an aluminum tractor with a detachable plow and steel chain for $1.65; second, in a colored metal version (which some later ads stated was green) for 98 cents; and third, in a colored steel version for 83 cents.

One of the colored metal versions is red with blue wheels and has a mesh-like grille. A farmer with a large-brimmed hat drives the tractor. The Huth patent, described above, is on the toy.

This tractor comes in an illustrated orange box showing a front view of the tractor and another view of the tractor going up a steep incline. Fancy large white lettering on the box reads, "Marx Tractor" and smaller lettering to the side says "Pulls, Climbs, Pushes". (Similar lettering was used for the Eccentric Coo Coo Car toy and box. See the Eccentric Cars chapter.)

Advertised along with the colored metal tractor, although it could be purchased separately, is a red- and blue-lithographed corrugated cardboard castle or fort. (It has also been seen in a red and green version.) The tractor was intended to storm the castle walls. The box front for this toy has "Toy

---

[1] *Playthings* magazine, January 1930, pps. 116-117. Louis H. Hertz, the well-known author and authority writes in *The Complete Book of Building and Collecting Model Automobiles* (Crown Publishers, Inc., New York, 1970, p. 211) that both Tootsietoy and Kilgore Manufacturing Company had licensing agreements with Marx under the Huth patent #1,334,539.

Good   Exc

Castle and Bridge" on a red background; the box back has an assembly diagram. Illustrated in the catalog are several tractors, including the industrial tractor set, and the turnover tank.

The toy castle comes in four pieces: the center "box," two ramps, and an undecorated top panel. The lithography on both sides of the castle consists of a red and tan stone pattern, trees, and several barred windows. The Marx logo appears on the window above the double doors. The doors on each side may be opened.

The tractor sold for 49 cents in the 1930 Montgomery Ward catalog and measured 40" long x 10-1/4" wide x 10-1/2" high. In February 1930 Marx filed patent #1,828,288 for this tractor. In fact, the patent illustration shows the tractor climbing over books, similar to the drawing in the advertisement.

                                                          80   175

INDUSTRIAL TRACTOR SET: 1930. 7-1/2" long. This Marx tractor with attachments is illustrated in a 1930 Butler Brothers catalog. The display box for the tractor is lettered "Industrial Tractor Set".

In the advertisement, this orange and red heavy gauge plate tractor appears flatter and more streamlined in design than the Climbing Tractor, though this may be due to the artist's rendering. There are no side exhausts, although illustrations in some catalogs show similar tractors with side exhausts. Also, the radiator appears to be unlithographed.

The tractor comes with two differently colored 4-1/2" trailers and a driver wearing a cap rather than a hat. The wholesale cost was $9.00 for a dozen sets.   **80   175**

YELLOW and GREEN TRACTOR: 1930. 8-1/2" long. Also described in the 1930 Butler Brothers catalog is this yellow and green tractor with three side exhausts, a mesh grille, 3" black disc wheels, and a driver wearing a cap.

Good   Exc

The toy comes in a box illustrating the tractor climbing up and over obstacles.   **80   175**

1931 TRACTOR

SUPER POWER REVERSING TRACTOR: 1931. 12" long x 4-1/2" wide x 5-3/4" high.
First Version: Sold by Montgomery Ward, this six-wheeled nickel-plated reversing tractor is embossed with a simulated motor on the side. The tractor has two shifts, one to start and stop, and one for backward or forward.

It comes with several attachments: a brush sweeper, metal scraper or plow, road roller, wrecking device, steel chain, and a metal wagon with a tongue. The tractor with attachments is listed for $2.89 and by itself for $1.49 in the 1931 Montgomery Ward catalog.

A similar tractor to the first version was sold with a disc harrow and rake instead of the two trailers.   **80   175**

Second Version: Advertised in 1931, this tractor has a nickel-plated finish, red wheels, and, compared with the first version, is shorter and has different side embossing. The driver wears a tan cap, white shirt, and blue overalls.   **80   175**

1932 TRACTORS

HILL CLIMBING DUMP TRUCK: 1932. 13-1/2". This truck with rubber treads is very similar to the more standard Marx dump truck manufactured a couple of years later except, of course, for the rubber treads (see the third Coal Truck on page 79). Like the dump truck, the climbing truck has litho-

The 13-1/2" Hill Climbing Dump Truck, manufactured in 1932, is similar to another Marx Dump Truck also made without treads. T. Riley Collection.

The Reversing Climbing Tractor has a nickel-plated finish. It was manufactured in 1931 and measures 12" long. Treads are missing from this toy. P. Rolin Collection.

	Good	Exc

graphed exhausts and "Marx" on the side of the hood. Unlike the dump truck, the climbing truck has red disc wheels (rather than black wheels with yellow hubcaps), a white un-lithographed dump bin (rather than striped and lithographed), and is red and orange (rather than predominantly red).

The spring-driven Hill Climbing Dump Truck has a black base and lithographed tin driver, cab hood, and grille. A lever on the driver's side raises the body, while a brake lever and the key for the windup motor are on the passenger side.

60 160

TRACTOR SET (Seven-piece): 1932. 8-1/2". To compete with the Montgomery Ward tractor with attachments (see the 1931 Super Power Reversing Tractor), Sears sold a similar tractor with three exhausts, a speed governor, and start/stop lever. Selling for $1.67, the set includes a steel wagon with wooden wheels, disc harrow, aluminum scraper, road roller, wrecker derrick, and a nickel-plated hauling chain.

90 225

ARMY DESIGN CLIMBING TRACTOR: 1932. 7-1/2" x 3-1/4". This new Marx tractor in army colors, advertised in the 1932 Sears catalog for 48 cents, comes with a doughboy driver, spring motor, and start/stop lever. **70 175**

1933 TRACTOR

TRACTOR with SCRAPER: 1933. 8-1/2". This windup tractor resembles the 1931 Climbing Tractor, but as advertised in the 1933 Sears catalog, it has a nickel finish, an aluminum scraper, and two exhausts lithographed on the side. It can haul heavy loads and has a speed governor. **60 140**

1934 TRACTOR

	Good	Exc

TRACTOR with PLOW and WAGON: 1934. Similar to the Tractor with Scraper, this enameled metal tractor also comes with a plow and a wagon. It sold originally for 89 cents.

55 125

1935 TRACTORS

TRACTOR SET (Five-piece): 1935. 8-1/2" tractor. This set resembles the 1932 Seven-Piece Tractor Set, but it no longer includes the road roller and disc harrow, has two rather than three exhausts, and is aluminum instead of enameled metal.

Another aluminum tractor with three exhausts, advertised in the 1935 Sears catalog, is described as having a new, more powerful motor and able to push loads bigger than itself. The toy sold for 94 cents; another version with lithographed metal housing and a less powerful motor sold for 59 cents.

60 125

MIDGET CLIMBING TRACTOR: 1935. 5-1/4" long. Though small, this new tractor has a spring motor, a brake, and a hook for pulling small objects. Commensurate with its size, the tractor sold for the tiny sum of 25 cents in the 1935 Sears catalog. [2] In 1935 these tractors had flat radiators and metal wheels. Later, the radiators would be curved and eventually the wheels would be plastic. Excellent price includes original box. **50 125**

---

[2] Knowledgeable collector John Ritter has pointed out that certain Marx tractors resemble the tractors of the British manufacturer Triang. For instance, the Marx "Midget" tractor resembles the 1933 Triang "Nippy" tractor, while some of the Marx "Climbing" tractors resemble the 1933 Triang "#2" tractor.

1936 TRACTORS

Good   Exc

In 1936 Marx again devised some new ideas for tractors, such as the self-reversing model.

SELF-REVERSING TRACTOR: 1936. 10" long x 5" wide x 6" high.

First Version: Advertised as if the world had been anxiously waiting for it, this tractor is described in the 1936 Sears catalog: "At last a self-reversing tractor . . . when front bumper hits obstacle, motor is reversed, causing tractor to go backwards. When rear bumper hits object, tractor goes forward again." Made of steel with a heavy-duty clockwork motor, it sold originally for $1.39 and was the largest tractor Marx had yet manufactured. The reversible principle is the same as the Marx Reversible Coupe which was advertised in the same catalog.

The tractor has black wheels, a scraper, and a flat radiator. The driver wears a red shirt, blue overalls, and a large-brimmed hat.   **60   125**

Second Version: 1940. This later version has a snowplow and an oval radiator, a type first produced in 1940. The driver, dressed in tan, wears a large-brimmed hat.

Good   Exc

The patent for the Self-Reversing Tractor is probably #2,091,004, applied for in 1935. The patent drawing looks substantially like the toy except that the toy's embossed simulated motor on the side is not shown.   **60   125**

TRACTOR TRAIN with TRACTOR SHED: 1936. 8-1/2" long tractor. Marx's most ambitious tractor toy set, it consists of a tractor with aluminum casing over steel, two 7-1/2" colored heavy gauge trailers, a steel road roller, a scraper, a derrick that lifts weights, a steel tow chain, and approximately 24 wooden blocks (that can be loaded into the trailers). The trailers are similar to those used in the Truck Train (see page 109).

Its lithographed cardboard box can be set up as a shed. The "brick" roof is labeled "Tractor Shed" and the Sears brand name "Allstate" is on one side. (This was the first time the name "Allstate" was used in conjunction with Marx tractors.) Next to "Allstate" is a lithographed farmer. The shed, measuring 11-1/4" long x 9-1/2" wide x 7-3/4" high, is featured in the 1936 Sears Christmas catalog.   **75   175**

TRACTOR SET (Four-piece): 1936. 8-1/2" tractor. The set is made up of a tractor with three exhausts, a plow, a trailer, a derrick, and a chain. The 1936 Blackwell Wielandy Company

The Tractor-Trailer Set, manufactured circa the late 1930s to early 1940s, measures approximately 8-1/2" for the tractor and 5" for the trailer. E. Owens Collection. G. Stern photograph.

Good Exc

catalog describes the tractor as finished in aluminum and silver and the extra pieces finished in silver. **80 175**

1937 TRACTORS

MIDGET TRACTOR and PLOW: 1937. As shown in the 1937 Montgomery Ward catalog, this tractor looks just like the Midget Climbing Tractor with a plow. The bright metal tractor is described as having enameled wheels and trim, a spring motor, rubber treads, and a stop/go lever. Curiously, the plow the tractor pulls is made of cast-iron, painted red, although the wheels are metal. It is likely that Marx made the tractor, but the plow was probably made by another manufacturer. (In the early years, Marx combined with another manufacturer, Daisy, to make some of the guns in the Marx Soldier of Fortune Sets.) **60 125**

SUPER POWER TRACTOR SET: 1937. 8-1/2" tractor. Advertised with the Midget Tractor and Plow and identified as Marx is the Super Power Tractor with a trailer, a snowplow, a lifting derrick, and a 31" log chain. The tractor and its aluminum accessories have an overall length of 17-3/8". The complete set is advertised for $1.69 in the 1937 Montgomery Ward catalog. **90 200**

TRACTOR with ROAD SCRAPER: 1937. 8-1/2" tractor. New in 1937, this climbing tractor has an aluminum case over a steel body, 1" rubber treads, and a steel road scraper. It sold for 94 cents and a colored metal version with a similar motor sold for 59 cents in the 1937 Sears Fall/Winter catalog. **80 175**

TRACTOR SET (32-piece): 1937.
First Version: Also new in 1937, this large impressive set consists of 32 pieces, including, for the first time in a tractor set, a 10-1/2" steel Dump Truck along with the 8-1/2" aluminum-cased steel tractor.

Other accessories in assorted colors are an 8" detachable derrick, two 7-1/2" steel trailers, a road scraper, a road roller, and a 24" steel log chain. The set was priced originally at $1.89 in the 1937 Sears catalog. Excellent price includes original box. **175 400**

Second Version: Also sold by Sears in 1937, but for $1.79, this set contains the new "Power House Tractor" (presumably 8-1/2" long — the length is not mentioned) which has an aluminum-over-steel case and a flat radiator with vertical indentations. The ad states, "Wind the powerful, speed-controlled clockwork motor, detach rubber treads from front wheels, jack up with block, attach pulley cord to 'power' wheel, release brake. With derrick attached, it pulls and lifts heavy objects." The tractor could lift its own weight, actually pull 33 times its weight, and climb 40-degree grades.

In addition to the jack block and 8" derrick, the tractor set includes a new 13" box lithographed as a Hip Roof Barn, a 10-1/2" steel dump truck, an 8" steel dump gravel trailer, a bag of wood blocks, a 30" logging chain, a disc harrow, a road scraper, and a pulley cord. These items together are listed for

Good Exc

$1.79 in the 1937 Sears Christmas catalog. Excellent price includes original box. **175 400**

1938 TRACTORS

TRACTOR with PLOW and SCRAPER: 1938. This aluminum tractor with plow and scraper, as advertised in the 1938 Montgomery Ward Fall/Winter catalog, has a removable driver, a brake, and a radiator with a vertical pattern.

The tractor with the plow measures 10" long and the scraper 5-1/2". It originally cost 94 cents. A smaller 8-1/2" colored metal version, without the plow, sold in the same catalog for 59 cents. **60 125**

TRACTOR SET (Five-piece): 1938. 8-1/2" tractor. Also advertised in the 1938 Montgomery Ward Fall/Winter catalog is an impressive tractor set consisting of an aluminum tractor with a brake and governor to maintain an even speed up and down grades. The tractor's radiator has a mesh-like pattern and a strip of color on the hood.

The tractor comes with a 5-3/8" detachable snowplow, a derrick with a crank for lifting and holding objects, a 5-1/2" detachable trailer, and a 31" log chain. With an overall length of 17-3/8", the set sold for $1.69. **80 175**

SUPER-POWER BULLDOG TRACTOR with V-SHAPED PLOW: 1938. This aluminum-finished Super-Power Bulldog tractor with a new detachable V-shaped plow, advertised in the 1938 Sears Christmas catalog for $1.59, is described as being able to go through snow, sand, or mud. With the plow attached, the tractor measures 13" long x 5" wide x 6" high and has a hook for pulling other objects. **60 140**

TRACTOR ROAD CONSTRUCTION SET (36-piece): 1938. This set has the same powerful 8-1/2" aluminum-cased tractor as in the 1937 32-piece set, but instead of a dump truck is a 9-1/2" cement truck with a crank to turn the mixing drum and a latch door that opens. The 11" tractor box has a different pattern consisting of "wood" siding rather than lithographed people.

Also in the set are a detachable steel road scraper, a 7-1/4" detachable sand scoop, a steel derrick with a crank handle, a 4-3/4" steel wheelbarrow with a spade, a new 8" trailer with a detachable sand sieve with a crank, about 26 blocks, and two steel signs, one of which says "Stop", the other "Men Working". (The sand sieve is also used on a Marx Sand or Gravel Truck and the small signs are used with other Marx toys.) The complete set is listed at $1.98 in the 1938 Sears Fall/Winter catalog. **150 350**

FARM TRACTOR SET and POWER PLANT (32-piece): 1938. This second tractor set, produced later in December 1938, has the same tractor as in the 1937 32-piece set, but the grille has a slightly different vertical pattern and is more rounded.

The set consists of an 11" milk truck without bottles and an 11-1/2" steel farm wagon with horse and driver. (The wagon,

This 8-1/2" No. 2 Tractor with scraper, manufactured in 1940, is missing its driver. Pictured with the tractor is the lithographed tin sheet measuring 10-1/2" x 6-1/4" from which the radiator for the tractor was made. W. Maeder Collection. R. Grubb photograph.

Good Exc

horse, and driver were sold the same year with Ferdinand the Bull in the wagon. See page 79 in Volume I.) In addition, it comes with a revolving lifting crane, a steel V-shaped plow, a disc harrow, a bag of blocks, a string pulley cord, a 30" chain, and a 10-1/2" long x 11" wide x 13" high cardboard barn box with "Tractor Set" lettered on the roof and "Allstate", the Sears brand name, on the side. The box, as shown in the 1939 Sears Christmas catalog, appears to have lithographed figures. The set sold for $1.79 in the catalog.   **150 325**

TRACTOR PROTOTYPE: 1938. 5-1/4". This red tractor has black trim, a flat grille with a mesh-like design with the Marx logo above it and "Licensed under patent No. 1,334,539" below. (This is the same Huth patent referred to on page 155.)

The tractor has a black strip on the hood, four exhausts on the side, and no driver.

The most noticeable features of the toy are the two small front and two large back wheels, all without treads. The front balloon-type wheels are white with red centers. The back wheels are black with green centers. The base of the toy reads "January 24, 1938 Erie".   **NRS**

1939 TRACTORS

Good Exc

Marx managed once again to come up with more new ideas for tractors; in fact, a whole page of them appeared in the 1939 Sears Christmas catalog! Also in 1939, and perhaps earlier, Marx became more conscious of the effect of its toys on furniture. Various ads begin to state that the rubber treads of the tractors would not hurt furniture.

TRACTOR, TRAILER, and V-SHAPED PLOW: 1939. This 8-1/2" copper-colored steel tractor has a trailer, a V-shaped plow, a speed-controlled clockwork motor, and a brake. It measures 20" overall and is listed for 98 cents in the 1939 Sears Christmas catalog which also advertised a colored metal tractor with a smaller motor without the trailer and plow for 49 cents.   **75 160**

TRACTOR-TRAILER SET: 1939. This is the same 8-1/2" copper-colored tractor described above with just the trailer. The box for this toy is lettered "Tractor-Trailer Set". The driver wears a blue shirt, red belt, and large-brimmed hat. The 5"

Good   Exc

white trailer has yellow-centered black wheels. (Marx sold tractors and trailers before, but usually as part of a larger set.)

A similar tractor was also produced with a red road scraper and a driver wearing a white shirt, blue pants, and a cap instead of a wide-brimmed hat. **60   135**

SUPER-POWER GIANT CLIMBING TRACTOR: 1939. Advertised on the same page in the 1939 Sears Christmas catalog is this Super-Power Giant Climbing Tractor for $1.49. Like the Super-Power Bulldog Tractor from 1938, the tractor has the same side embossing, but the ad illustration shows the radiator with a mesh pattern instead of vertical indentations. The tractor and plow together measure 13" long x 5" wide x 6" high. Attached to the tractor is a hook for pulling other items. Excellent price includes original box. **175   350**

MIDGET ROAD BUILDING SET: 1939. A good example of Marx ingenuity, this set marks a change in the company's large tractor sets. The set is described in the 1939 Sears Christmas catalog as: "5-1/2" tractor with coupling hook, road scraper, crank handle lift-derrick fits on tractor, 3-3/4" road roller, 6" dump trailer [now two-wheeled and tilting with solid sides instead of four-wheeled and stationary with cut-out sides], cement mixer truck, handle turns mixing drum, steel shovel 3-1/4" long, pick ax, two road signs, sand scoop wheelbarrow in proportion, copper-colored metal tractor has key-

Good   Exc

wind motor, brake." This entire set is listed at the bargain price of 98 cents in the 1939 Sears Christmas catalog. The two road signs read "Resume Speed" and "Road Closed, Detour" (with an arrow). Excellent price includes original box. **175   375**

FARM TRACTOR SET (40-piece): 1939. Ending the year is Marx's biggest set to date, the 40-Piece Farm Tractor Set. As shown in the 1939 Sears Christmas catalog, the set consists of the same 8-1/2" power house tractor as before but now copper-colored. The tractor has a lift block and a speed-controlled clockwork motor, which allows the tractor to run about 14 feet with one winding.

Also in the set is the Meadow Brook Dairy Truck which was also sold separately (see Buses and Trucks chapter for more information). Pictured inside are four wooden milk cans, four wooden barrels, two glass ice cubes, and a pair of tongs.

Another item in the set is a horse and driver with a steel, block-filled wagon. (The horse was used in another toy, the Horse and Car with Driver, which is pictured on page 43 in the Animal Toys chapter in Volume 1.)

As if this were not enough, also included is a revolving dumping steam shovel with a crank handle, a pulley cord, a steel road scraper, a gang plow, a 5-1/2" disc harrow, a 13" lithographed hip roof barn box, and a stone boat. (According to Charles Weber, a stone boat is used to haul stones away from

The 8-1/2" Tractor with attached scraper was manufactured circa 1941. W. Maeder Collection. R. Grubb photograph.

Good Exc

a field before planting, to help build a stonewall, or to put in gullies to prevent erosion. It looks like a sled with a hook on the front.) The set sold for $1.98 in the 1939 Sears Christmas catalog. Excellent price includes original box. **200 500**

1940 TRACTORS

Marx does it again! A whole page of new tractor ideas appears in the 1940 Sears Christmas catalog. The most noticeable change is the new curved radiator.

MIDGET TRACTOR: 1940. The little Midget Tractor, which originally appeared in 1935, is described as "New curved radiator front, 5-1/4" long x 2-1/2" wide x 3-3/4" high to top of driver's head, sure grip endless rubber treads, strong spiral motor, brake, removable man, rear hook." Surprisingly, the tractor still sold for its 1935 price of 25 cents. In the 1940 Sears Christmas catalog, drivers are shown both with and without caps. The fact that the drivers are removable has resulted in many being lost or replaced incorrectly in the wrong tractors.

The Midget Tractor comes in a number of versions and prototypes.

First Version: This copper-colored all-metal tractor has wheels of all the same size. The radiator is flat and unlithographed. **35 75**

Second Version: This variation is all metal with a curved, mostly red, lithographed radiator and sides and a green hood with yellow stripes. The black wheels are all the same size. **25 60**

Third Version: Though similar to the second version, this tractor has a red hood with yellow stripes and red wheels. The tractor has been seen with a hatless driver dressed in a white shirt and blue pants.

Later versions of the Midget Climbing Tractor have plastic wheels. **35 80**

Good Exc

First Prototype: This tractor has a yellow body with a curved striped radiator, a red stripe on the hood, and a lithographed motor on the side. Lettered "X-1493 Erie 12/49", this prototype has small front and large rear black metal wheels with red centers. The hatless driver wears a tan shirt and blue pants. **NRS**

Second Prototype: This prototype is similar to the first except that the small front wheels are rubber and the driver wears a white shirt and blue pants. Markings are "A-1483 1-5-49".

A yellow Midget Tractor fitted with two differently-sized wheels was also produced. The unillustrated box for the toy simply says "Mechanical Tractor". It has been seen with a white-shirted driver, similar to the second prototype. **NRS**

Third Prototype: Mostly red with a curved lithographed radiator and sides, this tractor has small rubber front wheels and large black metal rear wheels with khaki centers. There are no known markings. The driver has a cap and is dressed in tan. **NRS**

REVERSIBLE SIX-WHEEL TRACTOR: 1940. 11-3/4" long x 4" wide x 5-1/2" high. Also new in 1940, this bright red-colored steel tractor has a rounded radiator, either a black and white or silver, red, yellow, and black lithographed motor on the side, and blue or silver wheels. The grille has black polka dots across it. The treads are on the single and the rear two sets of wheels. The tractor also comes in military olive drab and may have come in other colors, too.

This strong tractor can actually pull a 35-pound toy since it can pull 20 times its own weight. Other features are a forward/reverse lever on the side of the driver's seat, a speed governor, brake, clockspring motor, and the capacity to climb 50-degree grades. The tractor sold for $1.89. **70 150**

TRACTOR with TRAILER and PLOW: 1940. 8-1/2" tractor. This tractor is the same as the 1939 copper-colored Tractor, Trailer, and V-Shaped Plow, but with the new rounded

A production variation of the Midget Tractor with rubber front wheels and tin rear wheels. C. and C. Weber Collection.

The Caterpillar Climbing Tractor has the same body shape as the 8-1/2" Tractor pictured on page 161, but it is more brightly colored. E. Owens Collection. G. Stern photograph.

	Good	Exc

radiator. Like the Reversible Six-wheel Tractor, it can pull 20 times its own weight. The trailer measures 8" long.

70 150

NO. 2 TRACTOR: 1940. 8-1/2" tractor. This red tractor with black wheels has a flat rather than rounded radiator. As shown in the 1940 Sears Christmas catalog, it has a large black "2" and black vertical stripes on the radiator. Above the stripes is a black Marx logo and, below, the Huth patent "Licensed under patent No. 1,334,539".

The tractor hood has a stripe and three exhausts on the side, all in taupe. A hook on the back of the tractor is used to pull loads.

Although not illustrated in the ad, the No. 2 Tractor comes with a dark gray scraper 5-1/2" wide.

A white-shirted driver with a gray wide-brimmed hat and gray pants has been seen in this tractor. Whether this is the original driver is not known. The tractor was not shown in catalogs after 1940, though it may still have been produced.

50 125

FARM TRACTOR SET (40-piece): 1940. This 40-piece set is different from the 1939 set. As shown in the 1940 Sears Christmas catalog, it no longer has the truck and stone boat, but includes the 8-1/2" copper-colored power house tractor with

	Good	Exc

a rounded radiator and horizontal ridges. Also in the set are the following steel implements: an 8" mower with moving teeth like a real mower, a 6-1/2" hay rake with a dump lever, a 6" two-gang plow, a 5-1/2" scraper, a 5-3/4" disc harrow, a 5" corn planter, and two steel trailers each measuring 5-1/2" long. In addition, there is a miniature shovel, a pitchfork, a hoe, and a rake, plus a bag of various-sized blocks. The 13" long x 9-1/2" wide x 9" high box can be set up into a tractor shed. The complete set sold for $1.98.

250 350

ALUMINUM BULLDOG TRACTOR SET: 1940. The N. Shure Company of Chicago advertised this set with a tractor similar to the 1939 Super-Power Giant Climbing Tractor. The tractor is described as having extra wide treads and measures 9-1/2" long x 6-1/2" wide x 5" high. The set includes, in addition to a V-shaped plow, a stake truck trailer, a steel dump truck, a derrick, a plow and chain, a road roller, and a bag filled with wooden blocks. The N. Shure catalog priced the set for $1.30.

200 300

1941 TRACTORS

Other than the two pieces described below, Marx did not advertise any more new tractors in 1941, but repeated the

Good   Exc

advertisements of the previous year. This is hardly surprising in view of the approaching war during which the company did not manufacture toys since it was involved with defense and war work.

8-1/2" TRACTOR: 1941.
First Version: This tractor has a flat radiator, embossed and lithographed with vertical and bar-like lines.

Priced at 59 cents in the 1941 Sears Christmas catalog, the tractor is described as being newly designed with lighter metal than the other tractors advertised with it (the others could pull 20 times their own weight). This lighter tractor retains all the features of other Marx tractors, such as rubber treads, a speed governor, brake, and strong motor.

The tractor, which is mostly orange and yellow with red, black, and white accents, has black wheels and an orange hood with a yellow strip. A lithographed motor and three yellow exhausts are on the side and a yellow and orange Marx logo and a hook for attaching objects are on the back. A lithographed dashboard displays various dials.

Less colorful than most Marx drivers, the driver is gray, black, and white, but it may have come in other colors. To the right of the driver is a start/stop switch. The tractor comes with a red scraper and a red trailer.   **70   160**

Second Version: This tractor, colored like the first version, has a rounded front, red or copper wheels, and a silver scraper. The driver wears a cap, white shirt, and blue pants.

70   160

Third Version: This mostly red tractor has a blue-shirted driver. As shown on its red, yellow, and blue illustrated box, the tractor has a rounded radiator, but the actual toy has a flat radiator. The box reads "Power Snap Caterpillar Climbing Tractor". A tractor with this name also comes in aluminum. Excellent price includes original box.   **70   200**

Fourth Version: Made in copper, this windup tractor measures 8-1/2" long x 5-1/4" high. It has an embossed three-pipe manifold and embossed exhaust on both sides. The yellow front comes with plow clips. The gray back has a nickel hanger. The tractor has a rear hook, four holes in each wheel, and wheel treads.

The driver wears a blue shirt with rolled-up sleeves, red pants and neck band, a gray hat with a black band, and blue boots. The red-, yellow-, and blue-lithographed box says "Have Fun With A Caterpillar Climbing Tractor, Strongly Built For Playtime Hauling, Logging, Farming, Building" with the Marx logo. The top and bottom of the box reads "Power Snap Caterpillar Climbing Tractor".   **70   160**

Prototype: This version, which is probably a prototype, has small black front wheels and large rear wheels without treads. At each side of the driver's seat are red guard pieces. The radiator is missing.   **NRS**

TRACTOR with AIRPLANE: 1941. This intriguing toy has a tractor with an attached dolly that pulls an airplane. The 1941 Sears Christmas catalog describes the $1.19 set as a

Good   Exc

"3-piece Air Liner, 27" wingspread plane. Dolly hitch on wheels, 5-1/2" airport tractor. Detach tractor and hitch, then play 'take-off.' Plane has tricycle landing gear, silvery steel, 21-1/2" long. With metal tractor attached."

As shown in the catalog, the tractor resembles the 1940 Midget Tractor prototypes described on page 162. The driver of the airport tractor wears a cap, but it may have come in a hatless version, as did this toy's prototype. The tractor has been seen in both red and yellow.

The tractor pulls a four-propeller monoplane with "AA" on the left wing and "NC-2100" on the right. This plane was also sold separately. Excellent price includes original box.
225   475

Prototype: 1941. This 5-1/2" mostly red prototype has large metal rear wheels and small, possibly rubber, front wheels. The black rear wheels have a red center design, similar to the wheels of some of the eccentric cars.

The prototype has a detailed motor lithographed on the side, a red hood with a yellow strip, and a curved radiator. The base reads "Erie 1/21/41 #174-B $ AOY DIE EST" with the Marx logo.   **NRS**

1942 TRACTORS

Because of the war, 1942 was the last big tractor sales year for some time. 1942 catalogs also showed a set with a farm wagon (trailer) pulled by two horses along with implements, but without a tractor.

8-1/2" COPPER-COLORED TRACTOR with SCRAPER: 1942.
First Version: In 1942, the 8-1/2" copper-colored Tractor with Trailer and Plow with the rounded radiator from 1940 was returned, no longer with a V-shaped plow but with a red scraper that could double as a snowplow. The tractor has the same powerful speed-governed clockspring motor and is driven by a figure wearing a wide-brimmed hat, white shirt, and white boots. A hitching hook at the back pulls other toys. This tractor is advertised in various catalogs, some describing it merely as being made of metal. Excellent price includes original box.
80   175

Second Version: This tractor is silver with a silver scraper and black wheels. The driver wears a tan cap, white shirt, and blue pants. A similar 8-1/2" aluminum tractor with a flat radiator and a scraper was also available at the same time in the 1942 Sears Christmas catalog. Excellent price includes original box.   **80   175**

TRACTOR SET (40-piece): 1942. 8-1/2" tractor. This set is similar to the 1940 set, but its orange tractor is like the 1941 8-1/2" Tractor with flat radiator. The tractor may also have come in red and other colors. The set includes wooden milk cans and barrels in the trailers. Excellent price includes original box.   **250   550**

The 1950 Automatic Steel Barn is part of a set which includes this Midget Tractor, manufactured in 1940. E. Owens Collection.

Good Exc

MECHANICAL FARM TRACTOR with NINE IMPLE-MENTS: 1942. This toy resembles pieces in the 1939 Midget Road Building Set, but, as shown in the 1942 Montgomery Ward Christmas catalog, some of the pieces are different. The Ward set consists of a 5-1/2" treadless tractor with a curved radiator and small 1-5/8" front wheels and large 2-1/4" rear tin wheels. This set may also have been made with the copper tractor from the 1939 set.

The tractor pulls the following all-metal implements: 6-1/2" hayrake which actually raises to "drop" load as wheels turn, 4" corn planter with a dummy marker which plants two rows at a time, 5-3/4" ten-disc harrow, 8-1/4" mower with a sliding cutting blade, 6-1/4" gang plow with two plow shares, 3-1/2" road scraper, 3-3/8" shovel, and 4-1/2" pitchfork. The complete set sold for $1.23 in the 1942 Montgomery Ward catalog.

The red tractor has a curved radiator, red hood with a yellow strip, plus a red, yellow, and orange lithographed motor on the side. It is possible that the tractor came in other colors.

The 1942 Montgomery Ward Christmas catalog shows the tractor with tin wheels, but the wheels later came in red plastic. The ad illustrates the driver wearing a hat, but the plastic-wheeled version has a hatless driver dressed in a white shirt and blue pants. Just as this tractor came in different colors, it probably had different drivers, too.

The plastic-wheeled silver tractor pulls a two-wheeled tilting trailer with red wheels. The trailers came in other colors as well.   **130** **275**

Good Exc

CATERPILLAR CLIMBING TRACTOR: 1942.
First Version: For the first time, in 1942, "Caterpillar" is on the tractor's side. (Actually, Marx Caterpillar-type tractors had been advertised as far back as 1929.)

Advertised for $1.69 in the 1942 Montgomery Ward Christmas catalog, the 9-1/2" Caterpillar tractor is able to climb 50-degree slopes and has a scraper and a hook on the rear for towing.

The yellow Caterpillar tractor has a rounded radiator with "Diesel" on the side. The motor is lithographed primarily in gray and black on the tractor sides. Under the motor is "Caterpillar" in red. It has red wheels and the Marx logo behind the front wheels. The tractor's driver has been seen either in a cap, white shirt, and blue pants, or in a brown hat, brown shirt, and tan pants.

Although the ad shows the tractor with a standard scraper, it also has a V-shaped plow. The tractor and plow together measure 13-1/2" in length. Excellent price includes original box.   **90** **220**

Second Version: This orange tractor has yellow wheels and "Caterpillar" in black. Excellent price includes original box.   **90** **225**

SUPER POWER CLIMBING TRACTOR and NINE-PIECE SET: 1942. 9-1/2" tractor. The 1942 Montgomery Ward Christmas catalog describes this brightly-colored metal tractor with red wheels with one-inch treads, and a curved radiator as the "Biggest most fanciful tractor of them all." The ad also states "We hitched this heavy duty climber and our smaller tractor ... often sold with sets of this price ... together back to back, wound them up and set them going. This one not

Good   Exc

only walked right off with the smaller job that was pulling against it, but pulled a 35 pound coaster wagon as well."

The tractor has many features, including a brake, a special governor for smooth speed, and a motor that cannot be over-wound. It climbs over obstacles and steep grades and "Hauls loads many toy tractors won't even budge."

Additional all-metal items in the $2.39 set are "Two trailers, each 7-1/2" long, 5-1/2" Road Scraper, 3-1/4" Road Roller, 5-1/2" Disc Harrow with revolving discs, 9" Derrick with Windlass that actually lifts loads, 30" Loading Chain and Shovel."

Sears sold a similar tractor in 1939, but it was chrome-finished with a flat radiator. Montgomery Ward may also have sold this tractor earlier than 1942.   **150   250**

1946 TRACTOR

From 1943 to 1945, Louis Marx & Company advertised no tractors, since the company was involved with war work.

TRACTOR TRAILER and SCRAPER: 1946. 8-1/2" tractor. This tractor has the same flat radiator with a vertical-patterned grille as in previous years, but it also has a road scraper and pulls a two-wheeled detachable tilting trailer. The trailers are either silver or red and have black wheels. The radiator patterns differ slightly on the two versions. The tractors were sold with or without trailers. Excellent price includes original box.   **75   150**

1947 TRACTOR

By 1947 the company, with its unique ability to gear up quickly, was able to produce a new set with a different tractor.

Good   Exc

STEEL FARM TRACTOR and IMPLEMENTS: 1947. 15" tractor. This imposing 15" steel bulldozer tractor with treads not only looks real, but sounds real, too. When pushed, it makes a motor-like noise.

The yellow and red tractor has a motor lithographed on the side in gray, yellow, and black. The large rear wheels measure 5-1/4" in diameter, while the small front wheels measure 2-3/4" in diameter. The rear wheels have yellow centers, surrounded by a red and black circular design and black-lithographed treads. The front wheels have the same treads, but a red and black design, similar to the design on certain Marx Eccentric Cars. The driver wears a yellow cap, white shirt, and blue pants.

The tractor has a hydraulic-type road plow which can be set in two positions by operating a lever. It also comes with an 11" three-gang plow.

Other implements in the set include a 10" wide hayrake with a dump lever and an 11-1/4" wide mowing machine with realistic automatically-moving teeth. All implements have a baked-on enamel finish. The tractor, road plow, and three implements sold for $3.98, while the tractor and road plow without the implements sold for $2.59 in the 1947 Sears Christmas catalog.   **150   250**

1948 TRACTORS

FARM TRACTOR and IMPLEMENT SET: 1948. The famous Marx ingenuity is at work again, as shown for $4.89 in the 1948 Sears Christmas catalog which advertised this diesel bulldozer tractor with a new hydraulic road scraper on the front. The hydraulic scraper extends almost the length of the sides, fits over the tractor hood like a handle, and can be snapped into an up or down position. The tractor, which is the

Reversible Six-wheel Farm Tractor Truck measures approximately 14" long and was manufactured in 1950. Tractor can go forward or backward or climb steep inclines. P. Rolin Collection.

Good Exc

same as the 1942 "Caterpillar" tractor, has a start/stop lever and a rear hook for attaching the baked-on enamel implements. The implements include an 11-1/2" wide mower which has an action cutter bar, a 9-3/4" wide hayrake with automatic dumping action by means of a dump lever, and an 11-1/2" long three-gang plow.

Marx tried something different with this set. Not only is there a driver for the tractor, but also one for the mower. The metal tractor driver wears a hat and the metal mower driver wears a cap.

The corrugated box repeated from previous years is 15" wide. The box is lithographed to resemble a farm machinery service station and reads "Tractor Sales Service, Farm Machinery".

In the same catalog, the Caterpillar tractor from 1946 continued to be sold, but with just the front scraper, for $2.69.

150 250

CATERPILLAR TRACTOR and HYDRAULIC LIFT: 1948. Montgomery Ward also sold this Caterpillar tractor with the hydraulic lift (hand-operated) which raised and lowered the scraper, but without implements, for $2.98 in its Christmas catalog.

45 100

TRACTOR and SIX-IMPLEMENT SET: 1948. This set, selling for $4.69 by Montgomery Ward, is similar to the 1948 Farm Tractor and Implement Set sold by Sears. In place of the Caterpillar tractor with the hydraulic- type road scraper, Montgomery Ward substituted the 8-1/2" aluminum tractor with the rounded front which had been brought out earlier. Like the Sears set, this one includes a three-gang plow, a scraper, a hayrake, and a mower, but no driver on the mower. Also added is an 8- 7/8" disc harrow with discs that really turn and a 6-1/2"

Good Exc

dumping trailer with two balloon-type metal wheels. The set comes in a corrugated box lithographed to look like a farm shop.

150 250

TRACTOR and MOWER: 1948. Marx used the "new" material, plastic, in this miniature set. The 5" lithographed steel tractor has a brake, a rear hook, wide plastic wheels with rubber treads, and a detachable mower. The mower bar moves back and forth (but does not cut). The two pieces together are listed at $1.17 in the 1948 Montgomery Ward Christmas catalog.

At the same time, Montgomery Ward sold the large tractor with a hydraulic bulldozer scraper from the 1948 Farm Tractor and Implement Set for $2.29. It had appeared a year earlier in catalogs with a V-shaped plow and also as part of a set.

35 80

1949 TRACTORS

Although plastic parts were used in the 1948 Tractor and Mower, Marx had not yet made an all-plastic tractor, trailer, or implement. It was not until the 1949 Sears Christmas catalog that this new feature was highlighted.

PLASTIC TRACTOR: 1949. Marx's first all-plastic tractor and scraper is headlined in an ad as: "New! Plastic Tractor — Latest design Diesel-type tractor, 8" long with road scraper attached. Molded of plastic in fine detail. Bright colors. Wide rubber treads. Clockspring Motor." The toy sold for 89 cents.

35 80

TRACTOR and EQUIPMENT SET (Five-piece): 1949. 16-1/2" tractor. Although Marx had made an all-plastic tractor,

Prototype of Reversible Six-wheel Tractor Truck in Army colors. P. Rolin Collection.

Good   Exc

it continued to make metal tractors. This steel set is mostly made up of items from the earlier sets. One new feature, however, is the high lift scoop loader attached to the tractor that raises, lowers, and dumps loads. The tractor, which was sold with a similar set in 1947, has embossed metal over-sized rear and small front wheels.

The three-gang plow, man with mower, hayrake, and corrugated building are the same as those in the 1947 Steel Farm Tractor and Implements. The new item is a 10-3/4" utility trailer, the largest two-wheeled type that Marx had yet made with a tractor set. The complete set sold for $4.89 in the 1949 Sears Christmas catalog.   **150   350**

1950 TRACTORS

TRACTOR SET (Two-piece): 1950. 19" tractor. This steel tractor with the rounded front is the same as in earlier years, but it has a steel grader attached to the back. The front wheels of the grader are swivel-mounted and the scraper part of the grader can be adjusted for angle and can be raised or lowered. It sold for $2.29.   **55   125**

PLASTIC TRACTOR SET: 1950. 6-1/2" tractor. Marx favored sparking toys so it was only a matter of time before sparking tractors were made. This tractor, as shown in the 1950 Sears Christmas catalog, has sparks that fly from the engine exhaust, which is actually a stack on the tractor's hood. Besides the sparks, the tractor has the usual features of rubber treads and a clockspring motor.

The set has a movable scraper attached to the tractor and an approximately 10-1/2" wagon with removable stakes and a tongue. The set sold for $1.39 in the 1950 Sears Christmas catalog. Montgomery Ward also sold this same toy and one without the wagon, the latter for $1.15.
With wagon: 25   60

AUTOMATIC STEEL BARN and MECHANICAL PLASTIC TRACTOR: 1950. 7" tractor. This clever toy features a red plastic tractor which runs up to the steel barn door. The door opens when the tractor touches it and then the tractor runs inside. The 10-1/4" barn has similar style lithography to the corrugated boxes sold with the tractor sets. One version of the barn (there may be others) has yellow paneling, a red shingled roof, and red bricks on the lower part of the building.

Good   Exc

The Marx logo is near the door. Farm scenes such as a farmer, horse, and farm equipment are lithographed on the walls.

The tractor has a spring motor and a fixed, simulated hand crank which serves to activate the barn door-opening action. The set is listed for $2.45 in the 1950 Montgomery Ward Christmas catalog.[3] This set may have been named "The Magic Barn and Plastic Tractor."

Instead of the 7" plastic tractor, the set also comes with the 1940 Midget Tractor (Third Version, described on page 162). The tractor may have come in other colors.   **75   150**

REVERSIBLE SIX-WHEEL FARM TRACTOR TRUCK: 1950. This reversible tractor has a stake bin attached and is described in the 1950 Sears Christmas catalog: "Simple lever controls direction. Move tractor forward or backward — change direction even while in action ... stake body in rear 7-1/2" long x 4-1/2" wide x 2" deep. Link metal chain for securing loads to stake body or for hauling." The climbing steel tractor measures approximately 13-3/4" long and originally sold for $2.94. The mostly red tractor has a lithographed yellow and black motor on the sides, a rounded radiator, yellow wheels, and a blue fixed stake bin. The Marx logo is near the middle wheel. The license on the front reads "W9116". The driver wears a large-brimmed yellow hat, yellow shirt, and brown pants.

In later years, this toy was manufactured with a solid bin and miniature tools. The same tractor also came with silver wheels and a lithographed movable bin marked "Coke" which was jointed at the end. This bin with different lettering was used on other Marx toys.   **75   125**

REVERSIBLE SIX-WHEEL TRACTOR TRUCK PROTOTYPE: 1950. This hand-painted prototype tractor truck has an olive drab Army-colored body with hand-painted markings which include a yellow "Army No. 671" on the side and "Engr's. Div. No. 671" on top of the hood. Other markings on the truck are "PFC". The driver of the truck is an Army corporal in blue fatigues.

A production toy was made that is similar to the prototype, but it has different markings. On top of the hood are "Army W-9116" over "1st Div. Engineers 7A". Other markings are "1st Div" above the Marx logo near the middle wheel.   **NRS**

---

[3] Marx also made a "Magic Garage and Auto," but the auto is friction.

Index

ABOUT THE AUTHOR

When asked how she became a toy enthusiast, **Maxine A. Pinsky** recalls: "I saw a Marx eccentric car at a train meet over 20 years ago and was so taken with it that I bought it and, subsequently, all of the Marx cars that I could find. One toy led to another and...toys became a passion." And as a result, she authored *Greenberg's Guide to Marx Toys*, Volume I and is presently working on Volumes III and IV of the Marx series.

Born in London, England, Maxine attended St. Maurs High School before coming to the United States. She earned her undergraduate degree at Temple University in Philadelphia and attended graduate classes at the University of Pennsylvania. Maxine worked in the "Get Set" program for pre-school children in the Philadelphia area. Her interests include tin toys, vintage clothing, and movies.